Military Justice in the Confederate States Armies

by
Jack A. Bunch

WHITE MANE BOOKS

This White Mane Books publication
was printed by
Beidel Printing House, Inc.
63 West Burd Street
Shippensburg, PA 17257-0152 USA

In respect for the scholarship contained herein, the acid-free paper used in this book meets the guidelines for permanence and durability of the Committee on Production Guidelines for Book Longevity of the Council on Library Resources.

For a complete list of available publications
please write
White Mane Books
Division of White Mane Publishing Company, Inc.
P.O. Box 152
Shippensburg, PA 17257-0152 USA

Library of Congress Cataloging-in-Publication Data

Bunch, Jack A., 1932-
    Military justice in the Confederate states armies / by Jack A. Bunch.
        p. cm.
    Includes bibliographical references and index.
    ISBN 1-57249-204-X (alk. paper)
    1. Courts-martial and courts of inquiry--Confederate States of America. I. Title.

KF7620 .B86 2000
343.75'0143--dc21
                                                              00-036648

Contents

Preface

As the delegates from the six states that had seceded to date met in Montgomery, Alabama, in February 1861, to form a new government, hope rode high that there would be no war. Nevertheless, the delegates had to address the possibility of a conflict, and it is ironic that they first considered Jefferson Davis not as president, but as commanding general of the army of the state of Mississippi.

Organization of the new government drew heavily upon that of the United States as well it might. For the secessionists were not bent upon overthrowing the government of the United States, but were determined to separate themselves from that government so that they could prepare their own laws to govern their future.

The structure of the new country's military, as well as its government, was closely patterned after that of the United States, and the system of military justice was adopted entirely after the examples of the old country.

The army regulations, the articles of war, and the custom of the service were carried over into the Confederacy virtually unchanged. And even though all of these had not been put to extensive tests, they were the best at hand. In the four years of bloody battle before them, both sides would find themselves sorely tested in their efforts to provide proper military justice. When fighting erupted in April 1861, neither side could foresee the overwhelming numbers they would face across courts-martial tables.

Comprehensive opinions have been written by military scholars on the many cases tried by the North during the war, but little beyond an occasional article or essay has appeared regarding the effort of the Confederacy to enforce such justice.

Proper codes and enforcement are essential to the function of a well-regulated army. Without such a system an army is a short march from becoming an unruly mob. The fact that both the North and the South did not lose control of their forces stands as a superior achievement. There were many examples of guerrilla depravations, but these were committed by outlaw bands, not soldiers under the command of properly commissioned officers.

The military justice system in the Confederate States Armies was well organized and functioned properly within the articles of war in force during the 1860s. A study of it has simply escaped the attention of scholars, no doubt because of the presence of more exciting topics such as Gettysburg and other famous battles. The Confederate government broke new ground in the creation of military courts. The organization of such courts was well planned by the Southern Congress, and the implementation was initially successful. Problems arose chiefly because of a lack of suitable manpower as the troubles of the South mounted during the closing months of the war.

The very nature of the war placed an unusual strain on the men and the high command. Secession took place because of divided opinions, then after the Southern states became a Confederacy, opinions were still divided among many of its citizens. All persons were not of one political mind; this was a leading cause for the high rate of desertions which placed an extraordinary burden on the military justice system. All of this makes fascinating reading and many theories can be put forward as to how the South might have fared under differing circumstances of military justice.

The most disappointing aspect of the study of the South's list of courts-martial is the lapse in material. Unfortunately the records of many soldiers are missing and will never be found, but as with all research, unlooked for surprises occur, and a few of those listed as missing may some day appear.

The written names of the soldiers in the ledgers of the Adjutant and Inspector General's Office were occasionally illegible, others were spelled differently from the names listed in the compiled service records. In order to bring consistency to a troubling situation, the spelling in the compiled service record was used. This was done without the intrusion of brackets or the explanation that other variations were found. In some cases such spelling may differ from that which the soldier's family recognizes. But even within families spelling sometimes varied; I found this to be true with my own ancestors.

The enforcement of military justice by the Confederate armies was conducted within the confines of the articles of war and was prosecuted according to army regulations. Some variations occurred by chance, others by design, but overall, prosecution was carefully monitored by army high command and by the government in Richmond. As the years went by a transformation took place within the armies of both North and South. The soldiers who met at First Manassas were not the same as those who stacked their arms at Appomattox. Both sides had matured into hardened veterans. This was one of the chief reasons that the final battles were so costly.

These veterans had come to recognize and accept the hardships of campaigning: long marches, short rations, incompetent leadership, the loss of cherished leaders, wounds, sickness, death, and sometimes bitter defeat. They had also come to accept the necessity of military justice. Most had by now witnessed many examples of courts-martial; like all veterans they grumbled about army life, but they knew that enforcement of regulations was needed. A dilemma was ever-present, soldiers rebelled at seeing their friends punished, but they knew that tough laws were needed, so for better or for worse the men in the ranks swallowed the harsh medicine of military justice.

Acknowledgments

It is not possible to thank all the people who contributed to this work; unnamed friends offered encouragement when I lost courage, others bolstered my confidence when it was falling. But I could not have finished the task without the support of my wife, ElDoris. Through the weeks and months that turned into years, she never once suggested that I abandon the project, even though I entertained the thought myself on more than one occasion. Long periods of separation were standards for us, and many "vacations" were journeys to libraries. So it is for her love and devotion that I am most deeply thankful.

All writers of history are unforgettably aware of their dependency upon the reams of information that must be pursued, explored, skewered by the pen, and transferred to the printed page. Without the help of hundreds of unrecognized librarians and archivists, the researcher's job would be virtually hopeless. To paraphrase the old real estate adage about location, military history's three most important elements are research, research, research.

With a feeling of embarrassment, I confess that I have overlooked more people than I have remembered, but I would begin my thank yous by recognizing John Slonaker and his staff at the United States Army Military History Institute at Carlisle Barracks, Pennsylvania. Also I wish to mention Ervin L. Jordan, Jr. of the Alderman Library at the University of Virginia in Charlottesville.

The advice and material furnished to me over the years by the old army team on 11 West of the National Archives would literally fill volumes. I cannot express enough appreciation to William Lind, Gary Morgan, Michael Meier, Michael Musick, and Stuart Butler for their help and encouragement.

I leave a special note of thanks to Henry Grunder, former special collections librarian at the Virginia State Library and Archives in Richmond. Henry spent several days with me in the rare books room in the basement of the old library researching all of the special orders of the Adjutant and Inspector General's Office; he then photocopied the hundreds of pages that I requested. His help made a difficult task achievable.

I owe recognition to Burrus Carnahan, an attorney from McLean, Virginia. He reviewed my manuscript and pointed out several inconsistencies with 19th-century military law. His suggestions helped save me from running off the rails on the central issue of my work.

I cannot say enough to express my appreciation for kindness and help that I received from the librarians and archivists throughout the Southern capitals; the one exception is the library in Alabama. I do not mean to say that I was neglected in Alabama, but rather that I was directed to the Birmingham Public Library instead of the Department of Archives and History in Montgomery. The films of compiled service records of Alabama soldiers are housed in Birmingham rather than Montgomery; the public library in Birmingham has an entire beautiful old wing devoted to genealogy and history.

I worked with the Arkansas History Commission in Little Rock; the Department of Archives and History in Atlanta, Georgia; the Department of Archives and Libraries in Frankfort, Kentucky; the Department of Archives and History in Jackson, Mississippi; the North Carolina Department of Archives and History in Raleigh; the South Carolina Department of Archives and History in Columbia; the Tennessee State Library and Archives in Nashville; and in addition to the Virginia State Library which I have already mentioned, I did extensive work at the West Virginia Archives and History Library in Charleston. That library carries films of the compiled service records of Virginia's Confederate soldiers as does the library in Richmond, Virginia.

Many of these wonderful institutions operate on limited budgets, and yet none skimps on the services offered. From the state libraries to the National Archives all should be given larger allocations to work with. Such money spent would be truly spent for the benefit of all citizens.

I cannot close without a mention of my home-town library of Cincinnati and Hamilton County; it has grown to become one of the outstanding libraries in our country one balanced by careful use of resource dollars, and one which I have been greatly dependent upon.

The staff at White Mane Publishing has furnished me with needed help and kind consideration for which I am indebted to them, and most of all I owe recognition to my indexer, Diane R. Gordon, for exploring that minefield that writers fear to tread.

Chapter I
Background

Before the first shot was fired toward Fort Sumter, Southern states' militia units were more than ready for a fight. The Confederate States possessed the nucleus of an army before the Confederacy was even created. However, the tremendous task of organization lay before them, and the Southern government struggled with that task until the very end of its existence.

As soon as the Congress of the Confederate States of America was formed, it began adopting legislation implementing the construction of a new government. Among the first provisions passed was the regulations for the army, along with the articles of war.[1] By necessity, most of the rules were copied verbatim from those of the United States.

The United States Congress made some minor revisions to the articles of war in July and August 1861, and approximately eight significant amendments were passed between 1806 and 1861; otherwise, the 101 articles governing military law were unchanged from 1806.[2]

The wisdom of the adoption of the United States Articles of War is apparent. Expediency notwithstanding, many of the officers of the Confederate armies were familiar with the United States articles. No time was wasted learning new rules, and the execution of military law under these articles worked equally well for the Confederate government as for the Federal government.

It is fitting to say that the employment of similar articles of war worked well for both the Union and Confederate armies; it is misleading to imply that the prosecution of courts-martial was an easy task. For both the North and the South, it was a time-consuming delay.

General courts-martial may be appointed only by a general officer commanding an army or a colonel commanding a separate department. These courts may consist of any number of commissioned officers, from five to thirteen inclusive, but should not consist of fewer than thirteen without manifest injury to the service.[3]

Most courts contained fewer than thirteen officers. It was often difficult to obtain the minimum of five. Courts with five, six, or seven members were always in danger of having a case dismissed because of loss of members during a trial whereby the remainder numbered fewer than five.

The president had the power to convene general courts, as well as the officers mentioned, but rarely did so. The officer appointing the court is referred to as the convening authority. Members appointed to courts were required to serve or petition the convening authority for relief, for only he or his successor had the power to grant such relief or appoint substitutes. Members were required to serve upon a court until it was dissolved by the convening authority.

Only commissioned officers of the line or staff could be appointed to courts; chaplains and surgeons were precluded from serving on Confederate courts.[4] Regular officers could not sit upon a court which tried "militia," but regulars could be tried by volunteers or militia officers. The term militia taken expressly from the United States Article #97 should have been amended to read militia or volunteer. Virtually all courts in the Confederate service were composed of volunteer or militia officers.

The convening authority was also responsible for appointing a judge advocate for each court. The judge advocate was the law officer of the court and while army regulations did not require him to be a commissioned officer, in virtually all examples, he held commission rank. He did not vote in the outcome of the trial, and his position was not determined by rank as it was for members of the court. He and the president of the court, who was the highest ranking member of the court, were the two persons responsible for proper court procedures. Both were required to sign the written proceedings at the conclusion of the trial; the president was responsible for decorum among the members and the voting by members for guilt or acquittal and for voting upon sentence if guilt was pronounced.

The judge advocate was both prosecutor for the government and guardian of the rights of the prisoner. He was responsible for the procurement of witnesses for both prosecution and defense; he was required to establish that charges and specifications were properly drawn. These were usually handed down from the officer preferring charges, and while the judge advocate had no authority to draw such charges, he clearly was responsible for seeing that the wording was accurate. It was also his responsibility to furnish a copy of the charges and specifications to the prisoner.

Upon the commencement of a trial, it was the duty of the judge advocate to swear all members of the court. Following this, the president of the court was required to administer the oath to the judge advocate. All of these details had to be entered into the written record, lest the proceedings be nullified for lacking these required facts.

The judge advocate then requested of the prisoner any objection he might have to any member of the court sitting in judgement against him. If any such objection was raised, the court retired to consider these claims and to determine the validity of the prisoner's request. If the court determined that the request should be granted, the member or members were excused. If the number of members remained at five or more, the trial continued; otherwise, the case was not heard until the convening authority appointed additional members to the court.

Objections were rarely raised by prisoners on this point, and when they were raised, were seldom accepted by the court; but a failure to perform this requirement and to include the wording in the written document nullified the proceedings.

Expenses connected with courts-martial were established by army regulations, and all concerned, from the convening authority to the judge advocate were required to keep such expenses under control. The judge advocate was expected to summon the necessary witnesses, but he was bound to show that the witness was indeed required. The court held the power to order a judge advocate to obtain specific witnesses if any dispute arose. Citizens were paid transportation fare and three dollars a day while attending the courts. Officers were paid one dollar per day when serving on a court or when appearing as witnesses provided the court was not held at their station. The judge advocate also received one dollar a day travel expense if required to travel; in addition, he was entitled to one dollar and twenty-five cents per diem for each day employed.[5]

The government did not provide travel expenses for soldiers appearing as witnesses or who were otherwise employed on courts-martial as recorders, interpreters, or attendants.

Regimental or garrison courts-martial were resorted to whenever possible. These courts could be hastily appointed and dissolved without the necessity of meeting stricter demands of general courts. They were often referred to as battalion courts-martial. The requirements were set forth in Article of War (AOW) #66:

> Every officer commanding a regiment or corps may appoint, for
> his own regiment or corps, courts-martial, to consist of three
> commissioned officers for the trial and punishment of offenses
> not capital, and decide upon their sentences. For the same pur-
> pose, all officers commanding any of the garrisons, forts, bar-
> racks, or other places where the troops consist of different corps,
> may assemble courts-martial to consist of three commissioned
> officers, and decide upon their sentences.

AOW #67 explained the limit of sentences imposed by these courts:

> No Garrison or Regimental court-martial shall have the power to
> try capital cases or commissioned officers; neither shall they in-
> flict a fine exceeding one month's pay, nor imprison, nor put to
> hard labor any non-commissioned officer or soldier for a longer
> time than one month.

These courts served a very useful purpose in quickly disposing of
minor cases, then getting on with the business of fighting the war.
A regimental commander could appoint a court by simply ordering
three of his officers to hear the case and by naming a judge advocate to prosecute. The court was bound by similar rules as general
courts, such as swearing in the members and the judge advocate,
allowing the accused to object to any of the members, etc.

The person appointing the court became the reviewing authority when cases were completed; he then had power to mitigate
all or a portion of any sentence handed down. Proceedings in such
trials were not required to be forwarded to the Adjutant and Inspector General's Office, but sometimes were. However, these
records needed to be preserved and were generally retained at the
division level. The 35th AOW allowed any soldier who felt himself
wronged by his company commander to appeal to the officer commanding the regiment, who was then required to appoint a regimental court to hear the case. If either party still felt aggrieved,
that person was able to appeal to a general court-martial.[6]

The United States service debated the application of this article of war during the first half of the 19th century and learned
that the wording of the article was less than clear. The meaning
was intended to give an enlisted man an avenue of appeal for grievances against his company commander. However, his complaint
was to be directed through military channels; he was required to
make his grievance known to his company commander, then if sat-
isfaction was not achieved, to his regimental commander, who was
expected to appoint a regimental court-martial to hear the case if
the issue were not settled. Such appeals were rarely resorted to
because the general court had the power to summarily punish the

person appealing if it determined that the appeal was totally without merit.

An example of an appeal that was successfully made from a regimental court to a general court was that of Sgt. John (Jonathan) R. Nash of Company F, 52d Virginia Infantry. The 52d was part of Brig. Gen. John Pegram's Brigade, of Maj. Gen. Jubal A. Early's Division, Second Corps, Army of Northern Virginia, when the case was heard on January 30, 1864.

Nash's compiled service record (CSR) shows that he was absent without official leave (AWOL) from July 27, 1863, to August 14, 1863, and that pay was deducted. There is no reference to a regimental court-martial in his CSR, nor is one listed in the ledger of the Adjutant and Inspector General's Office (A&IGO). The notation to the general court-marital that was held on January 30, 1864, which appears in the ledger of the A&IGO reads: "This was an appeal from a regimental court martial. The court find that Sgt. Nash has fully substantiated the grievances complained of by him."

Unfortunately, no orders were found covering the case and his grievances were not identified, so they can only be guessed at, but it would appear that his pay would have been restored if that was, in fact, the cause of his complaint.[7]

As a footnote to the case, the CSR shows that Sergeant Nash was killed in action at Bethesda Church, May 30, 1864, so any funds that might have been due him were doubtless spent by someone else.

General courts-martial were time-consuming undertakings. As the war wore on, cases mounted, other duties demanded officers' valuable time, and fewer qualified officers were available due to attrition. On October 9, 1862, the Congress of the Confederate States of America passed an act to organize military courts to attend the army corps in the field.

The new courts were to be appointed by the president, one for each army corps. Each court was to consist of three members, two of whom would constitute a quorum, with each member entitled to the rank and pay of a colonel of cavalry. The president would also appoint a judge advocate for each court with the rank and pay of a captain of cavalry. The military courts defined by the new act were to have jurisdiction over all offenses under the articles of war. The courts also had power to prosecute all crimes committed under the laws of the Confederate States by members of the army. In addition, they were empowered to prosecute any member of the army in cases of murder, manslaughter, arson, rape, robbery, and larceny, as defined by the common law when committed by a member of the army against another member of the army or against the property

or person of any citizen or other person not in the army. This gave
the new courts authority to take action against members of the
Confederate States Armies for major infractions committed within
the Confederacy, the border states, or the Northern states.[8]

The only limitation placed upon the military courts was the
inability to try general officers. Their authority extended only to the
rank of colonel.[9] Since all three members were colonels, the issue
of members of a court not being of inferior rank to the accused was
overcome. General courts-martial would still need to be convened
to try general officers, but the minimum number of such cases
made this requirement insignificant.

The creation of this newly designed tribunal was a wise decision; the practical employment of these courts was another matter.
Appointment of members rested with the president, by and with
the advice and consent of the Senate. Amendments to the act allowed the president to appoint additional courts in geographical
military departments and for various state regions.

The president made every effort to appoint qualified military
invalids to fill vacancies on these new courts, but as time went by,
fewer and fewer candidates became available. All in all, the retention of qualified individuals for these important positions did not
go as smoothly as expected. A later amendment requiring army
commanders to review the cases nullified much of the advantage of
the new courts. The burden of this review by the overworked staff
of each army raised the ire of all army commanders.[10]

The creation of these new courts should have not only relieved
the heavy pressure on military commands to convene courts-martial, but it also should have provided more consistently competent
members and judge advocates. The most important person on a
military court or court-martial was the judge advocate.

This unique position demanded a person with knowledge of
military law, command experience, perseverance, and patience. The
delicate task of prosecution of the military's case and protection of
the rights of the accused required the wisdom of Solomon.

The proper wording of both charges and specifications was
the duty of the judge advocate. Add to this the fact that he had no
voice in preferring charges; this was the responsibility of the person bringing such charges; that person was often a senior officer
while most judge advocates were junior officers, lieutenants or captains. But if the charges or specifications were improperly drawn,
the findings were likely to be disapproved by the reviewing authority. The many such examples of disapproval seen were proof of the
incompetency of numerous judge advocates.

When charges were preferred, they would have been signed by
the officer making them. He would then be termed the prosecutor;

this would remain the case except in those circumstances where a high-ranking officer names a subordinate to prefer charges. This prosecutor may not be a civilian nor may he be an enlisted soldier bringing charges against an officer. Such action is permitted, provided the complaint is delivered through proper channels. If a civilian were to charge a private soldier with stealing his livestock, such action would need to be prosecuted through the soldier's command and the charges preferred by a responsible officer.

If any infirmity exists in the presentation of charges, such as an absence of culpability on the part of the accused, it should be recognized by the judge advocate and further proceeding of the trial should be suspended. Moreover, no change or alteration in charges can be made after a plea by the accused.

Young volunteer officers could hardly be expected to know how to handle such responsibilities. The military justice system was designed to function within a well-organized regular service made up of qualified young officers who had graduated from military schools and who had had some experience sitting upon courts, and who had further enjoyed a few years of leisurely service to learn all about military custom and operations.

As cases backlogged, men awaiting trial were kept under arrest for long periods, contrary to the articles of war. Moreover, it was inconvenient to keep men under guard when the army was on the move. Some of the hard cases were sent to military prisons while awaiting trial, but this too was inconvenient for authorities as well as an injustice to the accused.

No accurate estimate of the number of desertions that occurred of prisoners awaiting trial can be obtained, nor for that matter of those who deserted between trial and sentencing or after sentencing was pronounced. Much has been made of the inconsistencies of trials, court sentences, pardons, remissions, and commutations. These criticisms are generally applied from a contemporary point of view. But to properly evaluate the performance of officers involved, one must understand the limitations under which they were laboring during the 1860s.

The system for recruitment in both the Union and the Confederate armies was made to order for undermining military discipline. At the beginning of the war, short-term service for volunteer units was standard procedure. This oversight was soon amended to receive volunteers for "during the war" enlistments, but thousands had to be induced to re-enlist at the expiration of their original term of service through bounties and furloughs. The Conscript Act was a disaster for both sides, but much more so for the Southern cause; as their manpower dwindled, they were required to rely more and more heavily on draftees.[11] Unfair exemptions for special persons caused further resentment; and bounties paid for enlistments and the act of allowing draftees to obtain substitutes further eroded discipline.

As desertions mounted, presidential amnesty was offered; another action that is easy to criticize, but desperation required the government to do anything it possibly could to get men back into the ranks. Nevertheless, the outcome of these offers of leniency was simply a further erosion of discipline.[12]

Thousands of deserters were either not prosecuted for their crimes or were acquitted under the various amnesties offered. The uncertainty that the offers created probably caused more additional desertions than the number of men recovered. In addition to the thousands forgiven of their crimes under amnesty, the president pardoned nearly all capital cases appealed to him. Political necessity took precedence over military discipline; consequently, a very large number of culprits escaped their just deserts in order to appease those voices of protest against the evils of war. Both Lincoln and Davis had similar records in the extension of pardons, and army commanders in both the Union and Confederate armies were compromised in their efforts to keep their men in the ranks. Military justice in the Confederate States Armies was a major issue affecting the efficiency of those armies; the importance of the subject has never been properly addressed.

The records of cases are spotty, as are many of the Confederate records, but a framework of cases exists in the files of the A&IGO. Copies of general orders listing general courts-martial were sent to Richmond, along with the proceedings of cases. Clerks at the A&IGO made handwritten records of these cases. The ledgers contain the name, rank, unit, and company of the accused, along with a summary of his sentence. The date of the trial is shown as well as the date the facts were recorded in the ledger.

These ledgers have been microfilmed in the National Archives under record group #109, chapter 1 (volumes 194–99). Military units were required to forward documents on general courts-martial cases to the attention of the judge advocate in the A&IGO. Copies of the regimental courts-martial were not required to be sent to Richmond. Nevertheless, several cases contained in record group #109 are regimental cases, and, of course, all general cases did not find their way to General Samuel Cooper's office. Approximately 20,000 cases are recorded in these ledgers; even though the information is limited, further facts can be uncovered from general or special orders whenever they can be located.

Various Confederate orders are contained in the National Archives. Those that can be located concerning courts-martial or military courts provide the necessary facts covering cases. Unfortunately, many of these important documents are missing, thus leaving hundreds and hundreds of cases to mere speculation.

Copies of the special orders from the A&IGO are contained in the rare books room of the Virginia State Archives in Richmond as well as in the National Archives. These important files contain the orders from the secretary of war on all important military matters, including the action of the president or the secretary on courts-martial cases that were referred to them.

The proceedings, which are the handwritten records of the trials signed by the president of the court and the judge advocate, have not been located. These valuable records were probably lost in one of the many fires in the fall of Richmond.

The compiled service records (CSRs) of the individuals often contain much valuable information. Many do not have any record of court-martial, but in a few examples of regimental courts, copies of the proceedings can be found in the CSR.

By employing and comparing these various records, conclusive evidence of cases tried can often be ascertained. In many examples, results can only be inferred, and in others, information is either contradictory or totally lacking.

Identification of some individuals is virtually impossible because of the lack of unit information. In other examples, proper identification is precluded by misspelling of names. For consistency, the accepted name shown on the CSR has been used when it differs from that in the ledger. Clerks in the A&IGO copied names onto the ledgers from general orders; many of these general orders list the soldier's name incorrectly. Variations occur in listing men's names in the CSRs, but these variations are often pointed out so that errors can be corrected.

Many individuals could not be identified in CSRs because of faulty records for some units. The 5th Confederate Infantry is one example of spotty recordkeeping; the 25th Virginia Battalion Local Defense Troops also misplaced the records of several men; the 22d Alabama Infantry is another, as is the 1st Louisiana Battalion of Zouaves. These are but a few of the organizations that had gaps in the CSRs. In some cases, such as the 5th Confederate, recordkeeping suffered from the consolidation from other regiments; the 5th was formed from two Tennessee regiments, then consolidated with another Confederate regiment and then became known as both the 5th Confederate and the 9th Confederate. Some organizations had the misfortune to lose records or have them captured, never to be found again.

For the majority of the hundreds of names that could not be found in the CSRs, the cause is simply missing records. A few cannot be identified because of misspelled names or possibly misidentified units, but these are limited. Given the circumstances of military recordkeeping during the Civil War and the collapse of the Confederacy with the fall of Richmond, it is nothing short of astounding that any valuable records were preserved by the Union and Confederate authorities.

No attempt has been made to identify the civilians tried. Many were employed by the army and therefore subject to courts-martial, such as teamsters, sutlers, storekeepers, and slaves working for their army masters. The other group of civilians culpable to courts-martial were those caught spying; these were classified as non-Confederate citizens and if tried under section 2 of the articles of war and found guilty of spying were then sentenced to death.

A few trials appear for Union soldiers prosecuted under Confederate courts-martial. Some of these were deserters from Union regiments who turned up in the Confederate lines and immediately became suspects; others were simply lost and found themselves in a Confederate camp when seeking their own bivouacs. Those who could not verify their actions would face court-martial charges. Most were acquitted and allowed to return to the Federal lines or to join Confederate units if they were so inclined. Union soldiers caught in the act of spying would be charged under section 2 of the articles of war, and if convicted would then be subject to a death sentence. Those charged with and convicted of breaking parole would also be subject to a death sentence.

The A&IGO records show 23 Union soldiers tried under Confederate courts-martial. One or two of these were civilians posing as soldiers, but the rest were doubtless soldiers, although approximately eight could not be identified.

Chapter II
Courts-martial and Their Origin

The first code of laws for governing an army within the American states was hastily passed by the Continental Congress on June 30, 1775. These original articles numbered 69 with 16 more added on November 7, 1775. These rules begin with a reference to an allegiance to King George III:

> Whereas His Majesty's most faithful subjects in these colonies are reduced to a dangerous and critical situation by the attempts of the British minister to carry into execution by force of arms, several unconstitutional and oppressive acts of the British parliament for laying taxes in America, to enforce the collection of those taxes, and for altering and changing the constitution and internal police of some of these colonies, in violation of the natural and civil rights of the colonies.[1]

On September 20, 1776, following the Declaration of Independence, the above articles were revised to include the words "The United States" wherever appropriate, along with other additions or amendments.[2]

These articles remained the rules for the United States Army, with some revisions imposed on May 31, 1786, until Congress passed the Articles of April 10, 1806, which were those in effect at the beginning of the Civil War.[3]

Just as the Confederate States adopted the code being used by the United States on March 6, 1861, the American colonies had copied the existing British code used by its ministerial army.[4]

The Articles of April 10, 1806, numbered 101, whereas the British Articles of War of 1765 totaled 111. The British articles were drawn in sections, with each section numbered and titled, then those articles pertaining to a section were listed under that section and numbered. Some sections contained only one or two articles, but others contained articles numbering in the twenties (see appendix 3).

Some of these articles were peculiar to the British service and contained rulings that were ignored by the American code, such as the single article under section 10: carriage; others were carried over into the American code in virtually identical language, such as Article #1 under section 6—desertion:

> All officers and soldiers, who having received pay, or having been duly enlisted in our service,[and] shall be convicted of having deserted the same, shall suffer death, or such other punishments as by a Court-martial shall be inflicted.

The 20th AOW of the Confederate States reads: "All officers and soldiers who have received pay, or have been duly enlisted in the service of the Confederate States, and shall be convicted of having deserted the same, shall suffer death, or such other punishment as, by sentence of a Court-martial, shall be inflicted."

In addition to adopting the many articles from those of the British code of 1765, the Americans also adopted the procedures for courts-martial. Most of the standards provided in the American articles were taken directly from those of Great Britain, such as naming general and regimental courts to convene, as well as setting forth the numbers for each. The British code restricted the meeting hours for courts-martial between 8:00 a.m. and 3:00 p.m. They established the vote of a majority for conviction and the restriction of announcing the verdict until approved by convening authority as well as the secrecy of the individual voting. And so it was with mostly all the procedures in the American code.

The English courts were originally established by William the Conqueror. They were first identified by various names such as "The King's Court of Chivalry," "The Court of the High Constable and Marshal of England," sometimes called "The Court of Arms," or "The Court of Honour." They were empowered to try "all matters touching honor and arms," the rights of prisoners of war, and generally the offense of soldiers contrary to the laws of the army. One of the unique characteristics of these sessions is that they were held outside in the open to establish a level of credibility as well as to show an example to observing members of the military.

The authority for the British articles rests with the Crown, but the American articles were rooted in the constitution, and the power to extend, change, or revoke them rested with Congress. The president of the United States and the president of the Confederate States held some special powers under the articles of war; the most consequential was the act of pardon, but these presidents had no power to change or suspend such laws, and just as passage of civil laws rested with the Congress, so did those laws governing the military forces.

Even though the authority to create the laws rests with Congress, the military court-martial itself exists as an extension of the powers of the president as commander in chief of the armed forces. Military courts of the 1860s were not law courts in the true sense; moreover, they had no relation to the judiciary of the United States nor did they have under the laws of the Confederate States. They were temporary tribunals called into existence to enforce order and discipline in the armed forces. They functioned, within the limits of the articles of war, as creatures of military orders.

During the 10 years preceding the Civil War, from 1851 to 1861, the United States Army tried approximately 7,550 general courts-martial cases; a few of these cases were courts of inquiry.[5] Several of the officers of the Confederate States Armies, who subsequently became senior officers, sat upon some of these courts. A few presided as presidents of the court or as judge advocates but this practical experience was limited to a handful of officers. These persons, most of whom became army or corps commanders, struggled throughout the war to properly enforce the requirements for courts-martial.

These commanders whose responsibility it was to approve findings and sentences were frequently required to disapprove the courts' actions and set the accused free because of mishandling by the courts. Orders are filled with criticism of the courts for sloppy work and the frustration of the commanders is obvious. But in all examples noted, the rights of the accused were paramount.

When the war began, there were only two major works in circulation covering the procedures for courts-martial:

1. *The Practice of Courts-Martial* by Major General Alexander Macomb, published in 1841,[6]
2. *Observations on Military Law and the Constitution and Practice of Courts-Martial* by William C. DeHart, Captain, 2d U.S. Artillery, published in 1846.[7]

Even this limited material was not available to most of those in need of it in the Southern armies. A few copies were carried by the Confederate officers who had served in the United States Army, but the typical volunteer officer had no access to such publications. Charles Henry Lee, a Virginia attorney, had been appointed assistant adjutant general with the rank of major on October 27, 1862. His duties were performed in the office of judge advocate in

the War Department. In 1863, he published his famous work outlining procedures for courts-martial; an expanded edition was
printed in 1864.[8]

Lee's work draws heavily upon DeHart, but addresses the current needs of the officers of the Confederacy. Both Lee and DeHart
emphasize the inconsistencies of the articles of war as well as the
vague wording in many instances. Lee did a good job of outlining
the requirements for courts-martial, and those officers fortunate
enough to obtain a copy of his work could face their duties on a
court with confidence.

The question of jurisdiction of a court-martial is sometimes a
serious issue. Outside the area of martial law, which was only occasionally imposed in limited areas of the Confederacy by the Confederate States Armies, military courts-martial can only try those
persons subject to military law. In most examples, this is a clear
issue; occasionally it is not. In addition to soldiers serving in the
army, those persons subject to military jurisdiction were liable.
These might be such people as teamsters driving army wagons, or
sutlers, or other civilian employees. In addition, section 2 of the
articles of war puts those persons "not citizens of or owing allegiance to the Confederate States of America" found lurking as spies
in jeopardy of trial.

Occasionally, a soldier would successfully plead in bar of trial
on the defense that he had been discharged prior to being charged.
If such a defense were valid, he would not be subject to a trial. The
soldier must have been a member of the military when the alleged
crime was committed and he must still be a member when brought
up on charges.

Private Richard M. Brooks of Company D, 47th Virginia Infantry, was charged with desertion in General Order (GO) #17, Army of
Northern Virginia, February 11, 1863. On the general order that
lists the outcome of the trial, Brooks is found not guilty because
"he was not properly in the service of the Confederate States at the
time he is charged in the specification."[9] Since the specification
does not appear in the general order it is impossible to identify the
dates, but it appears that Brooks was between enlistments when
he was charged with desertion. He enlisted June 4, 1861, and at
that time probably enrolled for a term of one year or less. The order
lists his company as "E," whereas he is carried on the rolls in Company D.

The 96th AOW as adopted by the Confederate States sets forth
a list of persons subject to courts-martial:

> All officers, conductors, gunners, matrosses, drivers, or other
> persons whatsoever, receiving pay or hire in the service of the

artillery, or corps of engineers in the Confederate States, shall be governed by the aforesaid rules and articles, and shall be subject to be tried by courts-martial in like manner with the officers and soldiers of the other troops in the service of the Confederate States.

In addition, the 60th AOW adds that "all sutlers and retainers in camp, and all persons whatsoever serving with the Armies of the Confederate States" are subject to orders and the rules and discipline of war.

Courts-martial tried 178 Confederate citizens and 14 slaves or free Negroes on charges that were almost always unstated; since those charges could not be ascertained a rather important question as to why they were tried remains unanswered.

When a court was assembled, the members took their respective places on the long side of the table opposite the judge advocate; the court was then proclaimed open. The prisoner was brought in attended by a guard if necessary, but usually not. He would then be seated to the right of the judge advocate at a separate small table and without fetters or irons.

The names of the members were called out by the judge advocate; the order for convening the court was read and the judge advocate asked the prisoner if he had any objections to any member of the court. Should the prisoner challenge any member, such comments were entered into the record and the court was cleared for deliberation with the named member abstaining and withdrawing from the discussion. Upon reassembling the court, the judge advocate announced the decision of the court and the challenged member either resumed his seat or retired from the court.

Although prisoners rarely challenged members, it was important to protect the prisoner's rights in this fashion. Such gross oversights as allowing the prosecutor (officer preferring charges) to be a member of the court would be valid grounds for a prisoner's objection.

On November 4, 1862, 3d Lt. Jesse L. Furguson, Company C, 32d N.C. Troops, was tried on two charges: (1) disobedience of orders, and (2) conduct prejudicial to good order and military discipline. He was acquitted of the first charge, but found guilty of the second, and sentenced to be suspended from command and pay for one month.

Furguson's unit was assigned to the Department of North Carolina at the time of his trial. Major General Gustavus W. Smith issued his orders as part of his review of the trial disapproving the proceedings, findings, and sentence because the officer preferring charges was a member of the court.[10]

Once the issue of challenge had been resolved and the court reconvened, the judge advocate would administer the oath to the assembled members naming each one but accepting their common oath together; remaining standing the members would await a similar swearing in of the judge advocate by the president of the court.

Members took their seats to the right and left of the president's chair in order of seniority. That is, the officer next to the president in rank would be placed upon his right, the second in rank upon his left and so on until all were seated. If a full court was present, six members would be on the president's right and six on his left.

On the opposite long side of the table, the judge advocate would be seated facing the president, the prisoner was placed at a small separate table to the right and slightly to the rear of the judge advocate. If counsel was provided for the prisoner, he would be seated at the prisoner's table. Upon the approval of the court, a prisoner may be accompanied by a friend who may act as counsel, usually another soldier, rarely a civilian. This person may not address the court, but he may assist the accused in writing out questions to hand to the judge advocate to direct toward witnesses or others. Occasionally, courts would allow counsel to read a prisoner's final statement at the conclusion of the trial.[11]

It was unusual for an enlisted man to have counsel at his trial. Officers, particularly high-ranking officers, were often accompanied by counsel; in complicated trials the judge advocate may be supported by such an advisor. But in no example was such advisor allowed to prosecute the case, and the defense counsel was only allowed to address the court where special permission was granted.

The ruling for courts recognizing counsel is illustrated by General E. Kirby Smith's comment on a case tried in his Trans-Mississippi Department in July 1864. Second Lieutenant Thomas K. Lowe was brought up on charges of (1) drunkenness, and (2) conduct unbecoming an officer and a gentleman. He was found guilty of the first charge and not guilty of the second charge. He was sentenced to be suspended from rank and command for four months, and suspension from pay and emoluments for a like period, and to remain with his command for the time suspended.

In his summation to the trial in his general order, General Smith indicates that the record shows that 2d Lt. T. K. Lowe asked until the following morning to prepare his written closing statement. This delay was granted by the court. However on the next morning the court reassembled, with all members and the judge advocate present, but with Lieutenant Lowe absent. The record indicated that the cause of absence was unknown, but the counsel for the accused informed the court that the accused would not present a written defense. The court was cleared, and proceeded to consider its finding and sentence.

General Smith disapproved the finding and sentence of the court with a lecture notifying them that the accused alone must waive his right to a closing defense and for the court to proceed with the trial without the presence of the accused nullified the entirety. He added an incisive comment on the role of counsel in the military courts of the 1860s:

> The record no where shows that the accused ever introduced any one as his counsel, and even if he had, the Court had no right to take any steps during the progress of the trial, (except when cleared for deliberation, from time to time, when necessary) without the personal presence of the accused. The trial is not deemed to be closed until the accused's defense and the Judge Advocate's reply, are in; or the parties announce that they have no statements to make. The counsel, when one is introduced, only *advises* the accused, and has no right to address the Court, for any reason whatever. [12]

Military courts of the 1860s considered the judge advocate counsel for the accused. He was specifically charged with protection of the rights of the accused under AOW #69, but concurrently was required to prosecute the government's case against the accused, an impossible dilemma.

Once the court was properly seated and sworn and any challenges dealt with, the judge advocate would read the charge to the prisoner in open court. The prisoner would be addressed by his proper rank and name and questioned: "You have heard the charge preferred against you; how say you, are you guilty or not guilty?"

The prisoner may plead guilty or not guilty or he may stand mute (refuse to answer), but he may not qualify his plea. He may plead guilty to a specification and not guilty to a charge. If he is to be found not guilty, he must be acquitted of the charge, or conversely if he is to be found guilty he must be convicted of the charge. Prisoners may also make special pleas in bar of a trial; reasons commonly cited for such pleas may be a former conviction or a former acquittal, or a pardon. Prisoners who felt themselves pardoned by the president's amnesty, for example, may plead in bar of a trial.

Another common defense for bar of a trial was the statute of limitations for offenses committed more than two years ago. This plea becomes a valid defense only provided that no converse action prevented prosecution of the case. A prisoner who deserted more than two years ago, but who was only recently arrested and brought to trial could not invoke such a plea as a bar to trial. [13]

Once the accused entered a plea, the case was ready for trial. The judge advocate would direct all witnesses to retire until called and all interested spectators to return. The first witness was then called and sworn by the judge advocate. The name, rank, and unit of the witness were recorded and the examination was conducted in the presence of the full court and the accused. Most testimony was given in response to questions delivered by the judge advocate. The prisoner may direct questions to witnesses by submitting them to the judge advocate in writing; the members of the court submit their questions in the same way to the judge advocate. If any question was objected to, the court would retire to decide whether to proceed to submit the question to the witness. If the majority of the court decided to proceed, then the question was put to the witness and it appeared as a question by the court.

After all the witnesses for the prosecution had testified, then the effort for the prosecution was closed. The prisoner was now ready to begin his defense. If extra time was needed by the accused, he would be allowed it by an adjournment if necessary. Once he began his defense, no further proof by the prosecution would be submitted.

If the witnesses for the defense had been called for, they would now be introduced. It was the responsibility of the judge advocate to procure such witnesses. Should they be civilians who refuse to appear, testimony may be obtained by a justice of the peace; however, this provision was of doubtful value in many trials.

Witnesses for the defense were examined in the same manner as those for the prosecution. After all examinations were closed, the prisoner was allowed to address the court to put his defense in the most favorable light possible. Such efforts attempted by the uneducated enlisted men were usually crude. An articulate person at this time could possibly influence the court to acquittal or in case of conviction, to the extension of a recommendation of mercy, but the average soldier undergoing such trials was rarely articulate; he was often illiterate, and was usually unfamiliar with the rules of military law.

At this time, any pleas to bar of judgement would be made. Though such pleas are unusual, the most commonly granted are those to the mentally incompetent. Several examples were seen whereby the accused was acquitted because he was of unsound mind.

Private John S. Wilson, Company F, 45th N.C. Troops, enlisted March 13, 1862, and deserted August 3, 1862. He was tried in October 1862, on a charge of desertion and found guilty of absence without leave. However, the court declined to punish Wilson because they were convinced that he was of unsound mind. They recommended that he be discharged, and his CSR indicates that he was given such a discharge on January 17, 1863.[14]

Other pleas of this type might be one of ignorance, of circumstance, or of laws. Occasionally a soldier had not been read the articles of war or he committed an act that was not truly criminal on his part. If a soldier could prove that he had not received the required reading of the articles, then he could possibly prove that he was unaware that the act for which he was convicted was contrary to military law. Such a defense for a veteran soldier was a weak one, but courts were lenient in passing judgement and sentence on new recruits, especially young ones. Again and again general orders show the compassion of the courts with comments to the effect of "due to the youth of the accused...,"or "due to the inexperience of the accused..." A similar plea of this type is that of an illegal order. Although soldiers are not required to obey illegal orders, courts seldom grant such a defense, for the qualification of an order being unlawful becomes a difficult point of law.

Probably the most frequently employed defense against judgement is that of intoxication on the part of the accused. The soldier who strikes his superior while in a drunken rage has no defense in a military trial. Courts would tend to regard the drinking as an aggravation rather than a defense.

Written entries into the proceedings were very important components. Whenever changes were necessary, it was required that erasures not be made, but rather a line drawn through the altered material.

Once all evidence was heard, the trial was closed. At this point, it was the duty of the judge advocate to perform what would be termed a summation of the whole case. In this responsibility the judge advocate has a difficult task. In lengthy trials, he may begin by reading the entire proceedings, at minimum a fair copy would be laid before the members. In many cases this reading was dispensed with, but the judge advocate would still be expected to inform the court of the legal implications of any evidence or testimony. This duty is a delicate one, for he may not attempt to influence the opinions of the members for or against conviction.

After all deliberation by the court was completed, a vote on guilt or innocence was taken. Voting proceeds on the specifications and then the charge; guilt of one does not necessarily imply guilt on the other. The charge is the offense that becomes punishable if guilt is concluded; thus a prisoner may be found guilty of one or more specifications, but be found not guilty of the charge. In some examples, he may be guilty of one or more specifications and found not guilty of the charge but guilty of a lesser charge. Such findings are not contrary to military law where the guilt of a lesser related charge is found. The example most frequently seen is that of finding a prisoner not guilty of "desertion" but guilty of "absence without official leave." On the other hand, it is improper to find guilt on an unrelated charge. If a prisoner is charged with "theft" and found not guilty, he may not be convicted of "absence without official leave" even though in the course of the trial it is proved that he was guilty of that offense.

The taking of the votes for guilt or innocence was an important procedure. The custom used during the 1860s was to poll the opinions of each member of the court (the court having been cleared of all persons except the judge advocate and the members) beginning with the most junior in rank. The judge advocate would address each member individually: "from the evidence in the matter now before you, how say you of the specification (or charge) ; is the prisoner guilty or not guilty?" The vote upon each specification was given and recorded, then the vote upon the charge was taken and also recorded. A written record of the voting was made and retained by the judge advocate. The custom of accepting the votes of the junior members first was done to prevent their being influenced by the voting of the senior officers.

A variation of the method of recording a verbal vote was to allow each member to record on a slip of paper "guilty" or "not guilty"; after these votes are polled by the judge advocate he announces the result. If that result is "guilty," the judge advocate then proceeds to accept a vote for punishment from each member in a similar manner as that for which guilt or innocence was taken; that is if individual slips were originally used, the members are again expected to record their vote for punishment on slips of paper.

The sentence is determined by simple majority, just as guilt or innocence was determined; but all members of the court must vote on both; no abstinence is allowed. If the sentence should be death, then at least two-thirds of the members must vote for death. Even though the judge advocate must keep a record of the voting, that record must be kept secret and in no manner divulged in orders. It is entirely improper for orders to state the number of votes cast for innocence or guilt, other than to state that two-thirds voted for the sentence of death, whenever such sentence is adjudged. That wording is an absolute requirement in the record.

Two examples illustrate the improper action by the court and the reviewing authority in divulging the voting record of the court in sentencing:

Privates J. Sullivan and H. M. Bishop both of Company B, 2d Battalion, S.C. Sharpshooters, were part of Gen. P.G.T. Beauregard's command in the Department of South Carolina, Georgia, and Florida. Sullivan had enlisted as a substitute for W. T.

Miller on February 19, 1862, and deserted on August 29, 1862. Bishop enlisted March 20, 1862, and deserted on September 13, 1862, in the course of which he stole the horse, saddle, and bridle of a Confederate trooper.

Both men were tried before a general court-martial during the month of December 1862 and both were convicted of desertion with Bishop also receiving a vote of guilty for the second charge of "stealing."

General Beauregard issued GO #17, Department of South Carolina, Georgia, and Florida, January 28, 1863, setting forth the charges, specifications, and findings in each case and adding the following paragraph to Sullivan's case:

> And the court does, therefore, unanimously sentence the said Private J. Sullivan, Company "B" 2d Battalion S.C. Sharpshooters, "to be shot to death with musketry, at such time and place as the commanding General may direct."

A similar paragraph is added to the details of Bishop's trial:

> And the court does, therefore sentence the said Private H.M. Bishop, "to be shot to death with musketry at such time and place as the commanding General may direct, there being but one dissenting voice in the Court."

The court should have stated that two-thirds of the members approved the sentence in each case and nothing more. But the greater sin falls upon Beauregard for divulging the voting record in general orders. Either he or his reviewing officer likely found the voting record as part of the trial information prepared by the judge advocate in the case, and decided to make it a part of the general orders. The added irony is that as a summary to his final paragraph in GO #17 where he sets forth his approval or disapproval of the various cases contained in the order, Beauregard admonishes the court for seven transgressions committed in their various trials.[15]

Both men were ordered to be shot one week later; however, their sentence was suspended and Bishop was pardoned by the president.[16] No records could be found on Sullivan beyond the suspension of the orders for his execution.

Just as the voting count must be kept secret, the findings and sentence of the court must not be made known until published in general orders. This nicety was routinely violated by officers; senior commanders often made it their business to learn the outcome of trials whenever possible.

The judge advocate was then required to complete the written proceedings by recording the findings of the court, and if guilty, including the sentence. At the end of the text on the last page of the proceedings, the president of the court signed at the right with the proper notation of his rank; the judge advocate signed below and to the left of the president's signature.

The pages of proceedings were then numbered if this had not already been done, and stitched together at the top with cloth string and forwarded to the general officer who convened the court. The prisoner, if a private soldier, was usually returned to confinement to await the announcement of the findings and sentence. If the prisoner was a commissioned officer, he was usually kept in the status of arrest, but sometimes this restriction was remitted by the officer placing him in arrest. That officer was usually the same as the one who preferred charges.

In the United States service, courts of inquiry were provided in the Articles of 1786; moreover, they had been used by Resolution of Congress during the American Revolution and by General Washington during that conflict. The articles adopted in 1806 provided for courts of inquiry in AOW #91 and #92. These were incorporated into the articles accepted by the Confederate service.

The 91st AOW sets forth the composition of such tribunals; they shall consist of one or more officers, not exceeding three, and a judge advocate, or other suitable person as recorder. It confers power upon the court to summon witnesses and to examine them under oath, but further adds that the members shall not make known their opinion of the case, except where required to do so by proper authority.

The 92d AOW contains the most important restrictions upon the appointment of such courts: "No court of inquiry can be ordered unless by direction of the President of the Confederate States, or at the request of the party accused." The necessity for such restriction cannot be overemphasized. Ambitious commanders could injure the reputation of a subordinate who would have little if any defense or protection against such inquiry.

The early use of courts of inquiry in the American service were not restricted by the Articles of 1806, and certainly the most famous trial of the American Revolution was performed by such a court. On on September 29, 1780, Gen. George Washington convened a court to investigate the case of Maj. John André, adjutant general to the British army. The court or "board" as named by Washington consisted of six major generals (Nathanael Greene, Lord Stirling, Arthur St. Clair, the Marquis de la Fayette, Robert Howe, and the Baron von Steuben), and eight brigadier generals (Samuel Holden Parsons, James Clinton, Henry Knox, John Glover, John Patterson, Edward Hand, Jedediah Huntington, and John Stark). John Lawrence was named judge advocate. The board was directed to report a precise state of the case, with an "opinion of the light in which he (André) ought to be considered and the punishment that ought to be inflicted."

The court reported that the accused "ought to be considered as a spy from the enemy, and that, agreeable to the law and usage of nations, he ought to suffer death."[17] Accordingly, Washington issued orders that André should hang, and the sentence was carried out at noon on October 2, 1780.

Courts of inquiry had no such power during the Civil War, they were merely an investigative body. They provided evidence to the president on important matters, following which he might order a court-marital or instruct one of his commanders to do so. In most cases, courts of inquiry convened at the request of the "party accused." This was typically done by the individual in an attempt to clear his name or to remove a cloud of suspicion. Both soldiers and officers could request such courts, but it was usually officers who did so.

The accused could appear at the proceeding of a court or he could decline to do so. It would seem to be in his best interest to be present, for he had the opportunity to not only give testimony, but to question or cross-examine witnesses. In addition, he was entitled to counsel if needed.

Courts-martial, except for deliberation and other special procedures, were open courts; however, it was unusual for a court of inquiry to convene with open doors. The nature of such bodies makes open courts potentially injurious to the reputation of the accused; for this reason these tribunals usually sit with doors closed. Furthermore, no time restrictions applied to courts of inquiry. Courts-martial were limited to meet between 8:00 a.m. and 3:00 p.m. unless expressly relieved from the time restraints by convening authority.[18]

Findings of courts-martial are published in general orders; results of courts of inquiry were not necessarily published. If a reason existed for doing so, it may be done. As will be seen in chapter 3, the Confederate Congress authorized courts of inquiry to deal with the special problem of drunkenness of officers.

After the reviewing authority decided upon the findings and sentence of each case, his orders were issued for either the punishment he decided should be inflicted, or if the accused were acquitted or the punishment disapproved then orders were issued for the accused to be returned to duty; or in some cases, the punishment was suspended, awaiting the action of the president. In any event, the proceedings along with a copy of the general orders were forwarded to the A&IGO to the attention of the judge advocate. Thus, all cases were to be routed to the War Department for review; those that required the action of the president were processed in his direction, but all others also were checked to see that proper procedures were being followed.

The records of garrison or regimental courts-martial were sent to division headquarters where they were retained. It was not required that these proceedings be forwarded to the A&IGO; however, many were sent simply because commanders were reluctant to impose sentences without the approval of the president or the secretary of war. This was a great waste of executive power, and it was one of the reasons for General Samuel Cooper's general order to commanders to assume their rightful responsibility.[19]

Chapter III
Charges

The charge is the formal written accusation which frames the offense the prisoner is considered guilty of. In military custom, the charge is supported or explained by the specification or specifications. The latter explains how the charge was committed.

The charge may be in general language, but the specifications must be drawn exactly, as to both enable the prisoner to defend himself or to allow the prosecution to expressly prove the charge. The language used in drawing charges should be succinct, and yet specific enough so as to allow no doubt of the offense committed.

The charge is framed by the prosecutor who is usually a superior officer of the accused. In the case of enlisted men, it is always a superior officer; in the case of officers, it can be an inferior officer, but it is very unusual for a subordinate to bring charges against his superior officer. In most such examples grievances would be made known to higher authority who would in turn prefer charges if warranted.

In military cases, the charge is similar to the indictment in civil cases, but the wording should be much more direct in courts-martial. The charge must specifically identify the military offense that the accused is considered guilty of. Military offenses are set forth in the 101 articles of war; however, not all articles specify the military offenses, some merely state procedures. It is an essential responsibility of all commanders to assure that a thorough reading and explanation of the articles of war be delivered to all soldiers upon enlistment.

The wording of charges need not expressly include the citation of an article of war. However, the practice of simply stating that a charge is a violation of a specific article of war was sometimes inaccurate. Charles Henry Lee is emphatic on the exact wording of charges.[1] DeHart covers the propriety of charges in one well-worded sentence:

> It is the duty of a court-martial, after being duly organized, and when the charges are read, to judge of their propriety, not only as to the nature of them with reference to their jurisdiction, but also to the precision of the language used, and the statement, or definition of the crime.[2]

Frequently, such wording resulted in the disapproval of proceedings. For example, to charge a person who had deserted the service with a "violation of Article of War #20," was unacceptable. AOW #20 merely sets forth the penalty for desertion, and so it is with several other articles. In this case, the simple word "desertion" would serve as a proper charge; the specification should then state the circumstances to describe the act of desertion committed by the accused.

Officers were discouraged from piling on charges to assure a conviction. The most frequently added charge was "conduct to the prejudice of good order and military discipline," under AOW #99. This catch-all offense was added to the articles to allow commanders to prosecute any offensive action that they wished to bring before a court-martial. When properly applied, AOW #99 is a useful citation; any general misconduct may be prosecuted properly under this article provided the offender is charged with "conduct to the prejudice of good order and military discipline."

Commanders would occasionally add the charge to other citations to try to assure a conviction. A soldier charged with "striking his superior officer" could be sentenced to death under AOW #9; such action on the soldier's part is obviously conduct to the prejudice of good order and military discipline. But it is unnecessary to charge a prisoner with a violation of AOW #99 if he is charged with "striking an officer."

More than 700 offenders were charged, in the examples where charges were identified, with "conduct to the prejudice of good order and military discipline." In the vast majority of these cases, no other charges were brought against the accused, which indicates a proper use of the charge. An additional 70 or so cases were cited with a "violation of AOW #99."

Among those charged was a large contingent of officers, so it proves to be a proper citation for officers who commit acts of misconduct that are not serious enough to be called "conduct unbecoming an officer and a gentleman."

There are examples of multiple violations committed by prisoners that warrant dual charges, or occasionally more than two. Sometimes an accused may be guilty of "absence without official leave" and "desertion" over a related period of time and then brought to trial on both charges.

The articles of war do not specifically define "absence without official leave" or "desertion." Articles #21, #41, and #50 refer to various forms of unauthorized absence, and AOW #20 spells out the punishments that may be inflicted upon conviction of desertion, but neither offense is properly described. The distinction between the two is one of intent. The courts of the 1860s dealt with the problem of unauthorized departure of individuals by trying to determine if the absentee returned to his command or intended to return to establish that he was only guilty of AWOL. On the other hand if the court determined that the accused did not intend to return, then he was considered a deserter.

The issue of charging more than one individual with a crime becomes more difficult to resolve. The accepted custom of the service was to try prisoners separately. There are situations which demand the common prosecution of two or more individuals because of the nature of the crime committed. But whenever the offense warrants, each accused should be tried separately.

Examples of both situations are found in cases tried by the Confederate States Armies. A clear illustration of a common prosecution occurred in January 1863; the general orders approving the trial were issued on January 23, 1863.[3]

The charge in the above case was a "violation of the 54th Article of War," and though the specifications are not contained in the general order, it may be inferred that the participants were disorderly in barracks or on the line of march. The members were all part of Brig. Gen. Ambrose R. Wright's Brigade of Maj. Gen. Richard H. Anderson's Division of the First Corps:

1. Bailey, W.—Pvt.—Co. E—22d Georgia Infantry
2. Belcher, O. R.—Pvt.—Co. D—3d Georgia Infantry
3. Bruce, James—Pvt.—Co. E—22d Georgia Infantry
4. Fostella, W. W.—Pvt.—Co. E—22d Georgia Infantry
5. Foster, B. F.—Pvt.—Co. E—22d Georgia Infantry
6. Gentry, J. D.—Pvt.—Co. E—22d Georgia Infantry
7. Hook, David R.—Pvt.—Co. E—22d Georgia Infantry
8. King, Elias—Pvt.—Co. E—22d Georgia Infantry
9. Oliver, L. K.—Pvt.—Co. E—22d Georgia Infantry
10. Pannell, Wm. B.—Pvt.—Co. E—22d Georgia Infantry
11. Samples, Jesse—Pvt.—Co. E—22d Georgia Infantry
12. Scott, J.—Pvt.—Co. B—48th Georgia Infantry

13. Shaw, Isaac—Pvt.—Co. E—22d Georgia Infantry
14. Taylor, N.—Pvt.—Co. E—22d Georgia Infantry
15. Webb, J.—Pvt.—Co. E—22d Georgia Infantry
16. Webb, J. M.—Pvt.—Co. E—22d Georgia Infantry
17. Whitten, W. L. A.—Pvt.—Co. D—3d Georgia Infantry

[Slight variations of spelling of some names occur in the general order].

Private O. R. Belcher was acquitted and restored to duty; all other prisoners were sentenced to 15 days of hard labor and confinement in the regimental guardhouse during the intervals of labor.

In the circumstances collective prosecution was necessary; the nature of the offense committed by the individuals was doubtless that of a group and warranted their being tried as a group. The British service handled a similar but more extensive example of riotous conduct in barracks in the 19th century by a battalion of the guards by simply shipping off the whole battalion to a tour of duty in Bermuda. After that, the battalion was aptly named by the sobriquet "The Onion Guards."[4]

Care must be taken in the framing of both the charge and the specifications so that the specifications properly support the charge. Moreover, prosecution should not lose sight of the importance of proving the charge. A classic example of this oversight is contained in the court-martial of Pvt. John H. Lee, Co. G, 8th Alabama Infantry. He was tried between July 16, 1862, and August 14, 1862, for the crime of desertion. The 8th Alabama was part of Brig. Gen. Cadmus Wilcox's Brigade in Maj. Gen. James Longstreet's Division. The specifications are set forth in the general order and it is necessary to review them to understand the example of conviction being based upon the specifications. The prosecution's case rested upon the specifications and failed to prove the charge. In his review of the trial, Gen. Robert E. Lee (or his staff members responsible for review of the court-martial) gives the court a valuable lesson in military law.[5]

Private Lee maintained that he was innocent of the charge of "desertion"; however he pleaded guilty to the two specifications:

CHARGE : Desertion

SPECIFICATION 1st: In this; that the said John H. Lee, Co. G, 8th Regiment Alabama Volunteers, left his Company and Regiment near Richmond, on the night of the 25th of May, 1862, without permission from proper authority, and did not return until arrested by Lieut. Ravesies, Co. E, 8th Alabama Regiment, in Richmond, on the 30th of May, 1862.

SPECIFICATION 2nd: In this, that the said John H. Lee, Co. G, 8th Alabama Regiment Volunteers, [sic] did, on the 31st May,

1862, break guard, while on a march from camp towards Seven Pines, and did not return to his company or Regiment, until arrested in Richmond, by Lieut. W. Sterling, Co. E, 8th Alabama Regiment, on the 14th of July 1862.

FINDING

OF THE 1st SPECIFICATION TO CHARGE: Guilty
OF THE 2nd SPECIFICATION TO CHARGE: Guilty
OF THE CHARGE: Guilty

SENTENCE

"And the court, two-thirds of the members concurring therein, do therefore sentence the said John H. Lee, a Private in the Co. G, 8th Alabama Regiment, to be shot to death at such time and place as the Commanding General may direct."

Upon his review of the trial at the end of GO #98, General Lee admonishes the court with these words:

In the case of Private John H. Lee, Co. G, 8th Regiment Alabama Volunteers, the proceedings are disapproved for the following reasons: I. It does not appear upon the record what crime the prisoner was charged with, inasmuch as the charge has not been embodied therein; nor, consequently, does it appear that the original charge which accompanied the record, is the charge which the prisoner was arraigned and tried. II. The prisoner when arraigned pleaded "guilty" to the first and second specifications, and "not guilty" to the charge; no testimony to sustain the charge was offered by the prosecution but the court proceeded to confirm the pleas of "guilty" as to the specifications and to find him guilty of the charge. The court cannot make a legal inference that the prisoner having pleaded guilty to the specifications, is by consequence guilty of the charge. The prisoner expressly makes an issue with the prosecution on that point; he admits the facts but denies the legal intendment, and his pleas are, and in Common Law under similar circumstances, equivalent to a general plea of "not guilty." Any plea on the part of the prisoner that does not confess all the facts and all the intendments of the law is virtually a plea of "not guilty," and throws the burden of proof upon the prosecution. As the case stands, the prosecution has in fact produced no evidence to support the charge, and it falls to the ground. Unfortunate as these errors are and guilty as the prisoner may be, he must nevertheless be released and returned to duty.

The charges do not appear in the vast majority of cases recorded in the journals of the A&IGO. Beginning in November 1864, the clerks recorded the charges in the "remarks" section. Unless general orders could be found for a trial or the CSRs contained such reference, charges could not be determined for prior cases. This is an unfortunate occurrence in that a thorough analysis cannot be made of the various charges brought.

One of the most important responsibilities of the judge advocate was to deliver a copy of the charges to the accused at the earliest practicable date. This would be done immediately following the acceptance of properly framed charges. The prisoner was entitled to a reasonable time to prepare a defense; if he needed to call witnesses it was the duty of the judge advocate to obtain such witnesses.

When the judge advocate presented charges to the accused, he was expected to properly explain these and to make the prisoner aware of the consequences. In many cases tried during the Civil War, the prisoners were unable to read; therefore, an added burden was placed upon the judge advocate to read the charges and specifications to the accused or to see that the adjutant or some other responsible officer from the prisoner's unit could act as an advisor.

Previous to the arraignment of the accused it was the duty of the judge advocate to establish that the charge or charges were properly worded and that the accused was subject to such charges. If there were any inaccuracies, it was his duty to correct them before proceeding to trial. Once the court had been sworn and the charges read, no changes or additions to them could be made.

Drunkenness has bedeviled armies since the first brew was concocted. Such problems troubled the Confederates, especially among the officers. Liquor was controlled to the extent possible in camps; sutlers and other civilians who smuggled it into bivouacs were prosecuted and their wares confiscated. Nevertheless, it became available, especially to officers, through various channels, and some took liberal advantage of its availability.

More than 200 cases were tried for intoxication in one or another form. The majority of such charges was "drunkenness." When the war opened in April 1861, "drunkenness" was not a violation of the articles of war. AOW #45 required that any officer found drunk on his guard, party, or other duty, be cashiered. The same article also provided corporal punishment for enlisted men guilty of such an offense.

The charge of "drunk on guard in violation of Article of War #45" was a properly worded charge. The specification supporting the charge must identify the person, the time, and the place:

> SPECIFICATION: In this that he, the said Private John Doe, Co. A, 1st Virginia Infantry, while on guard on the night of September 1, 1863, between the hours of 10:00 and 11:00 p.m. was

found in a state of intoxication in front of his picket post by the Sergeant of the Guard.

The problem of intoxication among the officer corps became such a concern for commanders that an act was passed by the Confederate Congress to address the situation. They approved on April 21, 1862, an act that provided that any commissioned officer found drunk, shall, on conviction of a court of inquiry, be cashiered, suspended, or reprimanded, according to the aggravation of the offense. In addition to the sentence of cashiering, he may be deemed incapable of holding any military office for the time specified. The findings of such courts were forwarded to the War Department, where sentence was pronounced.[6]

Most of the charges of "drunkenness" were drawn against officers and nearly all cases were tried after April 21, 1862. In these examples, a charge of "drunkenness" would be acceptable, for under the new act an officer could be cashiered for being drunk at any time whether or not on duty. Moreover, he may be convicted by a court of inquiry which affords him much less protection than does a court-martial.

The charge of "misbehavior before the enemy" was used to keep soldiers in the line of battle. As soon as a unit came under serious fire, the "coffee boilers" melted away. It was not unusual for a regiment of infantry to lose 50% of its manpower as soon as it moved into the attack. Effort by the officers and the NCOs to keep the files closed up was very difficult, and the truly clever shirkers always found a place to hide.

Those who could properly be identified after a battle might be brought up under charges of "misbehavior before the enemy." This offence covers various forms of cowardice, but the proper charge is important in order to set forth rightful punishment, for conviction can bring a sentence of death.[7]

One hundred ninety individuals were charged with "misbehavior before the enemy," and another 127 were cited as violators of AOW #52. The wording of this article includes not only the act of misconduct by the individual, but any effort by him to induce comrades to commit similar acts. Such inducement becomes second nature in tight situations; comrades need little persuasion to follow the soldier leading a retreat to the rear.

An example of a properly worded charge and specification is seen in the order which details the approval of the court-martial of Pvt. Sampson Collins conducted on September 1, 1863.[8] Collins, of Co. D, 37th N.C. Troops, is charged with "misconduct in the face of the enemy," under the following specification:

> In this, that he, Private Sampson Collins, Company D, thirty-seventh North Carolina Regiment, did, on or about July 3, 1863,

abandon his company and regiment, then in line of battle at or
near Gettysburg, Pennsylvania, in a cowardly, shameful, and dis-
graceful manner.

Collins was found guilty of the specification and the charge and
was sentenced to be shot to death with musketry. He was executed
on September 26, 1863.[9] At the date cited in the specification, the
37th was part of Brig. Gen. James H. Lane's Brigade, Maj. Gen.
William D. Pender's Division, Lt. Gen. A. P. Hill's Third Corps.

The subject of miswording of charges is such an important
aspect of courts-martial that examples need to be shown at the
risk of nitpicking. Many trials were disapproved by reviewing authority, but the errors persisted, and it seems that army command
eventually despaired of correcting them. A useful example of ad-
monishment is found in GO #95, A&IGO, July 7, 1863. The first
five paragraphs are quoted entirely:

I. Before a General Court-Martial, convened at the Camp of
Brig. Gen. Paxton, by virtue of General Orders, No. 128, of 1862,
per Headquarters Department of Northern Virginia was arraigned
and tried:

Private M. Ricket, Company H, 27th Va. Infantry, on the fol-
lowing charge:
CHARGE : Violation of the 52nd Article of War.
FINDING
| Of the specification, | Guilty |
| Of the charge, | Guilty |
SENTENCE
To be shot to death with musketry

II. Before a General Court-Martial, convened at the camp of
Brig. Gen. F. Lee's Brigade, by virtue of General Orders, No. 12,
current series, from Head Quarters Department of Northern Virginia, were arraigned and tried:

Privates Wm. G. Clarke and J. R. Humphreys, of Capt.
Buathed's [sic] Battery, Stuart's Horse Artillery, on the following
charge:
CHARGE : Violation of the 23rd Article of War.
FINDING
| Of the specification, | Guilty |
| Of the charge, | Guilty |
SENTENCE
To be shot to death with musketry

III. Before a General Court-Martial, convened at the camp of
Maj. Gen. R. H. Anderson's Division, by virtue of General Orders,

No. 133, of 1862, per Head Quarters Department of Northern Virginia, was arraigned and tried:

Private John Q. Childres, Company G, 5th Fla. Regiment, on the following charge:

CHARGE : Violation of the 52nd Article of War.

FINDING

Of the specification,	Guilty
Of the charge,	Guilty

SENTENCE

To be shot to death with musketry

IV. Before a General Court-Martial, convened at Savannah, Ga. by virtue of General Orders, No. 61, current series, Head Quarters Department of S.C., Ga., and Fla., was arraigned and tried:

Private Henry Smith, Company E, 22nd Battalion Ga. Artillery, on the following charge:

CHARGE : Violation of the 46th Article of War.

FINDING

Of the specification,	Guilty
Of the charge,	Guilty

SENTENCE

To be shot to death with musketry

V. The proceedings in the cases of Privates M. Ricket, Company H, 27th Va. Infantry, William G. Clarke and J. R. Humphreys of Capt. Buathed's [sic] Battery, Stuart's Horse Artillery; John Q. Childres, Company G, 5th Fla. Regiment, and Henry Smith, Company E, 22nd Battalion of Ga. Artillery, having been laid before the Secretary of War for the decision of the President, the following orders are made thereon:

The several Articles of War, with the violation of which the above named are respectively charged, neither prescribe any duty or define and prohibit any offense. They simply pronounce punishments to be imposed for certain offenses. The charge of a violation of such articles is too indefinite to justify punishment under it. The defect is fatal, and vitiates the whole proceedings; which are therefore set aside. The parties will be released from close confinement and returned to duty; and it is hoped that their future conduct will be such as to prevent any regret that they should have escaped the fate to which they were sentenced.

The orders from the A&IGO emphasize the position of the Southern command on the wording of charges. Ricket and Childres should have been charged with "misbehavior before the enemy";

Clarke and Humphreys of Capt. James Breathed's Battery should have been charged with "advising or persuading others to desert the service"; and Smith's charge should have simply read as "sleeping on post." The wording of charges is essential; the entire effort of a trial is expounded to prove that the accused did in fact commit the charge.

Major William Winthrop, assistant judge advocate general of the United States Army, refers to this issue in his classic work *Military Law and Precedents* which was first published in 1886. His section on the wording of charges deals with the variations employed:

> The charge, where specific, may consist simply of the name of the offence, as "Desertion," "Mutiny," "Misbehavior before the enemy"; or, referring to the article under which it is brought, it may be expressed as "Violation of the____ Article of War,"[98] or it may combine the two forms and be phrased as "False muster, in violation of the 14th Article of War."[10]

Winthrop's reference to the 14th AOW is applicable to the recently passed Articles of War of 1874, but can properly be inferred to also apply to the Articles of 1806 in effect during the war. He goes on to add in footnote #98 from the above citation:

> This form has occasionally been criticized as improper or unsatisfactory, (see G.O. 11 of 1862; Do. 32 Army of the Potomac, 1862; Do. 2, Dept. of the East, 1863; Do. 121, Dept. of the Mo., 1863; Do. 21, Dept. of the Columbia, 1885; O'Brien, 233), but it is sanctioned by the usage of the service, and is not open to legal objection.

Although the Confederate service did not have the work of Winthrop to refer to, nor the benefit of the sanction of the United States service during the war as a guide to their own trials, they continued to frame charges in all three of the ways cited by Winthrop, so that the end effect was that all three methods were sanctioned by their usage.

Chapter IV
Finding

Trials before courts-martial often involve the investigation of various charges and specifications. Each must be adjudged as to guilt. The procedure as required has been set forth in the previous chapter, but it is appropriate here to emphasize the importance of determining guilt on the charge as supported by information relating to the specifications.

Guilt in courts-martial findings is determined by simple majority. If a majority votes "guilty" on a charge, then the accused is found so; but if a majority does not thus vote, then he is acquitted. If a court were composed of five members, and three voted "guilty" upon the charge, then the prisoner is convicted; but if a court were composed of six members, and three voted "guilty" upon the charge, then he is acquitted.

The variation to the requirement of simple majority in determining guilt comes in those cases where conviction requires a death sentence: forcing a safeguard[1] and spying, under section 2. Although section 2 does not apply to members of the Confederate States Armies, if a person is prosecuted under such charges, guilt must be determined by two-thirds of the members of the court because a death sentence is mandatory.

The guilt of the prisoner is usually determined by the first ballot cast by the court, but since variations from the charge are possible, subsequent votes are sometimes necessary. Let us suppose that our six-member court is voting on the charge of desertion. Two members vote "not guilty"; two members vote "not guilty of desertion, but guilty of AWOL"; and two members vote "guilty." At this juncture of the deliberation, the judge advocate would announce the results without identifying the individual voters. The members would then begin a rediscussion of their findings, but not in three little groups of two. It is important that all members discuss their deliberations together and that one who expresses himself does so to all members and not just to one or two others.

On February 17, 1863, Pvt. John W. Smoke, Company H, 13th Virginia Infantry, was tried on a charge of violation of AOW #52 (misbehavior before the enemy) by a court convened by General Robert E. Lee. In GO #128, Army of Northern Virginia, dated November 25, 1862, Lee named the detail for the court of Brig. Gen. Jubal A. Early's Brigade (commanded by Col. James A. Walker at the time, for Early was in command of the division) as follows:

1. Col. J. S. Hoffman—31st Virginia Infantry
2. Lt. Col. F. H. Board—58th Virginia Infantry
3. Capt. G. A. Goodman—13th Virginia Infantry
4. Capt. C. A. Nelson—49th Virginia Infantry
5. Capt. J. Bumgardner—52nd Virginia Infantry
6. 1st Lt. Samuel Buck—13th Virginia Infantry
7. 1st Lt. Charles D. McCoy—25th Virginia Infantry

Lee named 1st Lt. Luther D. Haymond, 31st Virginia Infantry, to serve as judge advocate, and instructed the court to sit without regard to hours.

Smoke was found guilty of the charge and sentenced to 12 months of hard labor with ball and chain, to 84 days of solitary confinement when not at hard labor, and to forfeiture of 12 months' pay.[2]

In his regimental history of the 13th Virginia Infantry, David F. Riggs points out that an unofficial source reveals that "he [Smoke] came within one vote of being shot."[3] The unofficial source doubtless had access to the voting record of the court.

The court was composed of seven members, assuming that all of the members appointed were still serving when Smoke's case was heard. Four members had to vote for guilt, but in all likelihood more than four voted for guilt. When a vote for sentence was taken, four must have voted for death, whereas a vote of five was needed for approval. The court no doubt resumed the discussion of a proper sentence and settled upon the one handed down.

The original sentence of the court called for one year of solitary confinement when the prisoner was not at hard labor. General Lee remitted that portion of the sentence that exceeded 84 days, which are the maximum number of days allowed for such punishment within the space of one year.

The finding of a military court is the finding of all. Since guilt and sentence are determined by majority, it is important for members to understand that every member must support the finding, and every member must vote upon a sentence if guilt is determined. For these important reasons open discussion of the issues is essential, and after each member has spoken his thoughts and a vote has determined the finding by a majority of the members then each member is bound to support that finding.

In like manner, every member must support the sentence of the court. Even though procedures provide for the recommendation of mercy by individual members outside the written record of the trial, this does not detract from the total support of the court in handing down the sentence.

A prisoner may be found guilty of a lesser charge, but may not be adjudged so of a greater charge. As an example, officers were frequently charged with "conduct unbecoming an officer and a gentleman." Under AOW #83, conviction of such a charge under a general court-martial requires that the accused be cashiered. The finding in several cases judged the accused "not guilty" of the charge, but guilty of "conduct to the prejudice of good order and military discipline" as outlined in AOW #99.

Such a finding would be entirely proper if supported by the facts. AOW #99 is a lesser charge than AOW #83, but the improper conduct of the officer charged could very well be cited as "conduct to the prejudice of good order and military discipline." A totally improper action by the court would be a modification of the charge to find the accused to be guilty of part of it such as "conduct unbecoming an officer." The court would be exceeding its power to modify the wording of an article of war so as to find the accused guilty of only a portion of it. Moreover, they are bound to judge upon the validity of the charges as laid once the accused has entered a plea.

The most straightforward verdict is to find the accused "guilty" or "not guilty" of all specifications and the charge. However, since variations often occur, it is necessary to take notice of their implications. If a prisoner is found "not guilty" of all the specifications to a charge and then found "guilty" of the charge, such a conviction is most irregular, and could not be supported. It is possible that a prisoner could be found "guilty" of specifications, but "not guilty" of the charge.

Occasionally, a prisoner would plead guilty to the charge and specifications as stated; in these examples, the court would sometimes simply confirm the prisoner's plea. However, in many cases, the court would go on to prove for the record that the prisoner was indeed guilty. Care must be taken when accepting a guilty plea from a prisoner to ascertain that he is of sound mind. Were it found that he is incompetent, then he should be acquitted of the charge and discharged the service. In several examples, the courts made such decisions, but since the courts had no power to carry out any recommendation for discharge, it remained with the general commanding to issue orders for discharge. In all cases, such action was not taken.

Frequently, the finding stated by the court was "guilty, but without criminal intent," or similar wording. Such a finding was usually followed by a listing of "not guilty" to the charge. A more often employed exception was to find a prisoner guilty of a specification except for specific words. At variance with this, specifications were sometimes reworded as to guilt. First Lieutenant George McHenry Gish, of Co. I, 28th Virginia Infantry, was tried on October 20, 1862, on a charge of insubordination. At the time the 28th was part of Brig. Gen. Richard B. Garnett's Brigade, Maj. Gen. George E. Pickett's Division, First Corps.

The finding of "guilty" of the charge is recorded after a finding of "guilty" of the specification followed by these words: "of so much of the specification as follows, viz: 'On the 9th day of September, he was released from arrest by order of the Commandant of the Regiment, and his sword sent back to him. He sent it back by Lieut. Hoge of his company, broken in two pieces.'" The court sentenced Gish to be reprimanded by his brigade commander (Garnett).[4]

Modification of the wording of a specification in the finding is entirely acceptable. One of the most frequently modified specifications was that describing desertion that the court determined inaccurate; by rephrasing the specification a judgement of AWOL might be rendered.

A clear example is found in the case of Private George Taylor, Company C, 1st S.C. Artillery, P.F.C.S., who was charged with desertion and tried on January 13, 1863:

CHARGE

"Desertion"

Specification... In this; "That he, the said Private George Taylor, Company 'C,' 1st Regiment S.C. Artillery, P.F.C.S., did desert from Fort Sumter, Charleston harbor, on or about the 8th day of August, 1862, and did remain absent until brought back in custody of the Sheriff of Marion district, on the 17th day of October, 1862."

To Which The Accused Pleaded As Follows:

To The Specification: "Not Guilty."

To The Charge: "Not Guilty."

FINDING AND SENTENCE

The Court After Mature Deliberation, Finds The Accused As Follows: Of The Specification: "Guilty, with the exception of the words 'did desert from Fort Sumter, Charleston harbor, on or about the 8th day of August, 1862,' 'by the Sheriff of Marion district on the 17th October, 1862.'"

Of The Charge: "Not Guilty, but guilty of absence without leave." And the court does, therefore, sentence him "to be confined under charge of the guard for one month at hard labor, and that he forfeit four months of his pay from his next pay rolls to the Confederate Government, except the just dues of the laundress." The court is thus lenient in consequence of the prisoner having already been confined for three months at hard labor under the charge of the guard.[5]

The finding and sentence were approved by Gen. P.G.T. Beauregard, however the sentence was remitted on April 10, 1863, by Special Order (SO) #80, Dept. S.C., Ga., and Fla. As a footnote to the activities of Private Taylor, he was subsequently convicted of deserting from Morris Island, S.C., on July 6, 1863; the trial was heard in March of 1864, and Taylor was sentenced to be shot. The proceedings were referred to the secretary of war; although orders on the trial from the A&IGO could not be found it is certain that Taylor was not executed, for he appears in a third trial for desertion on March 14, 1865, where he was convicted of deserting the 3d N.C. Hospital on July 16, 1864. The court again sentenced him to be shot, but he was pardoned by the president's last general amnesty issued under GO #2, Armies of the Confederate States, February 11, 1865.

It is important to emphasize that the wording of charges may not be changed. The finding of guilt of a related but lesser charge is quite different from finding guilt on a modified or altered charge.

Under AOW #15, officers convicted of "knowingly making a false muster of man or horse" must be cashiered. If an officer were charged with such an offense and tried before a court-martial, the court would be bound to determine if the accused did in fact commit such a crime.

Let us suppose that during a trial, the facts clearly established that a false muster of man or horse was made. But as part of his defense the officer claimed to have been unaware that the report was inaccurate. The court on the other hand was convinced that he should have known that the records were incorrect and therefore handed down a finding of guilty of "making a false muster of man or horse." Even though the court determined that a false report was made, they would be totally out of line to modify the charge by deleting the word "knowingly." They would be bound to hand down an acquittal on the charge.

In such an example, the reviewing authority would doubtlessly deliver a strong rebuke to the accused in general orders when the results of the trial were printed. But the integrity of the court would have been maintained, even though a person who was probably guilty was set free.

In contrast to this ruling, a court may adjust a charge whereby the wording does not agree with the exact terms of the article of war. The trial of Brig. Gen. Jerome B. Robertson is a clear illustration.

On January 26, 1864, Robertson was brought up on charges: "conduct highly prejudicial to good order and military discipline," before a court-martial in Russelville, Tennessee. The charges were preferred by Brig. Gen. Micah Jenkins who was commanding Maj. Gen. John Bell Hood's old division in Longstreet's Corps which was on detached service in the Department of East Tennessee. Robertson was in charge of a brigade in Jenkins' division and Jenkins considered him guilty of neglect of duty.

Because General Jenkins was the prosecutor in the case, the court was convened by order of the secretary of war, through the A&IGO. The detail for the court consisted of Maj. Gen. Simon B. Buckner as president along with six brigadier generals: Charles W. Field, James L. Kemper, John Gregg, Francis T. Nicholls, George T. Anderson, and Benjamin G. Humphreys. Major Garnett Andrews was appointed judge advocate.[6]

When the charges were drawn, the wording was used "conduct highly prejudicial to good order and military discipline." The specification read:

> The use of language calculated to discourage his regimental commanders, and weaken their confidence in certain movements then in progress, and to create distrust in the minds of the troops as to the result of the campaign in which they were engaged.

The language that Robertson was accused of using was no doubt critical of Jenkins and when word got back to him, he preferred charges.

The court found Robertson guilty of the specification with the exception that his words were designed to weaken the confidence of the officers to whom they were addressed. They further judged him guilty of the charge, except for the word "highly." That is an important qualification to note. AOW #99 does not use the word "highly," and the court was therefore justified in determining guilt to the degree stated.

The court sentenced Robertson to be reprimanded and forwarded the proceedings to the A&IGO On February 25, 1864, General Samuel Cooper delivered the rebuke in GO #24, paragraph 3:

> The proceedings, findings and sentence are approved. The absence of a wrong intent does not change the obviously mischievous tendency of the remarks complained of. Officers cannot

be too careful in the expression of their opinion on such occasions; and this caution is the more incumbent, in proportion to their rank and influence. Hence, while the department is gratified that the Court has felt warranted in acquitting Brigadier General Robertson of improper motives, it altogether disapproves his conduct.

The custom of the service is to express acquittal in those cases where an accused is determined to be "not guilty" of the charge. Although this is in no way a requirement for establishing the fact that the prisoner is determined to be found "not guilty," it is customary to express such finding as: "and the court does therefore acquit the accused Private John C. Doe . . ." Sometimes the adverb "fully" or "honorably" is used to describe the acquittal; this adds but little to the court's judgement; it is merely a description that enhances the declaration of innocence.

A finding of acquittal is irrevocable regardless of errors of omission or commission made by the court. The commanding general may still disapprove the findings of the court; in doing so he would invariably admonish the court and perhaps the judge advocate, but this does not change the record of acquittal of the accused. Once he is tried by a court, he may not be tried again for the same crime, and he therefore is set free regardless of the errors of the court. If a finding of guilty is disapproved by the commanding general, the prisoner is also set free.

Disapproval of guilty verdicts occurs whenever the reviewing authority determines that improper procedures have taken place during the course of the trial or that the evidence did not support the findings. Sometimes the improper procedures are nothing more than oversights on the part of the court or the judge advocate, such as a failure to allow the accused to object to any member of the court before the trial begins. Nevertheless, such errors are fatal and require the general to disapprove the findings and set the prisoner free.

The accused stands in a similar position to acquittal in that he may not be retried for the crime, but he also stands outside the bounds of acquittal. The record must show that a finding of guilty was handed down, but was disapproved by reviewing authority.

Prosecution of violators of military laws and orders rests with courts-martial, except for minor infractions that are corrected by local commanders. Proper procedure for ordering such courts must be followed, and the rights of the accused protected. The court, on the other hand, has no authority for enforcement; that rests entirely with the general or other person, ordering the court-martial to convene. He is responsible for reviewing the proceedings and sentence to see that the regulations have been properly adhered to. In this capacity he is referred to as the reviewing authority.[7]

Except in those cases where the corps commanders were authorized to review cases under the act of October 9, 1862, for the organization of military courts; the reviewing authority for the armies in the field was the army commander, for all general courts-martial. Many cases were handled by these military courts for a period of time, but throughout the war, the bulk of the burden continued to rest with the army commanders: Robert E. Lee, Joseph E. Johnston, Braxton Bragg, John Bell Hood, E. Kirby Smith, and others.

No decision or sentence of a court possessed any finality without the approval of the reviewing authority. The entire principle of military justice through the system of courts-martial is to extend the authority of the commanding general. In the United States service, and similarly in the Confederate States service, the commander in chief is the president. Through his commanders, his authority over the armed forces is carried out.

The custom of the service that prevailed throughout the Civil War was for the courts-martial to act within the limits of the articles of war, and then leave the enforcement of the court's decision to the reviewing authority, the commanding general who appointed the court. In this respect, his authority was final, except for those examples that required referral to the president.

The reviewing authority occasionally returned the proceedings of a case to the court for reconsideration. This action could be entirely proper if the court had not been dissolved. The usual recommendation for reconsideration was in sentencing rather than in findings. If the general reviewing the case took exception to the finding, he would usually disapprove the proceedings thus nullifying all of the court's action. If he felt that the court needed to reexamine a segment of the case, it would be proper for him to refer the proceedings back to the court with a specific recommendation for such examination. But it is important to note that the court may not reopen the case. As long as they simply peruse the evidence and ponder their decisions such review could be acceptable, but they may not recall witnesses, nor question the accused or the prosecutor. They would require careful guidance by a competent judge advocate to reconsider their findings.

One of the best examples of the mishandling of cases returned for revision is contained in GO #35, Department of S.C., Ga., and Fla., March 2, 1863. Privates William Chastain, G. W. Rains, and Peter Burton all of Capt. T. B. Ferguson's S.C. Battery were tried on January 19, 1863, and January 20, 1863, on charges of desertion.

Chastain, Rains, and Burton left their battery between the dates of September 12, 1862, and September 15, 1862, and remained absent until captured and returned under guard on November 11, 1862. Each was charged with desertion and each pleaded guilty to the specification which described their absence, but not guilty to the charge of desertion.

In each case the court found them not guilty of desertion, but guilty of AWOL and sentenced each man to forfeit two months' pay and to serve two months at hard labor with ball and chain, alternating each week of labor with one week of confinement on bread and water diet.

General Beauregard explains his displeasure with his court in paragraph 2 of his general order:

> In the cases of Privates Chastine (Chastain), Burton, and Raines (Rains), the proceedings and findings are disapproved, and cannot be passed over without animadversion.
>
> The court in their proceedings in these cases, erred in not taking testimony after the plea of the prisoners, to show the precise character and degree of the offense committed. The charge against these men severally, was Desertion, that is, the crime of quitting their standard without lawful permission, and without intention to return of their own accord; the specification being that they had each absented himself without permission for a period of nearly sixty days. The crime clearly consisted in the intention of these men. Under the ordinary rules in force in the Army, so prolonged an absence would be taken as ample evidence of an intention not to return; that is, to desert, unless the prisoners should clearly show to the contrary; the mere averment of the accused themselves, assuredly, should not be taken as satisfactory, and yet such is really the effect of the finding of the court, in confirming the plea of the prisoners to the charge. The plea in these cases to the charge was in effect, however, one of "not guilty," and therefore evidence should have been taken in the outset.
>
> The second error of the Court was in taking testimony when these cases were sent back to be revised; their whole duty was to review the record, not to add to it; there was no power in the Court to reopen these cases.
>
> In the opinion of the Commanding General, the facts alleged in the specification made out a case of desertion, if proved; the plea of guilty to the specification established these facts, and should have been viewed as sufficient, in the absence of other evidence, to warrant the finding of guilty of the charge; therefore a reconsideration was directed. The evidence irregularly taken

confirms the views of the Commanding General, and he is constrained to disapprove both findings and sentence.

No good can come to discipline by such sentences, or by a lax view of the character of the military crime of quitting one's flag in the time of war, without leave or authority, a crime that will sap the efficiency of any army, if not properly regarded, held up to reprobation and subjected to prompt and radical punishments. Privates Wm. Chastine [Chastain], Peter Burton, and G. W. Rains, Ferguson's Artillery, P.A.C.S. will be released from confinement and returned to duty.

Throughout the lengthy review of trials, the prevailing action that appears again and again is that of protection of the rights of the accused. Courts sometimes gave too little attention to this protection, and in the circumstances of war, that is understandable, but the reviewing authority and the War Department intervened on behalf of the prisoner whenever the courts' findings were imperfect.

Captain William W. W. Wood of Company L, 44th Mississippi Infantry, was tried on April 14, 1863, on a charge of "conduct unbecoming an officer and a gentleman," by a military court in Lt. Gen. Leonidas Polk's Corps. The 44th was part of Brig. Gen. James Patton Anderson's Brigade, Brig. Gen. Zachariah C. Deas' Division, and the trial was held in Shelbyville, Tennessee.

Three specifications were laid to support the charge and the court found Captain Wood not guilty of the first and third specifications, and not guilty of all of the second specification except so much as charges him with "two days remaining away from his company at camp." However, the court found him guilty of the charge, and as required by AOW #83 sentenced him to be dismissed from the service.

The findings were submitted to the War Department for the president's action and the A&IGO issued GO #73 on June 2, 1863, which stated in part:

A portion of the 2nd specification is, therefore, all that in the opinion of the court sustains the charge. But this finding is altogether too imperfect and uncertain. If the 2nd specification refers to separate and distinct offenses, it is wholly defective, and should have been set aside before the trial; but if it embraces a single substantive offense, the Court cannot separate its parts, and find the accused guilty as to one portion and not guilty as to another, unless it is clear that the facts thus separated and established, of themselves constitute the particular offense charged. But this is far from being clear. The looseness and uncertainty of the 2nd specification, and the finding thereon, are a sufficient and fatal objection. The whole finding is moreover informal and irregular.

. . . Upon the whole, the proceedings are set aside, and Capt. Wood will therefore be released from arrest and returned to duty.

The findings in Captain Wood's case seem to be clearly misplaced, and a reversal of the decision of the court by the secretary of war was appropriate. A related outcome but one of entirely different circumstances involved Capt. John Q. Arnold, Company B, 12th Battalion Tennessee Cavalry. Arnold was tried on February 20, 1863, on a charge of violation of the 9th AOW, by a general court-martial in Knoxville, Tennessee. The 12th Battalion was part of the Department of East Tennessee at the time.

Arnold was accused in the specification of shooting to death with a pistol his superior officer, Maj. Thomas W. Adrien at Kingston, Tennessee, on November 16, 1862. Arnold filed a special plea of jurisdiction of the court which was overruled. He was found guilty of the charge, and sentenced by the court to be shot to death with musketry.

The proceedings were forwarded to the War Department for action by the president. His decision went directly to the findings first of all; that is, that AOW #9 forbids lifting up a weapon, or striking an officer in the execution of his duty. The response by the A&IGO points out that Major Adrien was walking across the street in Kingston when Arnold shot him, and not in the performance of some duty. It is the resistance to authority that the 9th AOW forbids and punishes, without that, an accused is not culpable under its requirements.

The department correctly determined that Arnold's objection to jurisdiction was valid, and that the court did not have the right to charge him. The findings and the sentence were set aside and the department suggested that the case be referred to the civil authorities of the state of Tennessee.[8]

A military court would have been the proper tribunal to hear the case. Such courts had the power to prosecute members of the army for the act of murder when committed against another member of the army or against a civilian.

It is not known if Arnold was indicted on a charge of murder by a Tennessee court, but his CSR indicates that he resigned his commission on December 12, 1864, so it would appear that he escaped punishment entirely.

Wherever competent authority reviewed the findings of cases the rights of the accused were adequately protected. Army commanders, without exception, were cognizant of these rights, and the authorities in the War Department were always vigilant in protecting the accused.

Chapter V

Sentencing

The sentence handed down by a court after a finding of guilty is voted upon by all the members and is determined by a simple majority just as is the verdict of guilty. The chief exception to the determination by a majority is in the event of a sentence of death; the articles of war require that at least two-thirds of the members of the court concur in the sentence of death.

It was important that the records of the trial showed that two-thirds voted for death. Occasionally, the records would state that the sentence of death was by a unanimous vote of the members. This was an improper procedure; the voting record of the members should never be divulged in such fashion.

In voting upon punishment, every member of the court must participate. If the sentence of death was an option and was voted upon by some members, but not by two-thirds of the court, then a new vote of punishment would be taken, until a simple majority can decide upon the same sentence.

The determination of a sentence was often difficult to achieve. An open discussion of the question would take place among all the members; individual opinions would be expressed and a fitting decision arrived at. Courts should refrain from handing down a combination of sentences to satisfy various members. On the other hand, multiple sentences were often justified. Such sentences consist of two or more modes of punishment. If a non-commissioned officer was sentenced to hard labor, he would also be reduced to the ranks; in addition if he has been convicted of desertion or absence without official leave, he would suffer forfeiture of pay for at least the time absent.

If an enlisted man was sentenced to be drummed out of the service, he typically would also have his head, or half of his head, shaved, and be branded on the left hip with the letter *D* if his offense was desertion.

In some instances, the articles of war demand specific sentences. As mentioned in chapter 4, two convictions require the sentence of death: (1) forcing a safeguard, and (2) spying. The first refers to violating protected property in "foreign parts." This would mean that during the course of the war, a member of the Confederate States Armies broke into and laid waste to some property in the United States over which the Confederate authorities had posted a guard and agreed not to violate such property. No examples of this crime were found in the cases reviewed. The other charge under section 2 of the articles applies only to persons not owing allegiance to the Confederate States convicted of spying. This charge was levied against several civilians and a few Union soldiers. In order for the courts to convict in these cases two-thirds must vote for guilt; the sentence then becomes automatic.

In other examples where death is pronounced, the court may declare it only for those violations that call for it in the articles of war. Thirteen additional crimes enumerated in the articles permit the sentence of death.

Table 5.1

Military Crimes Subject to the Death Penalty

Article of War	Violation
#7	Mutiny
#8	Failure to Suppress Mutiny
#9	Striking a Superior Officer
#20	Desertion
#23	Persuading Others to Desert
#46	Sleeping on Post
#49	Raising False Alarms
#51	Offering Violence to Sutlers
#52	Misbehaving Before the Enemy
#53	Making Known the Watchword
#55	Forcing a Safeguard
#56	Giving Aid and Comfort to the Enemy
#57	Giving Intelligence to the Enemy
#59	Forcing a Commander to Surrender
Section 2	Spying

A reference to the articles of war in the appendix will disclose the exact wording, but the above summaries give an adequate description of the crimes that a court is allowed to punish by execution.

As might be guessed, the charge of "desertion" brought, by far, the most prisoners before firing squads. An exact tally could not be achieved, because the charge remained unknown in many cases, but the crime of desertion was the overriding disciplinary issue for the Confederacy from beginning to end.

Another major sentence that is either permitted or demanded by the articles is that of cashiering of officers. Four articles allow the cashiering of an officer upon conviction of the crime mentioned, and 10 additional articles demand that the officer be dismissed the service.

Table 5.2

Military Crimes Subject to the Dismissal of Officers

OPTIONAL

Article of War	Violation
#5	Using Contemptuous Words Against the Government
#25	Sending a Challenge to Fight a Duel
#31	Charging Exorbitant Prices to Sutlers
#32	Failure to Keep Good Order on the March

MANDATORY

Article of War	Violation
#14	Signing a False Certificate
#15	Knowingly Making a False Muster of Man or Horse
#16	Taking Money by Way of Mustering Soldiers
#18	Knowingly Making a False Return
#33	Refused to Deliver Over Officer or Soldier Accused of Committing Civil Offense
#36	Conviction of Misuse or Embezzlement of Government Stores
#39	Conviction of Misuse or Embezzlement of Funds for the Payment of Men Under His Command
#45	Drunk on Guard, Party, or Other Duty
#77	Breaking Arrest
#83	Conduct Unbecoming an Officer and a Gentleman

The most important fact to keep in mind concerning sentences is that no sentence of a court contains any force until it is approved by the reviewing authority. The commanding general may disapprove the proceedings, which nullifies the finding of the court for the record. He may approve the proceedings but disapprove the sentence, thereby setting the prisoner free. If he approves the finding and the sentence, he may mediate the sentence by either shortening the term, or remitting all or a portion of the sentence except death or the cashiering of an officer. In the example of these two sentences, he may either carry out the sentence or refer the case to the president for his action.[1]

After a sentence was passed by the court, one or more members could make a recommendation of mercy. This was done on a separate page inserted after the final page of the proceedings and was signed only by those members electing to make such recommendation. The reason for the members' action would be set forth in the recommendation. Under military custom, it was the prerogative of the reviewing authority to weigh or ignore the recommendation.

Sometimes a reviewing officer would return the proceedings to the court and suggest that they reconsider the sentence. As long as the court had not been dissolved, this action was acceptable. One of the most unusual examples of such a recommendation occurred at a court-martial that sat on August 16, 1862, in Gen. P.G.T. Beauregard's command, the Department of South Carolina, Georgia, and Florida.

Sergeant J. R. Mosely of Company A, 1st S.C. Artillery, was tried on three charges:

1. disorderly and riotous conduct,
2. violation of the 9th AOW,
3. disrespectful language to a superior officer.

The specifications indicate that on July 10, 1862, Sergeant Mosely did disturb the camp on James Island, S.C., by offering violence to several members of the camp. When Capt. J. T. Youngblood attempted to quell the riot, Sergeant Mosely offered violence to him with his fists; he further spoke these words to him: "God damn you I ask you no odds."

Mosely was found guilty of the three specifications and the three charges. He was sentenced to be reduced to the ranks and to be shot to death with musketry. At this point the information seems to indicate that Beauregard thought the sentence too lenient and referred the case to the court for reconsideration. A closer reading would indicate that he considered the sentence too harsh; in either event, the court reacted thusly:

> Upon a reconsideration which was had by order of Genl. Beauregard, the court sentences the accused to be reduced to the ranks, to be confined in the charge of his regimental guard for the space of thirty days, to be put to hard labor, to wear a ball and chain weighing thirty-two pounds attached to his left leg by a chain three feet long and at the expiration of that time to be shot to death with musketry in the hands of twelve men.

Such a sentence could only be described as cruel and unusual—no other like it was seen in any of the cases of the Confederate States. However, Beauregard did not approve it; he referred it to the president for his action. On January 17, 1863, Beauregard issued an order which lists the details of the case and concludes with the general's remarks:

> The proceedings in the case of Sergeant J. R. Mosely, having been forwarded for the consideration and orders of the President, as prescribed by the 89th Article of War, and returned with the following endorsement: 'Respectfully returned to General Beauregard, who is authorized to commute the sentence in this case in such manner as to him shall seem best calculated to promote the interest of the service.' (signed S. Cooper, Adjutant and Inspector General)- the findings and sentence are now approved; but in consequence of the recommendation of the Court that the sentence of death be remitted, the Commanding General is pleased to commute the sentence to hard labor, with ball and chain attached to the left leg for the period of twelve months; a forfeiture of monthly pay for the same period of time; and confinement in the guard-house whenever not employed at hard labor. The order will be carried into effect under the direction of his district commander.[2]

The disclosure by Beauregard's order that the court recommended mercy adds more confusion to the issue. The entire sentence seemed inappropriate in the first example; relatively few men were shot for striking their superior officers, and no examples could be found where death was inflicted for only shaking one's fist in an officer's face. The referral by the A&IGO was certainly reasonable in the circumstances; however, it was entirely contrary to military law. No authority exists to substitute a sentence of 12 months' hard labor for a sentence of death.

The reviewing authority was limited in his power to mitigate sentences, and he had no authority to change a sentence. Even the president was bound by this limitation. However, many examples were seen where the president commuted death sentences to hard labor.

The reviewing authority may reduce the length of a sentence although he may never extend it. He may do this at any time before the completion of a sentence. For example, a prisoner may be sentenced to six months' hard labor; the reviewing authority may reduce the sentence to three months' hard labor. A more typical prerogative that was frequently employed was a remission of all or a portion of a sentence. The reviewing officer might examine a case where a prisoner is sentenced to six months' hard labor with a 12-pound ball attached to his left leg by an eight-foot chain. The general may approve the sentence, but remit the ball and chain.

General Thomas J. Jackson seemed to abhor those sentences which restricted the freedom of movement of his men. Again and again, prisoners would be sentenced to confinement or hard labor for AWOL; and, in addition, pay stoppage would be added. General Jackson would invariably remit all but pay stoppage. The accused would probably have preferred confinement to keeping up with Stonewall's troop movements.

General Robert E. Lee seemed to have an aversion to branding. Whenever the courts in the Army of Northern Virginia sentenced prisoners to be branded, Lee (or his judge advocate) would remit the branding. General Joseph E. Johnston was of a similar mind. He considered branding cruel and unusual punishment.

At various times reviewing generals would disapprove sentences because they considered them inadequate. In thus acting, the commander recognized that the prisoner was being set free with no punishment, but as was typically explained in his orders, the court was wasting the valuable time of the army, and such sentences were not worthy of being entertained.

In no other segment of the system of courts-martial in the Confederate States Armies was such variance found as in the approval of sentences. The performance of the courts was fairly consistent in their handing down of sentences. It was a general custom of the service during the mid-19th century to hand down a maximum sentence and leave remission in the hands of the reviewing authority.

This practice was usually followed by the courts of the Confederate armies; however, the commanding general would frequently remit a sentence upon what appeared to be a whim or urge. Moreover, hundreds and hundreds of cases were referred to the president or the secretary of war which wound up as pardons with the accused escaping punishment entirely, perhaps for a serious transgression. In other cases a lesser offender might spend the rest of the war working on the fortifications in Richmond with a ball and chain attached to his leg.

The most glaring lapse in military justice in the Confederate States was enforcement. Countless cases escaped punishment simply because the prisoner could not be found when sentence was approved. It was not unusual for a prisoner to receive a pardon from the president for a sentence of death for desertion, and to be found to have deserted again before the order of pardon was issued. Recovery of these people was certainly a time-consuming process as well as a hit-or-miss proposition at best. Bounties were paid for the return of deserters (typically $30).[3] Local law enforcers would often respond to broadsides posted or to notices in local newspapers to locate persons they were acquainted with. In such cases, the cost of the bounty would be deducted from the prisoner's pay once he was returned.

The system of communication in effect gave little support to tracing individuals beyond their home territory. Many deserters would attempt to go north where they would be relatively safe from recapture. The pressure of earning a living, however, often pushed them back into uniform, but into a blue one rather than a gray.

The act of deserting to the enemy became a greater problem for the Confederacy as the war wore on. During the final desperate year, many men went over just for the hope of getting three meals a day. The conditions in many Northern prisons were deplorable; some Southern prisoners were persuaded to join United States regiments to escape such conditions. One would suspect that most of those who did so were following the urges of their stomachs rather than any longing in their hearts. Such action was certainly risky, for any former Confederate captured in a blue uniform could kiss his stomach, heart, and derrière goodbye.

The procedure for handling prisoners in courts-martial cases contributed to the inconsistencies of enforcement. After a trial was completed, the commander of the prisoner was responsible for his safekeeping. The courts had no authority to retain prisoners. In most cases, the private soldiers were returned to the guardhouse. In some examples they were returned to military prisons to await the results announced in general orders. After the proceedings were completed and forwarded to the reviewing authority, he or his staff went over the cases carefully, then issued orders for sentencing or release of the accused. In the best of times this required several days or a few weeks. If a major campaign intervened, a much longer time was needed. In addition, if the proceedings were forwarded to the president for his action, the delay would turn into months. During this interval, private soldiers would often be serving in the ranks, and when sentence was finally issued through general orders, these rascals may be off on French leave once more.

It is certainly accurate to say that enforcement was uneven and therefore to that extent, unfair. The criticism of punishment of the innocent, however, is entirely unfounded. Not only did military commanders do their utmost to protect the rights of soldiers under courts-martial, they extended remission and forgiveness where it was frequently not deserved. It was a rare case whereby any innocent prisoner was convicted of a crime he did not commit, but frequently a guilty person was set free. The most commonly repeated transgression of this type was that of errors in the record. Again and again, prisoners sentenced to death were set free simply because the court failed to include the wording that "two-thirds of the court concurred in the sentence."

The issue of presidential pardon was frequently employed to set the guilty free. More than 600 cases were pardoned by the president after having been sentenced to death. Commanders were reluctant to forward cases to the secretary of war for consideration by the president because they knew that the accused would almost certainly be pardoned.

Under AOW #89, a reviewing authority has the power to carry out a sentence of death or the cashiering of an officer (except general officers) in time of war, but he may not mitigate such sentences, only the president may do that through his power of pardon. When the military courts were formed for army corps on October 9, 1862, these powers were ostensibly extended to corps commanders as reviewing authorities.

In the correspondence file of letters to the A&IGO an interesting epistle appears; this letter was sent to General Samuel Cooper by Lt. Gen. A. P. Hill on December 23, 1864:[4]

December 23, 1864—Gen. A .P. Hill
Hdq. 3rd Corps ANV
Copy of letter to Genl. Cooper
Genl-
I have the honor herewith to enclose the record in the case of Private David White, Co. D-15th, N.C. Regt. with the orders detailing Lt. Col. Butten as a member of the court and Capt. Cothran as Judge Advocate as required in your communication of the 2nd inst. I have always considered that the court had the right to adopt their own form of record under the 3rd section of the Act to organize Military Courts which gives to said courts the power to adopt rules for conducting business and for the trial of cases, nor do I conceive that there is any authority which is empowered to question the form of record adopted by them. Your communication was, however, referred to them and regarding it in the light of an order the record has been amended as directed. With regard to that portion of the communication from the Adj. and Insp. Genl. Office, War Dept. of Sept. 16th, 1864 which is as follows "The Secretary directs me to say that in all cases where the court adjudges the penalty of death or cashiering, coupled with a recommendation to executive clemency, whether the recommendation be addressed to the President or erroneously to the reviewing officer, it is the duty of the reviewing officer to suspend the execution of the sentence until the pleasure of the President

be known and to forward the record for his action in the premises." I beg leave to reply that in all cases where the recommendation for clemency has been addressed to myself as the reviewing officer it has not been done "erroneously" by the court but with a full knowledge of the fact that the President alone has the power to remit or commute the sentence in such instances and the intention of the Court in so addressing their recommendation has been to leave the matter entirely with me as to whether the sentence should be ordered to be executed or whether if in my judgement it is a case deserving of clemency, the record should be forwarded to the President for his action in the premises. That such was their intention I have been respectfully informed by each of the Presiding Judges of the Court and I have consequently declined to forward and to suspend execution of sentence when the recommendations have been so addressed, save in those cases where in my judgement executive clemency was desirable, or where some doubts or difficulties were presented upon which I was unwilling to decide, and I would beg leave to say that I have been strengthened in what I regard to be my duty in such cases by the pointed rebuke administered to reviewing officers by the Executive in Par. IV Genl. Orders No. 139, A&I.G.O. Oct. 28, 1863.

I have the honor to enclose also the record in the case of Private Emory Lunsford, Co. L, 14th Tenn. Regt. asking action in the case as requested in the recommendation of the Court addressed to myself. In ordering the execution of the sentence and not suspending it when the order announcing the approval of the Finding, Sentence, etc. is published to the command what I believe will be the most benefit to the service. The order suspending the execution of the sentence will be issued later.

Hereafter in all cases where the recommendation of the Court are not approved when the record will be forwarded immediately, the execution of the sentence will not be suspended unless an order to that effect in each particular case is received from your Department. As the reviewing officer of the Court, I consider this my right and shall continue to exercise it as long as I occupy that position.

I am very respectfully your obt. serv.

-A.P. Hill-

Lt. Gen.

The position taken by Hill is a firm one. The articles of war clearly indicate that it is the prerogative of the reviewing authority to carry out the sentence of the court when death is ordered or to refer the proceedings to the president for his action. This remains the procedure whether or not mercy has been recommended.

On the issue of a court's recommendation of mercy, DeHart takes a position that would even further exclude such recommendations from consideration:

> The manner in which a recommendation to mercy was presented for consideration formerly, was extremely variant; at times being embodied in the sentence, and at others appended to it. It was also frequently expressed as to the manner in which this merciful recommendation was to be carried out. This changeable and uncertain mode was, of course, objectionable and improper. The manner in which recommendations are to be made, is now prescribed by the regulations for the army. Paragraph 231 says, "No recommendation will be embraced in the body of the sentence, but will be inserted after the signatures of the president of the court and the judge advocate. Such members only, who recommend, will sign the same." The writer will add, that a court-martial ought not to point out any particular mode in which the clemency of the commanding general, or the president of the United States should be exercised.

> The recommendation is written, as directed, immediately below the sentence, and this is observed as a better way than that of writing it upon a detached piece of paper, or making it the subject of a letter,—as such papers are liable to be mislaid or lost.[5]

DeHart goes on to frame a convincing argument that there is something incongruous in allowing one or two members to express a recommendation to mercy. It then becomes the hope or desire of the individual members who sign such a recommendation and not the opinion of the court.

The court acts as a body and therefore the decision and punishment handed down is the work of that body. Any action or suggestion to subvert that decision compromises the unanimity of the court and to that degree is subversive.

He adds that where the judgement of the court is discretionary it is a contradiction to the sentence to offer to mitigate the sentence. The court had that option in passing the sentence and therefore should not second guess its own work and throw the burden upon the reviewing authority.

There are cases where the court is bound to pass specific sentences demanded by the articles of war. If such punishment were to seem unjustified by a court, a unanimous recommendation for mercy might be justified.

In the example that General Hill gives, one of the major issues is that of the direction of mercy or clemency. Even though it is conceded that in cases where death or the cashiering of an officer is handed down, only the president can mitigate such sentence, it is improper to infer that the court addresses the recommendation to the president. The court has no such power to circumvent the authority of the reviewing officer, and it is always his responsibility to approve or disapprove the findings and sentences of the court.

Hill cites GO #139, October 28, 1863, A&IGO, as a proper reference for his actions also. That order from General Samuel Cooper took exception with reviewing officers for bucking courts-martial cases to the president. Paragraph 4, the final paragraph, clearly reminds reviewing authority of their responsibility:

> IV. The 89th Article of War provides, that where the sentence of a Court Martial is death, or the cashiering of an officer, the officer convening the Court may suspend execution of the sentence till the pleasure of the President of the Confederate States be known.
>
> The intent of this article is not to relieve Commanding Generals of responsibility, but to enable them, in difficult and doubtful cases, to refer the question to higher authority. But it has been observed that in many cases, where the course to be pursued was rendered obvious by the evidence, commanding officers have nevertheless availed themselves of the privilege conferred in the article referred to, by sending on the record to be reviewed by the President. The duties of the Executive are sufficiently onerous without the accumulation of such matters for his attention, where they can be properly disposed of elsewhere; and while it is not designed to weaken the provisions of the articles of war, or interfere with the views of duty entertained by officers on this subject, it is proper to remark, that there are cases of capital punishment and dismissal, where the duty of the Commanding General is rendered by the Court record too plain to be doubted, and in which the responsibility "in time of war" being fixed upon him in the first instance by the law, should not be avoided.
>
> S. Cooper
> Adjutant and Inspector General

The file contains a response to Hill's letter penned by Major William S. Barton, Assistant Adjutant General (AAG), Secretary of War. The letter rambles on for four pages, giving a weak reply to Hill's charges except for the constitution of military courts under Article #3 of the act.

For the record, Pvt. Emory Lunsford, Co. L, 14th Tennessee Infantry, part of Brig. Gen. James J. Archer's Brigade of Maj. Gen. Henry Heth's Division, was pardoned under GO #2, Army of the Confederate States, February 11, 1865; he had been tried and convicted of desertion. Private David White of Co. D, 15th N.C. Troops, part of Brig. Gen. John R. Cooke's Brigade of Heth's Division, was pardoned under the same general order. White had deserted on July 31, 1863, and was apprehended on July 2, 1864, tried and convicted November 25, 1864.

In contrast to this approach, an excellent example of the need for a recommendation to mercy by the courts is found in the case of Lt. Col. Charles C. Flowerree, 7th Virginia Infantry. The 7th was part of Brig. Gen. James L. Kemper's Brigade, Maj. Gen. George E. Pickett's Division, First Corps. Flowerree was tried on March 12, 1863, on charges of "drunkenness on duty," by a military court attached to General Longstreet's Corps.

The court found Flowerree guilty, and, as required by the 45th AOW, sentenced him to be cashiered. As an addendum to the proceedings, the court attached this recommendation: (quoted in part)

> . . . The 45th Article of War prescribes that officers so offending [drunk on duty] shall be cashiered: and as that article is not repealed in terms, nor by necessary implication in the said act of the 21st April, they conceive that that article is still the rule of punishment for such offenses: but as before stated, they have come to the conclusion with reluctance. They find many inducements to a milder sentence. They find that the season and the service were so severe as to excuse to some extent the use of ardent spirits. They find that the "duty" upon which this officer was engaged was not such as to require any special exercise of care, conduct or capacity; and they find that he has established a character which is abundant of promise to the service and his state. For these reasons, therefore, they would have imposed a milder sentence and especially would not have deprived the Confederacy of his further services in the line of his profession. But in the absence, as they conceive, of such discretion, they can only commend him to the clemency of the Executive, which they hope may be exercised in such abatement of this sentence at least as will restore him to his command.

General Longstreet forwarded the proceeding to the secretary of war along with his endorsement of the court's recommendation; the president rightfully remitted the sentence.[6]

It is important to recognize that the president holds the power to pardon any sentence. As previously mentioned, this clemency was frequently used during the war, and nowhere as often as in the sentences of death or dismissal. The reviewing authority possessed the power to remit other sentences, but he held no power to pardon, even though the wording of AOW #89 uses the words "pardon" or "mitigate" in referring to this option.

Appeals for mercy were often made by avenues outside the court. After a sentence was announced in general orders, commanding officers of the accused or other members of his command would petition authorities to try to obtain clemency.

One example of such action involved Pvt. John Oscar Squires, Purcell Battery, who was tried for desertion on June 11, 1862; he was found guilty and sentenced to be shot.

The Purcell Battery was mustered into service on May 20, 1861, financed by a Richmond businessman, John Barry Purcell, and initially commanded by one of the South's most famous gunners, Capt. Reuben Lindsay Walker. At the time of the trial the battery was assigned to the Second Corps, Maj. Gen. A. P. Hill's Division, in the artillery battalion now commanded by Lt. Col. Reuben Lindsay Walker. Captain William J. Pegram was now in charge of the battery.

The battery had taken a front-rank position in Confederate artillery units and was known throughout the South for its gallantry after only one year of service. Members of the battery appealed to the president to spare Squires' life and on July 9, 1862, the president issued the following statement for the information of the army:

> In view of the representations made by members of the Purcell Battery in favor of Private John O. Squires, who is under sentence of death for desertion from that battery, and in consideration of the gallant service which that battery has rendered in the recent battles for the independence and peace of our common country, and especially with the hope that the great crime of which the said Squires has been convicted has been duly repented of by him, and that he will hereafter zealously perform his duty in defense of our sacred cause, the sentence of death is hereby remitted.[7]

In addition to the hundreds of individual cases dealt with by the president, he employed what might be termed blanket pardons by the extension of clemency to those who returned from absence without leave and to those serving extensive sentences of hard labor. Late in the war, the use of pardon was employed to try to put more men back into the ranks. The president virtually emptied the prison at Salisbury, N.C., in December 1864 of Confederate prisoners sentenced under courts-martial.[8] The extension of general amnesty that was authorized by the president in August 1863 was a failure; it certainly resulted in hundreds of cases of remission that were not deserved:

G.O. #109—A. & I.G.O.—August 11, 1863:

> I. A general pardon is given to all officers and men within the Confederacy now absent without leave from the army, who shall

(within twenty days from the publication of the address of the President in the State in which the absentee may then be) return to their posts of duty.

II. All men who have been accused or convicted, and undergoing sentence for absence without leave, or desertion, except only those who have been twice convicted of desertion, will be returned to their respective commands for duty.

A last desperate attempt to return men to the colors was issued under the heading of GO #2, Headquarters Armies Confederate States, February 11, 1865:

> . . . By authority of the President of the Confederate States a pardon is announced to such deserters and men improperly absent as shall return to the commands to which they belong within the shortest possible time, not exceeding twenty days from the publication of this order at headquarters of the district in which they may be. Those who are prevented by interruption of communications may report within the time specified to the nearest enrolling officer, or other officer on duty, to be forwarded as soon as practicable and upon their presenting the certificate of such officer, showing their compliance with this requirement, they shall receive the pardon hereby offered.
>
> Those who have deserted to the service of the enemy, or who have deserted after having been once pardoned for the same offense or those who shall desert or absent themselves without authority after the publication of this order, are excluded from its benefit, nor does the offer of pardon, extend to other offenses than desertion and absence without permission. By the same authority it is also declared that no general amnesty will again be granted. Those who refuse to accept the pardon now offered or who shall hereafter desert or absent themselves without leave, shall suffer such punishment as the courts may impose, and no application for clemency will be entertained . . .
>
> R. E. Lee, General

The response to this last offer of amnesty was negligible. Moreover, it had no effect on stemming the rash of desertions that commanders were struggling with daily. Such desperation is clearly spelled out by General Lee in a cipher dispatch dated February 28, 1865, to Richmond concerning Pvt. Samuel Thomas Huddleston, Co. E, 21st Virginia Infantry, who had been convicted of desertion and sentenced to be shot to death: "Private Huddleston's execution will be suspended as directed. Have reexamined case and he is not entitled to mercy under G.O. #2. Hundreds of men are deserting nightly and I cannot keep the army together unless examples are made of such cases."[9]

Other innovations were tried throughout the war to make use of these derelicts. Ward's Battalion and the Winder Legion are but two examples. The 100% of effort that went into these enterprises yielded only about a 2% return.

The success rate in all efforts to call transgressors to the colors was disappointingly low. The general malaise that worsened as the war wore on was the chief motive for desertion. Elements of induction added to the general discontent: conscription, special exemption from conscription, substitutions, variation in states' recruiting efforts, bonuses, and bounties. In addition divided loyalties prevailed in several states where the Confederacy was recruiting. The border states of Maryland, Kentucky, and Missouri offered a limited number of recruits for the Southern cause. In addition, Tennessee, although a Confederate state, was filled with Union loyalists. When some of these persons found their way into the Southern ranks, they became immediate candidates for desertion. The South experienced some strong Union sentiment in North Carolina also, to the extent that it was dangerous for Confederate recruiters to go into some North Carolina counties.

When these elements are weighed along with the deteriorating fortunes of the Confederacy during the last year or year and one-half of the war, it is little wonder that the desertions reached such high levels. The wonder of it is that more did not leave the ranks. Given the circumstances, the Southern government had little choice in choosing the options that it did for strengthening the cause.

Chapter VI
Punishments—
Not Capital

Punishment handed down by courts-martial or military courts ranged from reprimands to hanging. Enforcement of these punishments was usually left to the commanders of the division or brigade to which the prisoner belonged. However, this varied greatly with the extent and nature of the punishment.

Most sentences were multiple, that is, two or more types of punishment were inflicted. For example, a soldier sentenced to 30 days' confinement for AWOL would doubtless also suffer pay stoppage; an officer sentenced to suspension of rank and command may also be reprimanded. In order to properly classify sentences, a numbering system was used to indicate punishment. Numbers ranged from Code #00 for acquittal to Code #17 for hanging. Even though a man may receive two or more punishments, only the highest number is shown; thus, a prisoner sentenced to hard labor and pay stoppage would simply appear as Code #09.

Table 6.1
Numerical Codes for Sentences

Code	Sentence
00	Acquitted
01	Sentence remitted, disapproved, or no sentence
02	Reprimand
03	Fine or Pay stoppage
04	Suspension from rank and command
05	Company punishment
06	Confinement
07	Confinement on bread and water diet

Code	Sentence
08	Reduced to the ranks
09	Hard labor
10	Flogged
11	Cashiered
12	Drummed out of the service
13	Death, remitted or pardoned by president or other authority
14	Death, sentence not carried out, accused died, escaped, etc.
15	Death, but evidence sentence was carried out inconclusive
16	Shot to death with musketry
17	Hanged

Even though the numbering system does not tell the complete story in each case, it allows an accurate classification for the main category of each prisoner's sentence. Variations are not indicated by the numbered sentence; thus, a person put to hard labor for 15 days appears as Code #09, just as does one who is sentenced to six months.

Category 00

More than 16% of the cases recorded resulted in acquittal. This is a reasonable percentage. Higher numbers would indicate that too many unfounded charges were laid, and a lower rate of acquittal would call into question the impartiality of the courts. Barring the few examples of prejudice and jealousy among some officers, charges were brought in general courts-martial cases only where firm examples of transgressions were present.

The finding of acquittal by a court was final. If the court erred in its procedure, or if its judgement was misguided, no change could be made in its finding. The reviewing authority could castigate the court or the judge advocate or both, but he could not change the verdict. The accused must be restored to duty without punishment.

Category 01

The majority of cases in this category are those disapproved by the reviewing authority. If either the finding or the sentence was disapproved, then the accused was returned to duty and suffered no punishment. Other situations brought about a classification of Code #01, such as no sentence. A sentence is not demanded by military law unless the soldier is found guilty of a violation of an article of war that requires a specific sentence. In some examples, courts simply adjudged that the nature of guilt in a case deserved no punishment. In other examples, courts were aware of long terms of confinement that prisoners had been subjected to between arrest and trial. If the sentence contemplated by the court was of a similar nature, the court often awarded no sentence at all. The typical comment added by the court was "sentence none, the prisoner has already been sufficiently punished." If the reviewing authority disagreed, he could return the proceedings and request the court to reconsider the sentence, if the court was still sitting. However, if the court was adamant, his only option was to disapprove the sentence. This had no effect upon the prisoner's fate, it merely registered the commander's displeasure.

A reviewing authority was powerless to establish a sentence in a court-martial case. Within limits, he could mitigate sentences, but he could not change or substitute sentences. His power to remit all or portions of sentences was usually employed. The most frequent violation of military law was the substitution of one type of sentence for another. The chief example was the substitution of hard labor for a death sentence. This was done on several occasions by the president when he felt somewhat uncomfortable with extending an outright pardon to the accused. Late in the war, this misguided effort was also performed by army commanders.

A reviewing authority could always disapprove a sentence, thereby nullifying it and setting the prisoner free. The proper procedure for such action was for the commander to explain in his orders the reason for disapproval; however, no rule required him to set forth his reasons. The commander would occasionally issue orders at a later date remitting the unexpired portion of a sentence. This was usually done when punishment was being enforced within the prisoner's command structure. In such examples, the sentence code did not revert to Code #01, but remained its original classification. If a man were sentenced to three months at hard labor, and after serving one month, had the remainder of his sentence remitted, the sentence code stays as Code #09, hard labor.

Category 02

The mildest form of punishment awarded by the courts was the reprimand. This was done by either immediate superiors, such as "the colonel of the prisoner's regiment," or by a reprimand in general orders. The accused could be admonished privately or in front of his regiment or brigade at parade. The reprimand would be issued in orders if delivered at parade. The origin of these orders could be determined by the court. The reviewing authority was often the author of the reprimand; sometimes a lower commander was instructed to deliver the rebuke, and on occasion General Samuel Cooper issued the official dressing down from the adjutant general's office.

This mild form of punishment had little lasting effect, even for officers. The consequences for enlisted men were primarily a source for jokes. Early in the war, several enlisted men were sentenced to military tongue-lashings, but soon commanders extended the word to the courts to cease issuing such worthless punishments. After 1862, the habit of reprimanding enlisted men virtually disappeared.

Category 03

Fine or pay stoppage was another example of mild punishment. The proper terminology used in the articles of war is "fine." Enlisted men were usually fined a number of monthly payments to equal the term of their absence when convicted of AWOL or desertion. In addition they were often required to pay extra fines for lost articles of government property or for authorized bounties paid for their capture and return. Courts would order their pay stopped to satisfy the costs of fines handed down. A garrison court was limited to stoppage of one month's pay, no more.[1] For extended absences, soldiers were tried by general courts-martial or by the new military courts to assure that on matters of guilt, the required amount of pay could be forfeited.

Early in the war, the A&IGO issued the order to all commanders to enforce pay stoppage in all cases where the accused was convicted of absence without authorized leave.[2] Other types of fines were also provided for. Deserters forfeited the costs of bounties paid to civilian sources for their return ($30). The loss or destruction of arms and equipment resulted in a fine against the guilty party. If a man deserted with his weapons and accouterments, these items were seldom recovered upon his return. His sentence may result in a fine for the cost of such equipment.

In some examples, officers were required to repay large sums for misappropriation of money or property. Occasionally an officer would waste or sell stores belonging to the government; following a court-martial, if he were found guilty he would be cashiered and often fined a sum established by the court as the proper amount to be returned to the government.

Soldiers were sometimes found guilty of wasting military property; in such examples they may be fined the value of the property in question. Private John Kafelmann (Kaufleman) was tried by general court-martial in April 1863 on a charge of embezzlement of public property.

Specification 1st: "in that while acting ordnance sergeant at Battery Marshall he made away with ordnance stores entrusted to his care, March 7, 1863."

PLEA:

To the specification: "not guilty"
To the charge: "not guilty"

FINDING:

To the specification: "guilty"
To the charge: "not guilty, but guilty of gross neglect of duty"

SENTENCE:

That he forfeit to the Confederate States of America so much of his pay as will be necessary to reimburse the Confederacy for the property lost by his neglect.[3]

The forfeiture of pay for time lost was enforced throughout the war as evenly as the accounting records would permit, and commanders were careful to see that this rule was obeyed. For most transgressors it had little deterrence; the pay that was due them during their absence was not yet issued to them, so upon their return, following a court-martial, the court would order pay stoppage for time lost and any additional fines for apprehension or lost equipment.[4]

Category 04

The suspension from rank and command was frequently employed to punish officers convicted under courts-martial. This action was seldom imposed against non-commissioned officers; typically the court would reduce the NCO to the ranks, an act that rarely occurred with regard to officers. However, it was not unfounded for officers to be so punished, and late in the war it became standard procedure for officers who were cashiered to be immediately conscripted as privates.[5]

If an officer was suspended from rank and command for a specified length of time, the court could also suspend or forfeit his pay for that time period. This step was not automatic, but under AOW #84, the court had the power to invoke this added punishment. Generally, pay was not stopped for short suspensions (one month or less); but longer periods of suspension would usually be accompanied by pay forfeiture; in some such circumstances officers would apply for leave during the suspension.

Captain William B. Wade, Company D, 10th Mississippi Infantry, was tried on December 10, 1861, on a charge of AWOL; he was found guilty and sentenced to be cashiered. At the time of the trial the 10th Mississippi was part of Maj. Gen. Braxton Bragg's Army of Pensacola, Brig. Gen. Samuel Jones' Brigade.

After the proceedings were forwarded to the A&IGO, the president commuted the sentence to suspension from rank, pay, and allowances from December 31, 1861, to March 23, 1862.[6] No information on Captain Wade's duties during the suspension could be found. In all likelihood he remained with his company in an inactive capacity for these 81 days.

The fate of the accused is usually spelled out by the courts in such sentencing. An example is seen in the case of Capt. Seneca McNeil Bain of the 16th Mississippi Infantry who was tried in December 1862 on a charge of AWOL. At the time of the trial the 16th Mississippi was part of Brig. Gen. Winfield Scott Featherston's Brigade; Featherston was a fellow Mississippian, affectionately known as "Old Sweat," who had originally commanded the 17th Mississippi Infantry. His brigade was part of Maj. Gen. Richard H. Anderson's Division in the First Corps. Bain was declared guilty and his sentence was clearly set forth in GO #8, Army of Northern Virginia, January 23, 1863, paragraph 15: "And the Court does therefore sentence the said accused, Capt. S. McNeil Baine [sic], 16th Miss. Regiment, to be suspended from rank and pay, for six months; and during the said period, not to be allowed to leave the Regimental lines, except under orders."

An officer remaining with his command while under suspension of rank and command would function as a man temporarily without power. He could not perform his function as a commander of his troops, nor could he perform other military duties normally required of him, such as serving on courts-martial. He is not in arrest, per se, but he must operate much as an officer placed under arrest. He might be limited in his movements by his commanding officer.

Category 05

A frequently employed punishment under courts-martial was that of company punishment. That general term is used to describe the various methods employed within companies or regiments to inflict pain or embarrassment upon the accused to such an extent as to reform his indiscretions. Many of these forms of discipline were excruciating, while others were merely hilarious.

A typical sentence was to require the accused to walk in front of a sentinel with a sign attached to his back stating his offense: "chicken thief," "straggler," "drunk." An extension of this same punishment was developed to place the violator upon the head of barrel for a period of time with similar signage. Further employment of the barrel was used frequently in what was referred to as a "barrel shirt" or a "barrel jacket." This device was arranged from a common oak barrel with the head and floor knocked out, leaving only the outside staves and hoops; two straps were affixed to the top of the barrel so as to fit over the victim's shoulders. He was then required to wear the barrel on his walks before a sentinel; a clever sign would usually be attached.

Private Lewis B. McKinney, Co. C, 41st Georgia Infantry, was tried on December 28, 1863, for misbehavior before the enemy. At that time his regiment was part of Maj. Gen. Thomas C. Hindman's Corps, Maj. Gen. Alexander P. Stewart's Division, Brig. Gen. Marcellus A. Stovall's Brigade, Army of Tennessee. General Joseph E. Johnston issued GO #6, January 18, 1864, outlining McKinney's sentence. The court found him guilty and sentenced him to wear a barrel shirt two hours each day for 10 days, to be marched up and down in front of his "regimental parade ground." The barrel was to have attached a large sign reading "hasty retreat."

Sometimes a wooden horse would be constructed from a log and four wooden boards with a makeshift wooden head; the offender would be mounted backwards with two bayonets tied to his ankles as spurs, and a sign affixed to his back "joined the cavalry."

Bucking and gagging were used summarily for minor offenses as well as by garrison courts-martial. The offender was seated on the ground with his ankles bound and his wrists bound; his knees would then be brought up between his arms and a stick inserted underneath the knees and above the elbows. In addition, the victim may or may not be gagged. Such as awkward position became very uncomfortable after a short period of time; those left bucked for six hours or more could not walk immediately after being released.

Private John Riley was part of Capt. John T. Levi's Virginia Battery in the Department of East Tennessee. He was charged with "violation of 27th Article of War," by a court-martial on July 20, 1863. The specification states that he was guilty of disobedience of orders and of riotous conduct on June 14, 1863, at New Market, Tennessee.

Major General Simon B. Buckner, commanding the department, issued GO #101, dated August 4, 1863, outlining the results of the trial. Riley was found guilty of the specification and charge. His sentence was rather severe in that he was to serve 60 days at hard labor with ball and chain. Then, he was to be confined on bread and water diet for 14 days, and for one hour of each of these 14 days he was to be bucked and gagged, "between the hours of eight and nine o'clock, A.M."

Apparently the same court tried Pvt. Edward Ferry, of Capt. Edmund Winston's Company of Sappers and Miners, on the same charge and specification. He also was found guilty and was sentenced to be chained by the right leg in the guardhouse for 30 days and that during that period he was to be bucked and gagged for one hour each day from "8 o'clock until 9 o'clock, A.M."

Prisoners were occasionally tied up by the thumbs. Rope anchored to the wrists and knotted around the thumbs would be tied to a strong post or tree limb at a height to suspend the prisoner to the tips of his shoes so that his toes barely touched the ground, a very painful position.

Stocks were also employed to arrest either the victim's hands and neck so as to leave him standing as a public spectacle, or to fasten over his ankles with his back braced in an upright position, which soon became rather tiresome.

The artillery troops in both the Union and Confederate armies were some of the best disciplined units in service. It was no coincidence that the Confederate gunners were such outstanding performers, especially field artillerymen. Promotion for officers was limited; captains and majors were men of high rank. One of the positive results of this limited promotion was the cohesiveness of several commands; most veteran units were tightly controlled.

Straggling was often punished by tying the prisoner to the rear of a gun or caisson on the march. A dry day spent behind the wheels of a caisson had a sobering effect on the victim.

A more severe type of punishment was sometimes employed for habitual offenders. The prisoner would be bound by both wrists and both ankles to the fifth wheel of a caisson. That wheel is a spare which is mounted on the rear of the caisson at approximately a 60-degree angle.

Private William Shea, of Captain David D. Waters' Battery (Co. B, 2d Battalion Alabama Light Artillery), was tried by a battalion court-martial on April 27, 1863, on charges of conduct to prejudice of good order. He was found guilty and sentenced to be tied to the fifth wheel of a caisson for 12 hours per day for four days and to be fed upon bread and water during the term of his sentence. Waters' Battery was attached to Lt. Gen. Leonidas Polk's Corps in the Army of Tennessee.[7]

A variation to this type of punishment was sometimes employed to give the prisoner a very unpleasant ride. After the victim was bound, the wheel would be given a quarter turn and retightened, leaving him essentially trussed by one leg and one arm in a horizontal position. A short ride down the road would rattle the teeth of the offender.

Soldiers were frequently required to carry heavy logs while marching in a compound or "bull-ring"; sometimes the load was modified to a number of rocks in his haversack. These marching efforts were forms of public displays before the accompanying troops to convey the meaning of discipline to them as well.

A typical form of company punishment employed throughout the war was that of branding. This almost invariably accompanied another sentence such as "hard labor" or "drumming out of service." As a deterrent to reenlistment, an offender convicted for desertion who was sentenced to be drummed out of the service was branded on the left hip with the letter D; courts generally specified the size of the brand. At the beginning of the war, hot irons were used, but as the ill effects of these became apparent, indelible ink was substituted.

Several cases were tried by courts in the Army of Tennessee early in January 1864. The courts meted out punishments of branding that accompanied other sentences, such as confinement, drumming out of service, hard labor, or others. Many cases directed that the brand be placed on the left hip, D for desertion, but others were to be placed on the forehead or the left cheek.

General Joseph E. Johnston issued GO #6, dated January 18, 1864, and GO #7, dated January 26, 1864, wherein he remitted all the branding. He also informed the court that he considered branding cruel and unusual punishment and that they should restrict their punishments to the "usual" modes.

Branding was employed for other offenses than desertion. The letter T was sometimes used on prisoners convicted of theft, or C for cowards and D for drunks.

The use of these various forms of company punishment had a positive effect on other members of the command as well as an expedience of action. Locally enforced punishments eliminated the need for transferal of the prisoner to other areas. Therefore, commanders could expedite the sentence and then return the prisoner to duty as quickly as possible. Garrison courts would always invoke such limited punishments as their sentences. They also employed confinement and hard labor, but for terms of one month or less. These were invariably served locally.

Category 06

The sentence of confinement has been a standard for courts-martial for hundreds of years. During the Civil War, sentences for confinement ranged from one day to 20 years. Even though a 20-year sentence could not have been enforced, given the limits of the endurance of the Confederacy, at the time of the sentence, that limitation could not be foreseen. A few serious cases were given such lengthy terms. Courts would occasionally sentence prisoners to confinement in a state penitentiary; army commanders would usually disapprove such sentences with the reminder that the military had no such authority. The most sensible long-term confinement was for "during the war."

Private George Enseroth was brought up on charges on November 13, 1861: violation of Article of War #6 (twice), #9, and #45. He was found guilty of all charges. He was doubtless found drunk on guard (AOW #45); then displayed disrespect for his superior officer (AOW #6); and then struck or lifted up a weapon on his superior, perhaps the sergeant of the guard.

The court handed down a stiff sentence for him; he was to be confined with a 32-pound ball with a three-foot chain attached to both legs for the duration of the war. In addition, he was to be deprived of all pay and put into solitary confinement on bread and water diet the last seven days of every month during the time of his confinement. That would total 84 days during a year which is the maximum allowed by army regulations.

At the time of the court-martial the 1st Louisiana Battalion of Zouaves was part of Maj. Gen. John Bankhead Magruder's Army of the Peninsula. GO #122, dated December 21, 1861, lists Enseroth as a member of "Louisiana Zouaves"; however, no such name could be found in the *Louisiana Military Records* or for that matter in any Confederate index. But the accused must have been a member of the 1st Louisiana Battalion of Zouaves, an organization that had a dearth of recordkeeping.

In his approval of the trial Magruder expresses his preference for the term of confinement as "during his enlistment" rather than "during the war." He thereby remitted Enseroth's sentence to the term of his enlistment. At this early stage of the war, troops were not being enrolled for terms of enlistment as "during the war" as they were at a later date.

These long confinements required that the prisoner be shipped to one of the military prisons. The two most famous were Castle Thunder in Richmond, Virginia, and Salisbury Prison in Salisbury, North Carolina. Castle Thunder was a former tobacco warehouse and Salisbury was an abandoned cotton factory. Men were sent to these or other prisons to serve long confinements handed down by courts-martial or to await trial by courts-martial. Retention of many of the persons accused of crimes was a major problem for company and regimental commanders. Therefore, the military prison was often resorted to. Not that the prisons were escape proof; when orders were issued for the return of an accused to stand trial, he was occasionally not to be found.

Local confinement was used whenever possible for short sentences. Most regiments or brigades constructed guardhouses and these were used for confinement of prisoners. These facilities were temporary quarters for units serving in the field. When an army went into winter quarters, such facilities would be constructed by the men much in the same way that they would build their own shelters. During active campaigns, no such facilities would be available; company or regimental commanders would have to resort to tents to hold prisoners. Fetters, or "irons," would often be used to bind prisoners to tent poles, iron balls, or large blocks.

Category 07

Confinement on bread and water diet was used whenever the court deemed the seriousness of the offense warranted the added punishment. The sentence of solitary confinement on bread and water diet required the prisoner to be fastened in a dark cell (solitary confinement) and fed only on bread and water. The effect of such a sentence was recognized by authorities, for the limitation set forth in Article 873 of the *Regulations of the Army of the Confederate States* was taken directly from the United States regulations; that is, no more than 14 days at a time, with intervals between the confinement of not less than 14 days, with total days in such confinement limited to 84 days per year.

Despite these limitations in the regulations, violations were occasionally seen. Two such examples appear in Beauregard's Department of South Carolina, Georgia, and Florida. On May 25, 1863, Privates John B. Spradling and William H. Mayo of Company E, 46th Virginia Infantry, were tried on unknown charges and sentenced as follows: "To be confined in Castle Thunder or some other place, on bread and water alone for 30 days and forfeit pay for one month."

Private Pinckney H. Kennedy of the 14th Mississippi Infantry, Company C, was tried by a court in the Department of Mississippi and East Louisiana on May 8, 1863, and again on May 9, 1863. He faced two trials on the three charges of (1) sleeping on guard, (2) drunk on guard, and (3) quitting guard. He was found guilty by the first court and sentenced to 12 days on bread and water diet. At his trial on May 9, 1863, he was also found guilty and sentenced to 20 days' confinement, 10 days on bread and water diet, 6 days on regular diet, and the final 4 days on bread and water.

Undergoing solitary confinement (in a dark cell) on bread and water diet was a very unpleasant experience. The armies in the field, of course, did not have access to solitary prison cells. Men were usually confined to tents or to rudely constructed guardhouses if the army was in winter quarters. Nevertheless, such a diet could be injurious to the prisoner's health over long periods of time.

The sentence was liberally used, for more than 840 cases were tallied, without considering those that were added as supplements to hard-labor sentences.

72Chapter Six

Category 08

The sentence of reduction to the ranks was usually accompanied by added punishment when handed down by courts-martial. Military regulations required that NCOs be reduced to the ranks before suffering some punishments. Imprisonment and flogging could not be inflicted upon a non-commissioned officer; therefore, he automatically would be reduced to the ranks before undergoing such a sentence. No such requirement existed for the sentence of death.

Frequently a court would limit the punishment to a simple reduction to the ranks. Or, perhaps the reviewing authority would remit additional sentencing, leaving only the punishment of reduction. The general attitude of intolerance for violations by NCOs prevailed in most courts. If an NCO were adjudged guilty, he would usually lose his stripes. Sometimes a court would fail to add this to his punishment and the reviewing authority would simply put that omission in orders, since he had the authority to summarily reduce any non-commissioned officer.

Such action would often create a rogue for the service, especially in situations where the former NCO judges himself innocent of the charges. In other examples, the violator bounces back to recover his stripes in short time. Many examples are found in the CSRs of sergeants undergoing reduction two or three times.

The sentence of suspension from rank and pay, Code #04, could also be handed down for NCOs but seldom was. Only six examples were tabulated for sergeants or corporals who were suspended; this punishment would have been resorted to for mild infractions. Any serious misbehavior would result in a reduction to the ranks.

The total number of such sentences recorded was less than 300. That figure is misleading in that it only reflects those cases whereby a reduction was the most serious punishment inflicted. It does not contain all of those who were sentenced to hard labor for whom the reduction was subordinate to the greater sentence.

Category 09

The sentence of hard labor was the most frequently employed punishment inflicted by the courts in the Confederate service. In the many examples, the extent of the punishment varies greatly; the term might run to only one week in one case, whereas it might extend to "during the war" in another. A few unfortunates were sentenced to such terms as 10 years or more, although these were obviously inoperable once the war ended.

Short sentences were served locally and included any tasks that required strong backs, such as the burial of dead horses, grubbing of stumps, cutting wood, or corduroying roads.

Long sentences, generally those running to terms greater than three months, were usually performed at one of the military prisons; that is, the prisoners were incarcerated there. The labors performed were usually done on military works. For example, those sentenced to hard labor from the Army of Northern Virginia were sent to Richmond to build defenses around that city.

Alabama built a camp of correction for Alabama troops. This post was located in Mobile and most unfortunates in the western commands who were sentenced to hard labor served their time on the government works in Mobile and were confined in the camp of correction.

Probably 50% of the long-term sentences were accompanied by a provision for the prisoner to wear a ball and chain. This added attraction greatly increased the misery of the accused. The court would specify the weight of the ball (usually between 20 and 32 pounds) and length of the chain (usually 8 to 12 feet); the shorter the chain and the greater the weight, the more the prisoner was limited in his movement. Little could be done to prevent the manacle from rubbing the ankle raw and keeping it that way. Prisoners would attempt to wrap rags or bandages around their legs, but little space was available for such attempts.

Occasionally the reviewing authority would remit the ball and chain. Many such recipients did not realize how valuable such a remission would prove to be. A few unfortunates were sentenced to wear a ball and chain attached to each leg; and one or two examples were seen whereby the court directed that the chain be attached to the victim's neck.

One of the more interesting cases involved 2d Lieutenant William H. Starling of Company M, 9th Alabama Cavalry (Malone's, aka, 7th) of Brig. Gen. John T. Morgan's Brigade of Maj. Gen. Joseph Wheeler's Cavalry Corps. Starling was convicted on or about December 14, 1864, of AWOL by a general court-martial, having originally been charged with desertion. He was cashiered and further sentenced to six months' hard labor with ball and chain. Not only is the sentence of hard labor for an officer unusual, the imposition of the ball and chain is unprecedented.

General Wheeler sent Starling to the Department of the Gulf to labor on the works at Mobile. General Dabney H. Maury, who commanded the department, refused to invoke the sentence without higher authority. Telegrams were exchanged between Maury and his superior, General Beauregard. Maury claimed that the sentence was unlawful in addition to being contrary to the best interests of the service. Since the court had cashiered Starling, Maury claimed that he then became a civilian and not subject to further punishment.

Beauregard dodged the issue by declaring that Wheeler had no authority to send the prisoner to the Department of the Gulf since it was not part of his command. He directed Maury to return the prisoner to Wheeler, but no evidence is seen as to the disposition of Starling's sentence. It is a safe assumption that Wheeler simply allowed the disgraced officer to depart with a forfeiture of his pay.[8]

A similar case appears to have had a somewhat different outcome. On May 7, 1863, 2d Lt. Roger Tamure (Tammure), of Company I, 13th Louisiana Infantry, was tried before a court-martial convened by Polk's Corps at Tullahoma, Tennessee, on a charge of desertion. He was found guilty and sentenced to be cashiered and to be confined in such penitentiary as the commanding general may direct for the term of five years at hard labor. General Braxton Bragg approved the sentence and directed that Tamure be confined in the penitentiary at Wetumpka, Alabama, under the direction of the provost marshal of the Army of Tennessee.[9]

The initial reaction for these prisoners is one of sympathy, and it is certain that theirs was a pathetic lot. The living conditions in the Confederate prisons were deplorable; hard labor claimed more lives than the firing squad and the gallows combined. But the reality of those trying times gives one pause, and demands a reflection upon the devotion of those who remained in the ranks to face the horror of the Wilderness; the race with death at Spotsylvania; the bitter months in the trenches of Petersburg; and the heartbreak of Appomattox. Fully 90% of those undergoing hard labor and similar sentences were deserters who shrank from those unpleasant duties that their more loyal brothers in arms were facing; many had been convicted of desertion two or more times. It is easy to condemn the whole war as a needless waste of lives which it truly was, but without harsh discipline men cannot be kept in the ranks to face their grim duty.

Category 10

For the first two years of the war, the courts of the Confederate States Armies made extensive use of the lash in punishing offenses. The United States articles of war had undergone a variety of changes as regards flogging since their adoption in 1806.

As originally entered in AOW #87, flogging was limited by the simple phrase "nor shall more than fifty lashes be inflicted on any offender, at the discretion of a Court-Martial." Whipping was entirely repealed on May 16, 1812:

> So much of the Act for establishing Rules and Articles for the
> government of the Armies of the United States, as authorizes the

infliction of corporal punishment by stripes or lashes, shall be, and the same is hereby, repealed.[10]

The prohibition remained in effect until 1833, when it was modified. On March 3, 1833, flogging was once again an acceptable punishment for any enlisted soldier convicted by a general court-martial of the crime of desertion. On August 5, 1861, the United States Congress again banned flogging for all offenses.

When the Confederate States government adopted the United States articles of war, AOW #87 still read in part, "nor shall more than fifty lashes be inflicted on any offender, at the discretion of a court-martial." The amendments passed in 1812 and 1833 were cited at the end of the articles. The Confederate Congress simply removed all reference to stripes from AOW #87 and left it to read:

> No person shall be sentenced to suffer death but by the concur-rence of two-thirds of the members of a general court-martial, nor except in the cases herein expressly mentioned; and no of-ficer, non-commissioned officer, soldier, or follower of the army, shall be tried a second time for the same offense.[11]

The Confederate Congress went on to adopt Article #38 of the regulations for the army and in section 873, listed the legal pun-ishments for soldiers by sentence of courts-martial:

> . . . death, corporal punishment by flogging; confinement; con-finement on bread and water diet; solitary confinement; hard labor; ball and chain; forfeiture of pay and allowances; discharge from the service; and reprimands. Solitary confinement, and con-finement on bread and water shall not exceed fourteen days at a time, with intervals between the periods of such confinement not less than such periods, and not exceeding eighty-four days in one year.

The result of all these citations and amendments was that the Confederate States not only authorized the infliction of stripes, but they threw out the limitation of 50 that was written into the origi-nal article in 1806. Courts routinely sentenced prisoners to more than 50 lashes, rarely at one time, but frequently over a period of time. The usual such sentence was for "Pvt. A.B. to receive 39 lashes on his bare back, and to then serve six months of hard labor, and at the end of his term of labor to receive 39 additional lashes on his bare back."

One extreme case was brought to the attention of the secre-tary of war by the members of the House of Representatives on January 27, 1863, whereby they inquired into the sentence of Pvt. L. B. Seymour of Company E, 50th North Carolina Troops.

Leonidas B. Seymour, private of Co. E of the 50th North Carolina Infantry, was tried on October 14, 1862, for the crime of desertion, in

a court under the appointment of Gen. Gustavus W. Smith, Headquarters Richmond. At the time of the trial, the 50th was part of the
troops in North Carolina under command of Maj. Gen. Theophilus
H. Holmes, in Brig. Gen. Junius Daniel's Brigade. General Smith
approved the sentence on January 13, 1863:

> Private L. B. Seymour is to receive thirty-nine lashes on his bare
> back, every three months, for the period of the war, to be branded
> in the left hand with the letter D, and to be put to hard labor in
> Richmond, with ball and chain, for the balance of the war.

The secretary of war forwarded the inquiry to General Cooper.
His reply to the secretary explains the procedure whereby the Con-
federate Congress passed on February 9, 1861, all laws of the United
States in force on November 1, 1860, not inconsistent with the
Confederate constitution. He then cites the original AOW #87 from
the act of April 10, 1806, and all of the amendments referred to
earlier. However, he goes on to add that he is unaware that the
United States abolished flogging on August 5, 1861; he cites the
United States Army regulations, a copy of which he doubtless possessed. His reaction is reasonable in that he assumed that the
United States service dropped the punishment because of the in-
flux of volunteer units:

> It may be proper here to observe that while I am not aware of any
> law having been passed by the U. States abolishing the punish-
> ment by flogging yet in the enumeration of 'legal punishment for
> soldiers' in the regulations adopted in 1861 for the army of the
> U. States, this punishment is not referred to. The omission was
> no doubt made for the benefit of the volunteer service now orga-
> nized—an example, which I am of opinion, might very well be
> followed to that extent at least by our Government. For without
> determining between the arguments pro and con upon the gen-
> eral question it may safely be affirmed that in an army of volun-
> teers, composed of Southern soldiers, and in a country where
> punishment by stripes is perhaps seldom if ever inflicted on white
> citizens by the judgment of the civil tribunals, such punishment
> is naturally regarded as degrading, and had better be suspended
> at least during the existence of our present military organization.

Although General Cooper's facts are slightly flawed, his observations are incisive; three months later, the Congress of the
Confederate States abolished flogging.[12] General Cooper informed
the armies under GO #44, A&IGO, April 16, 1863.

It is likely that Seymour received his first round of flogging
and was sent forth to his term of hard labor, but he apparently did
not serve out his entire sentence. His CSR indicates that he was
returned to duty on "November 1, 1863, or prior."[13]

During the two years that the punishment of stripes was in force, the courts handed down 209 decisions awarding stripes to be inflicted upon the prisoners, three of whom were slaves and one a free Negro. In addition, 43 soldiers were ordered to be drummed out of the service after receiving lashes. If all sentences were carried out, then 248 Confederate enlisted men were whipped.

It was not unusual for courts to award a variety of sentences, stripes, hard labor, and to be branded and drummed out of the service. Yet the custom of the United States service, when flogging was employed, was to not accompany it with a sentence of confinement or hard labor. DeHart clarifies this issue by explaining the procedure in effect in the 1850s when flogging was authorized for the crime of desertion only.[14]

Since the regulations set forth by the Confederate Congress did not specify that the punishment of flogging was limited to the crime of desertion, it could legally be applied for other offenses. Moreover, as DeHart explains, for the United States service, where articles of war leave the punishment to the discretion of the court, such as for desertion, it was not unusual for courts to award both stripes and hard labor.

Only one poor fellow was sentenced by two different courts to face the lash, Pvt. Layton G. Meadows of Company C, 36th Virginia Infantry. On December 8, 1862, he was tried for desertion from his regiment, which was part of Col. John McCausland's Brigade in the Department of Western Virginia and East Tennessee. He was sentenced "to be struck on the back with 23 stripes."

Meadows was tried again on March 16, 1863, for desertion. This time the court sentenced him to receive 30 lashes, to forfeit 12 months' pay, to 2 months' hard labor, and to 14 days of solitary confinement on bread and water diet.

The number of lashes rarely exceeded 39; but if properly administered, that was sufficiently unpleasant. The procedure was not standard; sometimes the prisoner would be tied to three stacked muskets that were lashed together at the muzzles. A strong rope was used to bind his wrists to these rifle muzzles and the stripes would be laid on by some member of the brigade or regiment. The custom of the service was to use the drummer, but if only boys were available, another choice was needed. The strokes would typically be counted by taps on a drum, and a surgeon was usually present to assure that the victim did not receive more punishment than be could bear. In place of muskets, a more stable structure was a wooden tripod bolted at the top and anchored a little further down with one cross piece (forming a capital *A*) upon which the prisoner could lean his chest.

The usual instrument for administering the whipping was the cat-o'-nine-tails, which was constructed of nine lashes of whipcord, each knotted in three places. Each cord was from 16 to 18 inches long and fastened to a wooden handle approximately 14 inches in length. Rawhide was sometimes substituted for the whipcord.

The most expeditious means of arresting the prisoner was to lash him to the wheel of a gun or to the fifth wheel of a caisson. As time went by, such punishments were met with jocularity rather than any trembling. Men came to make light of the worst of circumstances. Those confined in dismal prisons viewed life as a cheap commodity and took their own passing or that of their companions with little regard.

Officers were not sentenced to receive lashes because such action would be injurious to the service. Also non-commissioned officers could not be flogged. Three sergeants and five corporals received such sentences, so prior to the laying on of the stripes, the NCOs would be reduced to the ranks.

The custom of inflicting stripes was handed down by the British service. The lash was the most convenient form of discipline for both the army and the navy in Great Britain long before the United States became an independent country, and such custom continued for more than 100 years after our independence. It was not until 1881 that Great Britain abolished flogging in service. The maximum number of strokes was limited to 50 in 1846, but prior to that no limit was established. Courts would routinely award 100 lashes for minor infractions and, in more serious offenses, several hundred. Such extreme punishment was often a death sentence.

The duke of Wellington was a firm believer in the liberal use of flogging. His influence in military decisions was quite powerful for the first half of the 19th century, and it was only after his passing that serious reforms in the British army began to take shape.

Category 11

The sentence of dismissal from the service, or cashiering, was the most extreme punishment awarded to officers. The act of cashiering an officer is the same as dismissal and the two terms are synonymous. Most of the articles of war that refer to this action use the term "shall be cashiered." The term usually employed in general orders is that "Captain A.B. is hereby dismissed the service, and as of this date ceases to be an officer of the Confederate States."

Comparatively, the Confederate courts dismissed far fewer officers than did those of the Union service. Incompetency among Union commands required the president to summarily dismiss hundreds and hundreds of officers; late in the war he delegated this authority to army commanders. This had no lasting effect on some. Before the ink dried on the orders, some rascals would return with a promotion from their governor.

The total number of approximately 530 cases for the Confederacy is explainable in one word: desperation. The indiscretions of anyone with merit were overlooked again and again. And in the final analysis, such action was justified. Valuable service was obtained from dozens and dozens who, in another army in another time, would have been dismissed. The few scoundrels who hung on when they should have been discharged where limited in number. It is hard to imagine how the Confederate cause could have been improved by the loss of Lafayette McLaws, William Barksdale, William E. "Grumble" Jones, and others who might have been dismissed from the service.

An added insult to cashiering was to publish the offense as the 85th AOW provided:

> In all cases where a commissioned officer is cashiered for cowardice or fraud, it shall be added in the sentence that the crime, name, and place of abode, and punishment of the delinquent, be published in the newspapers in and about the camp, and of the particular state from which the offender came, or where he usually resides; after which it shall be deemed scandalous for an officer to associate with him.

Cashiering was the ultimate punishment for an officer. In regular service, it meant the end of a career and, of course, for the older, higher ranking officer, it was even more devastating. For the volunteers of the Civil War, it often was of little consequence. Many who were dismissed had no business wearing shoulder straps in the first place, the service was surely improved by their departure. The system of electing officers within a regiment was greatly flawed. Many popular individuals were incompetent to hold such positions, and in several examples, the men paid dearly for their poor choices.

On a few occasions the incapable officer recognized his own limitations and voluntarily stepped down into the ranks. Persons with such wisdom often went on to serve as good soldiers. Most ambitious individuals who were looking merely for added privilege and then wound up being cashiered before a military court were rarely contrite; most were simply glad to be leaving the service. Manpower shortages later in the war required such individuals to be immediately conscripted into the ranks, often in another unit.

One example involved 2d Lt. H. Healey [Healy], Co. G, 1st Louisiana Volunteer Infantry, who was convicted by a court convened at Atlanta, Georgia, Army of Tennessee, on May 20, 1863. Healey was charged with presenting himself to the paymaster at Atlanta

as Capt. John Hendrix of Co. C, 1st Louisiana Volunteers and drawing pay for $130. This was committed while Healey was AWOL from
his command, but he was not charged with being absent by this
court. He was found guilty and sentenced to be cashiered and "sent
to his command to be conscripted and placed in the ranks of Company 'C' of the 1st Louisiana Volunteers, Army of the Potomac [sic]."

General Braxton Bragg forwarded the records to the secretary
of war after approving the findings and sentence, since he had no
authority to assign Healey to the 1st Louisiana Volunteers, which
was part of the Army of Northern Virginia, Second Corps, Maj. Gen.
Edward Johnson's Division, Brig. Gen. Francis R. T. Nicholls' Brigade. The A&IGO issued SO #170, July 20, 1864, paragraph 7,
whereby the sentence was approved, but added that the "accused
is permitted to select the company to which he may be conscripted."

It is uncertain as to how many officers who were dismissed by
courts found their way back into the commissioned ranks, a few
certainly did. It was not nearly as prevalent for governors to reap-
point such officers in the Confederate armies as it was for Northern
governors to do so, but it did occur.

An interesting example exists in the case of John Dunovant,
who had been a captain in the 10th United States Infantry. He
resigned to return to his native state of South Carolina and was
soon made colonel of the 1st South Carolina Regulars.

In June of 1862, the 1st South Carolina Regulars were part of
the Department of South Carolina and Georgia. His regiment was
ordered to make the advance on John's Island, South Carolina,
and to capture the bridge to the island on the night of June 9.
When Dunovant arrived with his infantry, he was so drunk that he
was unable to execute any orders. His brigade commander, Brig.
Gen. Nathan G. "Shanks" Evans, came up to find Dunovant lying
in the road, in front of the brigade, passed out. Evans was no
stranger to John Barleycorn, but he could not disregard such in-
competence; Dunovant was brought before a court of inquiry and
was recommended for dismissal.

The proceedings were forwarded to the president who caused
GO #83, A&IGO, November 8, 1862, to be issued in which he stated:

> The offense is of too grave a character to be overlooked in an
> officer of such high rank, and is aggravated by the circumstances
> under which it was committed. Colonel Dunovant will be dis-
> missed from the service.

This should have been the end of Dunovant's military career;
however, the 5th South Carolina Cavalry was organized in January
1863, and Governor Francis W. Pickens appointed Dunovant colonel.
It appears that the colonel had taken the cure, for he performed

yeoman service in the Department of South Carolina, Georgia, and Florida.

The regiment was transferred to Brig. Gen. Matthew Calbraith Butler's Brigade of the Cavalry Corps of the Army of Northern Virginia in time for the battle of the Wilderness, and by mid-summer, after Butler had been given command of a cavalry division, Maj. Gen. Wade Hampton elevated Dunovant to command of the brigade, and Davis approved his temporary rank of brigadier general on August 22, 1864. The record shows that he served ably until he was killed in action on the Vaughan Road on October 1, 1864.

This is but one story of many in which the Southern government made do with whatever resources were at hand.

Clemency for cashiered officers was often urged by brother officers outside the court. In addition to any recommendation for mercy that the court might make, fellow officers often petitioned the reviewing authority to suggest clemency. If the army commander was so persuaded, his endorsement on the proceedings that were forwarded to the secretary of war would carry considerable weight.

The power to pardon or remit the sentence of cashiering rested only with the president, in most cases where the court recommended mercy, proceedings were forwarded to the president for his action. However, in the majority of rulings, the commanding general simply approved the sentence of the court and announced in orders that the accused ceases to be an officer in the army of the Confederate States.

Category 12

The sentence of drumming out of service was a standard form of discharge for private soldiers convicted of crimes by the courts. The reviewing authority sometimes remitted the drumming out; however, 166 cases were found that received such sentences. Early in the war, courts frequently awarded such discharges, often accompanied by lashes to be inflicted.

Conviction of a charge of theft was almost automatically followed by a sentence of drumming out with or without flogging. It was generally the custom of the service to rid the army of such undesirable characters. In addition, the thief was usually branded with a letter *T*, often in the palm of the left hand.

Deserters were sometimes given such discharges early in the war and were branded on the left hip with a hot iron to show the letter *D*; this was done to preclude their reenlistment. Such sentences became ineffective for the typical deserter as the war wore on; consequently, reviewing authorities often remitted the drumming out. The true deserter was only too happy to be released from the army by whatever means were at hand.

Courts frequently exceeded the intent of military law by awarding multiple sentences. It was not unusual to find a man sentenced to receive 39 lashes, to be put to hard labor for six months, and to be drummed out of the service upon expiration of his hard labor after being branded on the left hip with the letter *D*. Reviewing authorities who approved such sentences were remiss. As the war progressed, more and more commanders would remit all but the hard labor.

Several examples were found whereby the prisoner was sentenced to hard labor during the war and then to be dishonorably discharged. At the end of the war, the second portion of the sentence, of course, became inoperable.

Several CSRs reflect the fact that the soldier was indeed dishonorably discharged, others do not indicate the facts. Private W. H. Giddings of Company A, 2d Arkansas Cavalry, stole a gold locket from a lady in town and was sentenced to receive 39 stripes and then to have his head shaved and be drummed out of the service. His last card shows he was whipped and drummed out on August 5, 1862.[15]

When a sentence was properly carried out, the regimental or brigade troops were assembled; the prisoner was brought forward in charge of the guard; the orders were read aloud for all to hear. The facings and buttons were removed from his uniform; he was then uncovered, and if so ordered, his hair was shaved off half his head; and he was marched out between files in front of the guard who had bayonets fixed while the drums and bugles played the "Rogue's March." The prisoner was escorted beyond the confines of camp and forbidden to return.

Officers were not subjected to this ignominy in the United States service or the Confederate States service; however, it was not unknown in other civilized armies of Western Europe.

One of the most troubling actions found in the records was that of the president substituting one sentence for another handed down by the court. The president performed such acts under his broadened interpretation of his pardoning power. No such authority rested in the hands of army commanders or other military convening authority.

Three members of the 1st Missouri Infantry were tried for desertion, two on July 22, 1862, and the other on July 23, 1862: Pvt. Farron Gray of Company H, Pvt. William Black of Company B, and Pvt. Henry T. Blaylock, of Company G. Each was sentenced to be shot to death. No notation was contained in the ledger records of trials to indicate that the proceedings had been referred to the secretary of war and no orders concerning the sentence could be found in those issued by the A&IGO. However, the CSR of Blaylock shows that he received 50 lashes and was drummed out of the service on September 2, 1862.[16] Black's record simply states that he was discharged by sentence of court-martial on September 2, 1862.[17] Gray's record states: "Drummed out of the Service by GCM Sept./Oct. '62."[18] It is reasonable to assume that all three men received the same punishment on September 2, 1862.

At the time of the trial, the 1st Missouri Infantry was part of Brig. Gen. Benjamin Hardin Helm's Brigade of Maj. Gen. John Cabell Breckinridge's Reserve Corps, Army of the Mississippi, under the command of Gen. Braxton Bragg, who reported to Gen. P.G.T. Beauregard. In the absence of orders, it is impossible to identify the authority who changed the sentence of the court, but since the ledger in the A&IGO shows the entry of the death sentence, it would appear that some instructions came from Richmond.

On February 5, 1862, Pvt. John Kennealy of Company H, 2d Alabama Infantry, was tried on an undetermined charge and sentenced to be shot to death by the court convened under GO #39, Department of Alabama and West Florida dated January 31, 1862. The 2d Alabama was part of the Army of Mobile, under the command of Brig. Gen. Jones M. Withers; that wing, plus the Army of Pensacola under Brig. Gen. Samuel Jones, made up the Department of Alabama and West Florida under the command of Maj. Gen. Braxton Bragg.

No orders could be found from either the Department of Alabama or the A&IGO concerning Kennealy's case, but the last card in his CSR simply states "discharged 4/23/62."[19]

Private William Cottrell, Company B, 35th Arkansas Infantry, was sentenced to death by a court on November 4, 1862, on an unknown charge. Notation in the trial ledgers of the A&IGO shows the sentence was "commuted by General Hindman to 39 lashes on his bare back." At the time of the trial, Cottrell was listed as a member of "Col. McRae's Regt. Trans-Mississippi Infantry." Dandridge McRae held several Arkansas commands. At Wilson's Creek he was colonel of the 21st Arkansas Infantry, but this regiment was later reorganized. McRae subsequently became colonel of the 28th Arkansas Infantry which was also called the 2d Trans-Mississippi Infantry. The index to the CSRs shows Cottrell as a member of the 35th Arkansas Infantry. All of these units were part of Maj. Gen. Thomas C. Hindman's Confederate First Corps of the Trans-Mississippi Army stationed at Prairie Grove, Arkansas.

A clear example of the substitution of one sentence for another by order of the secretary of war is contained in the trial of Pvt. Benjamin Staten, Company D, 36th Virginia Infantry, who was tried

December 8, 1862, for desertion and sentenced to be shot. The 36th was part of Col. John McCauseland's Brigade in the Department of Western Virginia and East Tennessee. Maj. Gen. Samuel Jones forwarded the proceedings to the secretary of war. The notation in the ledger of trials shows, "This sentence was commuted to the following: 'To receive 39 lashes on his bare back with a raw hide well laid on—to have his head shaved and to be drummed out of the service.'"

Enlisted personnel were unlikely to register a complaint after having a death sentence reduced to one of hard labor or flogging. Moreover, many of them may not have known the exact details of their case; the fact that most had a very limited knowledge of military law and the practice of courts-martial also played a part.

Action of commanders in the Trans-Mississippi differed somewhat from that of other generals. Early in the war, Richmond did not devote a great deal of attention to the region, and after the fall of Vicksburg, access to the area was very limited. The half-dozen examples of changes of sentences cited are but a few of those that occurred. Details were lacking in most, but the CSRs in many cases of soldiers sentenced to be shot simply indicate "discharged" alongside a date. In many of these court-martial cases, the War Department could not communicate with the commanders, so any action on the part of these officers was often left to their discretion.

Military law is very clear on this issue. The president alone holds the power to pardon; he can exercise this power to forgive any sentence handed down by a court. Reviewing authority may remit any sentence awarded by the courts except that of death or the cashiering of an officer. Remission has a similar effect as does a pardon, but it is important to recognize the proper terms; for military crimes only the chief executive has pardoning power.

The debatable issue here is the substitution of one sentence for another. Only the court may do that, and only if requested to do so by the reviewing authority while they are still sitting. Once the court is dissolved, it is too late for them to reconsider their sentence. It would be out of the question for another court to consider the sentence, for that would subject the prisoner to double jeopardy.

Reviewing authority has the power to remit all or part of any sentence except death or cashiering, or to mitigate the severity of other sentences. For example, a man may be sentenced to six months at hard labor; the reviewing authority may approve the sentence but reduce the terms of the sentence from six months to three months.

Although the president holds the power of pardon as well as the right to mitigate sentences, he may not increase sentences nor may he substitute one form of punishment for another. In addition, the president holds no power to approve the sentence of a court unless he is the convening authority. He holds the power to convene (appoint) courts, but rarely exercises it. This is the job of his army or corps commanders. After the court completes a case, it must be forwarded to that convening authority who then becomes the reviewing authority whose job it is to approve or disapprove the court's findings.

The president may not usurp the power of the reviewing authority; he becomes involved only in those cases whereby the general who reviewed the trial and approved the sentence forwards the proceedings to the president for his action on the sentence. This was usually done upon sentences of death or cashiering whereby the reviewing authority felt that mercy was applicable.

It is important to remember that the Confederate government was operating under the same articles of war as the United States and that their military law was based upon the lucid interpretation handed down by Captain DeHart. His writing on the subject of mitigation of sentences is so clear that it should be included to enlighten this issue:

> The law has clearly given the power to the officer who orders a court-martial, except in cases of capital punishment, or the cashiering or dismissing a commissioned officer, to pardon, or to mitigate any punishment ordered by such court-martial. To pardon is to absolve from punishment: to mitigate the punishment is to make it less in degree, but of the same species. Beyond this the reviewing officer cannot go. Any attempt to change the punishment in kind would be illegal, and such an exercise of authority would be the assumption of exclusive judicial, as well as to a certain degree, of legislative power. To commute punishment, is to substitute for the one ordered, another of a different kind, to change the species by the mere will of the individual, without any reference to judicial sanction.[20]

DeHart goes on to explain the unique characteristics of two sentences which will bear no mitigation: they are death and cashiering of an officer. Each of these sentences has only one degree of enforcement. The president holds the power to pardon either of these punishments, but he may not substitute other forms of punishment for either.

Moreover, military law in some examples demands the punishment of death or cashiering; for the president to substitute another form of punishment is not only a violation of the sanctity of the court that handed down the sentence, but a direct violation of the law that stipulates such punishment.

The president's power as commander in chief of the military gives him authority over all persons within the military, but that power is not unlimited. He may not perform acts that are not authorized by the United States Constitution and approved by the Congress. His power as supreme commander is limited; it is granted by the Constitution to give control of the armed forces to the nation's chief executive rather than to any general, but at the same time a framework of laws are laid down within which he must operate.

DeHart admits to controversy on the question of the president's pardoning power. He concedes that "opposing views have been sustained by able and distinguished legal gentlemen." He goes on to cite cases reviewed by Attorney General William Wirt of President Monroe's cabinet and Attorney General John McPherson Berrien who served under President Andrew Jackson. But he refers to a ruling in 1845 by Attorney General J. Y. Mason to support his conclusion regarding the limitations of the power to substitute sentencing.

Commander William Ramsay, of the United States Navy, was tried by a general court-martial and sentenced to be suspended from all rank and command for the period of five years.

President John Tyler reviewed the case in July 1843, and ordered the sentence commuted to suspension for six months, without pay. After expiration of the sentence, in April 1845, Commander Ramsey made application for his pay, and the question arose, had the president the power to deprive him of his pay? Attorney General Mason ruled that the president did not exercise his pardoning power; he went on to add:

> When an officer is brought to trial, and is sentenced to be punished, the executive may mitigate the severity of that punishment,—but there is a guide "the discretion is a legal discretion" and the mitigation must not be according to a capricious will, but must have the sanction of the judgment of the court "it must inflict a part of the punishment awarded by the judgment, with the exception of those cases in which there is no degree." When the whole punishment must be inflicted, or no part of it can be "such is the case of a sentence of death."
>
> I am constrained to the opinion therefore, that Commander Ramsay is entitle to pay during the period mentioned in the 4th auditor's letter, notwithstanding the term in which the president commuted his sentence.[21]

Charles Henry Lee addresses this troubling question in his guide for Confederate judge advocates. He reviews the material of DeHart's work cited above and concludes that absolutely defining the president's power is all but impossible. This portion of his work doubtless influenced the actions of the Confederate War Department and President Davis in the broad extension of executive clemency.[22]

Both Lincoln and Davis routinely resorted to the substitution of sentences of courts-martial cases referred to them, and for Lincoln, the issue of incompetent officers was so troubling that he frequently dismissed those acquitted by courts-martial. In cases where he adjudged the officer guilty of the infraction, even though the court found him not guilty, Lincoln would dismiss him. This was not truly a violation of military law, but simply a violation of military custom, for the president possessed the power to remove any officer.

For both presidents the terrible weight of military sentences, especially those extending to death, was a constant burden. Each took the avenue of least resistance by pardoning all cases referred to him that in any way deserved such mercy, and by substituting a less severe sentence in other cases to placate his army commanders.

Chapter VII
Punishments—
Capital

Capital punishment is the bedrock of military justice. Without it, or the threat of it, some of the demands made upon soldiers would be unachievable. In war, victory is the ultimate goal. To attain that goal an army must often make multiple sacrifices. When these sacrifices rise to a level so as to become overwhelming to the men in the ranks, their natural urge is to escape such horrors.

Duty, honor, country are the motives that keep most faithful to the task, but beyond that a code is needed to provide a path or a required road to travel upon. Just as civil laws are necessary to keep, or try to keep, all people honest, the "code of arms" is necessary to keep the soldier faithful to his task. It is true that such laws alone could not create great armies; mercenaries do not achieve greatness, such only comes from those devoted to their cause above and beyond the call of duty. But the terror of the execution is put before them to urge them to accept the responsibility of facing the daily terror that their duty demands of them.

Civil wars place an extra burden on military courts. Divided loyalties bring about a quicker breakdown of soldiers' duty; this invariably leads to a greater than expected recourse to capital punishment by courts-martial. And so it was with the American Civil War, both Federal and Confederate courts began extending sentences of death at a high rate. Their governments then made desperate attempts to mollify this situation, for it became a threat to the stability of the cause for which each was fighting. In the end each was forced to make compromises that would not have been made under differing circumstances.

Category 13

The sentence of death was so frequently pardoned or remitted that a separate code was provided for that occurrence so that a reasonable tally of the exercise of such clemency could be obtained.

The examples of the sentence of death emanating from a court-martial that is disapproved by the reviewing authority does not appear in this classification Code #13; such cases are simply part of classification Code #01. A death sentence by the court is an inactive occurrence until it is approved by the reviewing authority. His action and his orders are required to put it into force, until he acts the sentence is inoperative.

Army or corps commanders had no authority to remit or pardon death sentences, but they were required to disapprove them if any part of the sentence was infirm. If the proceedings were improper, then the findings would be disapproved, which nullified both the verdict and the sentence. If only the sentence is somehow improper, then the accused still stands guilty, but is set free because of the impropriety of the sentence.

The case of Pvt. Elijah L. Thompson, Company C, 28th Alabama Infantry, provides a clear example of the responsibility of the reviewing authority. The 28th Alabama was part of Gen. Braxton Bragg's Army of Tennessee, Polk's Corps, Maj. Gen. Benjamin F. Cheatham's Division, Brig. Gen. Daniel S. Donelson's Brigade. Thompson is charged with desertion, but the specification is worded that Thompson "did absent himself without leave on the march from Harrison's Ferry, Tennessee to Bardstown, Kentucky on or about the 5th day of September 1862, and remained absent until arrested by Lt. H. H. Green of Company C, 28th Alabama Vols. on the 11th day of November 1862."

The court found Thompson guilty of the specification and guilty of the charge, and sentenced him to be shot to death. Bragg disapproved the finding by properly noting that the specification does not allege desertion, but only absence without leave, further stating that desertion was not proven. The proper finding of the court should have been "not guilty of desertion, but guilty of AWOL." In the circumstances, a sentence of death was unauthorized, so the entire proceedings were nullified.[1]

General Bragg has been improperly portrayed as totally incompetent and a martinet who summarily had his soldiers executed for shooting chickens. No such examples exist in these records. Bragg was irascible, and he mismanaged all his battles, but he was a solid administrator, and where courts-martial were concerned he followed the rules of law. He put the interests of the soldiers clearly under the protection of the articles of war where they belonged.

Several death sentences were commuted to lesser sentences, usually hard labor, by the president. If the president commuted a sentence of death to one of hard labor, regardless of the impropriety of such action, it becomes a sentence of hard labor rather than a sentence of death, so these are merely tallied as sentence Code #09.

The proper use of the power of pardon was employed by the president again and again, even though unwarranted in many examples. A clear case where such power was properly exercised is illustrated in GO #139, A&IGO, October 28, 1863.

I. The President, having commuted or remitted the sentences pronounced by General courts-martial in the following cases, his decision is published for the information and guidance of all concerned:

1. Lieut. E. M. P. Brown [Bowen], Company B, 8th Battalion GA Volunteers. Charged with failure to suppress mutiny, and exciting and joining therein.
   Sentence—Death.
2. First Sergt. Abner Underwood, Company D, 8th Battalion GA Volunteers; also,
3. Private T. P. Wood;
4. Private T. W. Cannon [J. W. Cannon];
5. Private Wm. Garner; and,
6. Private T. Roberts, of Company B, 8th Battalion GA Volunteers. Charged with exciting and joining in mutiny.
   Sentence—Death.
7. Private Daniel Hollis, Company B, 8th Battalion GA Volunteers. Charged with exciting and joining in mutiny.
   Sentence—Confinement with ball and chain for twelve months, and forfeiture of pay.
8. The afore said parties were all tried by General Courts-Martial, convened under General Orders, No. 3, of 1863, Department of South Carolina, Georgia, and Florida. In view of the evident want of discipline in this battalion, the President has remitted the sentence of all the parties. Lieut. Brown, Sergt. Underwood, and Privates Wood, Cannon, Garner, Roberts, and Hollis will therefore be released from confinement and returned to duty.

The Department observes with regret the absence of a just military discipline in the above named battalion. Had this been properly observed and enforced, there is reason to believe these trials would have been obviated. The officers in charge are responsible for these evils, and must correct them. At the same time, they should observe towards the soldiers in their command a proper degree of consideration and kindness, which is generally a sure means of securing obedience and respect.

As the war progressed, army or department commanders would remit death sentences. Although this is contrary to the authority established in AOW #89, such action was tolerated by the War Department to lessen the burden of referrals to the president. It was not unusual to find corps commanders remitting death sentences handed down by the military courts of their corps in the last year of the war. Even so, these cases were exceptional, and any routine recommendation for clemency was still forwarded to the president for his action up until the termination of hostilities.

More than 600 death sentences were pardoned by the president or remitted by other authority. Many examples were worthy of the clemency extended, but a very large number went on to desert the service again, and in some cases, to desert to the enemy. These 600-odd trials do not include the hundreds and hundreds of deserters who were pardoned under the president's act of clemency. These persons were not tried by courts-martial upon their return, or if they were tried in error, the reviewing authority would disapprove the sentence.

Category 14

Another special category for death sentences was needed to identify those cases whereby the sentence was not carried out for reasons other than pardon or remission.

One hundred and one soldiers were identified as being under sentence of death when other events transpired to prevent the sentences from being carried out. In many examples, the individual disappeared between sentencing and execution, usually as a result of his having deserted the service.

Occasionally a soldier was killed in action while awaiting publication of the sentence of his court-martial in general orders. Others died from various illnesses. Some were captured by the enemy, often without too much resistance. For a few, the war ended before the ruling of the court was made known.

Private S. J. Andrews, Company E, 15th Alabama Infantry, Army of Northern Virginia, First Corps, Maj. Gen. Charles M. Field's Division, Brig. Gen. Evander M. Law's Brigade, was tried on March 28, 1865, for desertion and sentenced to death by Longstreet's orders issued March 31, 1865. Fortunately for Andrews, the 9th of April arrived before his sentence could be carried out. He appears on the Appomattox Roster under the name of Andrens, S. J.[2]

Several soldiers appearing on the Appomattox Roster were under a death sentence and, of course, others in similar circumstances were taken by United States forces throughout the war. Others escaped their commands or deserted, but do not appear on any prisoner of war records.

Private John Edwards of Company F, 1st Virginia Artillery, which was part of Lt. Gen. Thomas J. Jackson's Second Corps, was tried for desertion in early 1863. He was sentenced to be shot to death in GO #6, Headquarters Second Corps—January 22, 1863; however, Edwards made his escape on January 22, 1863.[3]

Circumstances surrounding trials varied. Some prisoners awaiting sentences continued to serve in the ranks, others were under guard in company tents or guardhouses (if available). Others were confined in military prisons. Private Benjamin E. Bentley, Company H, 55th North Carolina Troops, was tried for desertion on February 25, 1864. The 55th North Carolina Infantry was part of Brig. Gen. Joseph R. Davis' Brigade, Maj. Gen. Henry Heth's Division, Third Corps, Army of Northern Virginia. Bentley had been confined in Castle Thunder awaiting the results of his trial. He was scheduled to be shot to death but committed suicide on Tuesday, March 15, 1864.[4]

Further irony is added to the case by SO #216, A&IGO, September 12, 1864:

> IX. Private Benjamin E. Bently [sic], Company H., Fifty-fifth Regiment North Carolina Troops, against whom sentence of death was pronounced by military court for Third Corps, Army of Northern Virginia, is, upon the recommendation of the court, pardoned by the President, and will be released from confinement and returned to duty.

If the facts stated in Bentley's CSRs are true, the case is not unique. Upon receipt of the proceedings and general orders, the A&IGO would review cases and in those examples where warranted, orders would be sent to the commanding general by telegraph to suspend the execution of a particular prisoner until the decision of the president is made known. In a few examples, such orders arrived too late to save the condemned.

If the reviewing authority was following a recommendation by the court for mercy, or if he felt that a pardon was warranted, he would issue orders that a sentence be suspended until the pleasure of the president can be made known. In such cases, the accused was safeguarded from hasty execution before he could be pardoned.

Confirmation of executions in the CSRs is often a disappointing enterprise. In many examples, the records are simply inconclusive. Occasionally, diaries or other publications will reveal valuable insights into these mysteries. An enlightening example is found in Brig. Gen. Edward Porter Alexander's book *Fighting for the Confederacy.*[5]

Alexander speaks to us from the pages and vividly portrays the happenings of his experiences. He tells the story of two members of his command sentenced to death. He explains that he was president of a court-martial convened during the month of March 1863. He refers to two prisoners tried who were from Woolfolk's Battery (Capt. Pichegru Woolfolk, Jr.'s Va. Lt. Arty.); he identifies them as Howard and Wilson.

The first was Pvt. James Howard who was tried for desertion on March 14, 1863, found guilty and sentenced to be shot. The second was Pvt. Daniel Cavanaugh (alias William Wilson) who was also tried for desertion and sentenced to be shot.

Alexander's account of the trials and outcome of the two examples is fascinating because it explains procedures that can only be learned from such firsthand renditions. Howard was a deserter who had gone home and was captured by a conscript guard. Woolfolk believed that Howard had intended to return and had only gone home to see his folks and perhaps a sweetheart, and Alexander confesses his sympathy for him. He goes on to reveal the problems that commanders faced in holding prisoners. He realized that the processing of the cases would take some time, and that they would soon be breaking camp and launching a campaign. He further adds that "my men had no muskets to guard prisoners with, but only swords, and I was afraid, on an active campaign, the prisoners might escape." So he sent both prisoners to Castle Thunder with special instructions to the provost marshal to hold them until he sent for them.

Cavanaugh, who was enlisted under the name of Wilson, was a bounty-jumper. He had enlisted as a substitute for another of Woolfolk's men who had paid him $1,000. The money was initially given to Alexander with an agreement that it be paid to "Wilson" in installments. When Alexander met "Wilson" and explained these terms he said that he recognized him for what he was and warned him that if he deserted he would offer all of the remaining money he was holding as a reward for his capture. This did not deter "Wilson," for as soon as he got the first installment ($300), he deserted. However, in a matter of hours the men of Woolfolk's Battery had captured him.

Alexander moves forward to the middle of July 1863 on the retreat from Gettysburg, when he met Col. Henry Edward Young, Lee's judge advocate general. Young told Alexander that the proceedings had been approved in the two cases, and that an order was being issued for the execution of the two men. Alexander goes on to state that the battalion went into camp that afternoon, and no sooner than his tent was pitched, Howard walked in and reported for duty. Alexander's words were "my heart sank at the sight of him, orders were already signed directing me to shoot him."

Howard told Alexander that he had simply been turned loose from Castle Thunder and told to come and meet the battalion, so he walked from Richmond to the battalion, which was camped near the Potomac River. He added that he knew nothing of "Wilson."

Alexander stated that he believed that if he went to General Lee and begged him to commute Howard's sentence that he would do so, especially if he had "Wilson" to make an example of, but with "Wilson" gone, Alexander had second thoughts about approaching Lee. Lee was a stern disciplinarian and he knew that if his plea were denied by the commander, he would be forced to shoot Howard. So he determined that Howard should escape.

When Howard reported, Alexander told him he could not return to duty, but must be kept under guard until his sentence was published, so he placed him in the guard tent, but not in irons. Captain Woolfolk was officer of the guard that night and Alexander told him how he wished Howard would escape, and sure enough, the next morning he was gone.

No record of "Wilson's" release could be found; he was surely sent off the same time as Howard, but of course he traveled in another direction, probably to enlist for more bounty and to desert again.

Alexander confesses to the unmilitary nature of his action, but reveals a vivid appreciation for the value of the lives of the men who served under him.

Courts-martial and the punishments handed down by the courts had to take a back seat when the army was on the move. Private Houston Shirley, Company K, 24th Georgia Infantry, part of Brig. Gen. William T. Wofford's Brigade, Maj. Gen. Joseph B. Kershaw's Division, First Corps, Army of Northern Virginia, was tried on April 4, 1864, on an unstated charge and sentenced to be shot to death. While awaiting publication of orders, the Wilderness campaign was launched and Private Shirley was killed in action on May 6, 1864. The records show that the case was referred to the secretary of war on July 9, 1864, with recommendation for pardon.[6]

Frequently, only inference can be made from information available. An individual may be sentenced to death in April 1864, and no further orders or records can be found. He then appears on the Appomattox Roster of those paroled after April 9, 1865. It can reasonably be inferred that the execution was not carried out, but the exact reason why is not evident.

Category 15

A more puzzling category is contained under sentence Code #15. This is the inconclusive group. Nearly all the citizens condemned to death under courts-martial are contained in this group as are four slaves who were sentenced to be hanged. All of these persons were no doubt prosecuted for spying or giving intelligence to the enemy. Three persons in Category #15 are listed as "an alien enemy." These are individuals who could not be properly identified, but were prosecuted for being Northern spies.

The vast majority of persons listed in sentence Category #15 are Confederate soldiers; three Union soldiers are listed as sentenced to hang, but could not be found in the CSRs of United States forces. More than 300 Confederate soldiers are a part of this mysterious group. In many examples, the individual could not be identified in either the index or the service records. In other examples where records were found, information was limited. For example, the record on Pvt. John Doe may end on a June/Sept. 1863 card with the comment "NFR" (no further record); but the courts-martial record from the A&IGO will show that he was tried in August 1864, and sentenced to be shot.

The liberal use of aliases accounted for some of the missing names and in a few cases the unit may be incorrectly listed, but most are simply part of that group whose records were somehow lost or never properly recorded.

Doubtless the most fascinating story in this category is that of Pvt. Isaac D. Rosonbalm of Company F, 37th Virginia Infantry. Court-martial records show that he was tried on or about February 5, 1864, and sentenced to be shot. At that time, the 37th was part of Brig. Gen. George Hume "Maryland" Steuart's Brigade of Maj. Gen. Edward Johnson's Division, Second Corps, Army of Northern Virginia. The records from the A&IGO do not show the charges, and no general orders could be found covering the trial.

Thomas M. Rankin, in his history of the 37th Virginia Infantry, shows him present from April 30, 1864, to December 31, 1864, with no further record. The CSR may be incorrect, but of course if it is not, Rosonbalm could not have been shot to death during 1864.[7]

The account of "Rosonbaum's" execution, as told by Lt. McHenry Howard, AIG of Steuart's Brigade, gives strong evidence that the condemned man was Pvt. Isaac D. Rosonbalm.[8] His account begins one day in January or February 1864, when he was at the brigade guardhouse when a few prisoners were brought in.

He remarked that Col. Titus V. Williams, of the 37th Virginia Infantry, was present and spoke to one of the prisoners by name, "Rosonbaum." The colonel told Howard that the man was a bad soldier who had deserted, been picked up by conscript officers and was now returned to his command under charges.

Howard stated that "Rosonbaum" had been tried by military court assigned to the Second Corps. After his conviction, "Rosonbaum's" company officers asked Howard to check the case to see if somehow "Rosonbaum" could be saved. Howard found that the proceedings stated that a majority of the court agreed upon the sentence. He recognized that a majority of such three-member courts is two-thirds and that a plea on such a technicality was futile. Nevertheless, he addressed an appeal to Col. Henry E. Young, judge advocate general of the Army of Northern Virginia. Young agreed to send the appeal on to Richmond, but no stay of execution was ordered, the date was fixed for March 3, 1864.

Howard related that military activity made it impossible for the brigade to carry out the sentence on March 3; he explained this to Maj. Edward L. Moore of General Johnson's staff, who agreed to change the date to one week hence, that is, March 10, 1864. He asked the major to put it in writing, so he wrote it out on the back of an envelope, "by command of Major-General Johnson."

On the new date, the brigade was on picket duty on the Rapidan in an open valley. "Rosonbaum" was tied to the stake and a bushel bag was placed over his head and the firing party performed their duty. Howard explained that a storm was rapidly approaching and the men were hurriedly returned to their bivouac. That evening, he rode back to the place of execution to see that the prisoner had been properly buried.

In conclusion, he related that sometime later, an order came down from division headquarters suspending the execution. Howard responded that "Rosonbaum" had been executed. A courier came back from division at full speed with a request demanding by what authority the man had been shot. Howard returned a copy of the order that had been written out on the back of the envelope, and stated that nothing more was heard on the subject. Throughout his narrative, Howard only refers to the condemned man as "Rosonbaum," thus leaving his true identity a mystery.

Category 16

The general mode of execution in the military is the firing squad. This is the method by which the majority of those executed met death. Sentence Code #16 indicates that the victim was shot to death with musketry.

Reviewing authority approved more than 1,300 death sentences handed down by the courts during the war; many more were adjudged by the courts but were disapproved for one or another reasons. The majority of these sentences were not carried out for the reasons already explained. However, 204 Confederate soldiers plus one civilian were confirmed as having faced firing squads.

The first executions found in CSRs occurred on November 8, 1861, in the Army of Pensacola under the command of Maj. Gen. Braxton Bragg. Private Charles Lappin of Company C, 1st Louisiana Infantry (Strawbridge), was shot to death for striking a superior officer. On the same day, Pvt. Newton J. Mullen, Company E, 10th Mississippi Infantry, was executed; the charge could not be determined.[9] Both men were part of Brig. Gen. Samuel Jones' Brigade, but were probably tried under different charges since their trials occurred more than two months apart.

General E. P. Alexander describes the first military execution he witnessed. The victims were from Maj. Chatham Roberdeau Wheat's 1st Special Battalion Louisiana Volunteers; Alexander explains his admiration for Bob Wheat, but correctly identifies his battalion as "wharf rats" and goes on to relate that they were more trouble than they were worth. He adds that the shooting was for forcing a guard to release a friend of theirs who had been arrested. This occurred near Centreville in the fall of 1861.[10]

The two individuals that Alexander does not identify were O'Brien and Cochrane of Company B. Private Michael O'Brien, Company B, 1st Special Battalion Louisiana Volunteers, which was part of General Joseph E. Johnston's Army of the Potomac. O'Brien was tried on December 6, 1861, for violation of AOW #7 and AOW #9.[11] Private Dennis Cochrane, Company B, also tried on December 6, 1861, for violation of AOW #7, AOW #9, and assaulting a sentinel on duty.[12]

AOW #7, mutiny, was the basic charge applied to both prisoners, in that they created a riot to free their friend who was confined in the guardhouse of the 7th Louisiana Infantry, which was also part of the Army of the Potomac. Lieutenant Andrew E. Knox, the officer of the guard, was attacked by both Cochrane and O'Brien in his attempt to quell the riot, hence the charge of AOW #9. Cochrane was also found guilty of attacking Pvt. Joseph Kochler, a sentinel on duty at the guardhouse. All of this activity took place on November 29, 1861, at Camp Florida, Virginia. The sentence was carried out on Monday, December 9, 1861, under the direction of Maj. Gen. Edmund Kirby Smith.

The custom of the service prevailed for the procedure of carrying out execution by firing squads. The number of men selected varied, but was usually 12. A sergeant was detailed to load the muskets, two of which he would typically leave with no lead balls or conical bullets. The reason this was done was to theoretically allow any member of the firing squad the consoling thought that he had not fired a fatal bullet. Such consolation was misdirected, for veterans knew immediately if their weapon contained only powder from the recoil. Moreover, as the war wore on, the feeling of the members of the firing party was one of indifference.

The prisoner would usually be brought before the firing squad in a wagon, along with his coffin; the coffin would be placed alongside his grave, which was already dug. The regiment, or brigade, or division would be drawn up on a three-sided square with the file of riflemen facing the open side of the square where the prisoner is placed. He was usually seated upon the coffin, and after the chaplain spoke a word of prayer, the squad of riflemen delivered the volley. In most cases, the victim died immediately, but if he survived, a back-up squad was called forward to deliver another volley.

It was unusual for a prisoner to be tied to a stake, but some witnesses wrote vivid accounts of prisoners shot at the stake. An excellent firsthand account is provided in Capt. William J. Seymour's journal. Seymour's father, Col. Isaac G. Seymour, was colonel of the 6th Louisiana Infantry. He was killed at Gaines Mill, Virginia, while William J. Seymour was still in New Orleans running the family newspaper, *The Commercial Bulletin*. The younger Seymour published a patriotic obituary of his father and was promptly arrested by order of Maj. Gen. Benjamin Butler. Soon after his release, he joined the Confederate army as an aide to Brig. Gen. Harry T. Hays, who commanded the brigade of which his father's regiment had been a part.

In November 1863, Seymour was serving as assistant adjutant general in Maj. Gen. Jubal A. Early's Division of the Second Corps, Army of Northern Virginia, and was assigned the duty of carrying out the execution of Pvt. John Connolly of the 6th Louisiana Infantry. Connolly had been tried on November 6, 1863, for "desertion and joining the rank of the enemy," found guilty and sentenced to be shot seven days after the publication of GO #100, Army of Northern Virginia, November 20, 1863. Seymour describes the execution:

> On the 30th of November, while we were in line of battle at Mine Run, I had a most unpleasant duty to perform, viz.—the execution of Private John Connolly, of the 6th La. Regiment, a man who had deserted more than a year previously, had joined the Yankee Army—was captured at Bristow Station by a detachment from his old Regiment, tried by Court Martial, found guilty

and sentenced to "be shot with musketry." He was about twenty years old and had formerly been a newsboy in New Orleans—a sullen, cross, ugly fellow, who seemed to be entirely devoid of pride or sensibility. In my official capacity as Asst. Adj. General I had to direct & superintend the execution, and a more unpleasant and revolting duty it had never been my misfortune to discharge. The orders came from Division Head Quarters in the morning and soon after the prisoner arrived at our lines, securely manacled and guarded. I sent to the Field Hospital for a Catholic Priest, who arrived at 4 o'clock in the afternoon and administered spiritual consolation to the culprit. Half an hour later I ordered the Brigade to form on the breastworks, officers & men with only their side arms. A grave was dug fifty paces in advance of the centre [sic] of our Brigade line, at the head of which the prisoner was placed, his shackles having been removed and his arms pinnoned [sic] behind his back. Ten paces in front and facing him stood the firing party, consisting of twelve men of the company to which he had belonged. The Priest was by his side, talking to him & uttering prayers, at the same time holding before the prisoner a small crucifix of our Savior, which he kissed several times. After the good Priest had concluded the duties of his holy office, I read to the prisoner the charges against him, the findings of the Court Martial and the sentence of death. Connolly, apparently unmoved, listened attentively & after I had finished said that he had never pulled a trigger against his old comrades and that notwithstanding he had joined the Federal Army, he had resolved never to do so. He then remarked that he had no hard feelings against me for the part I was taking in his execution, for he was fully aware that I was but discharging my duty. After telling the men that it would be an act of mercy to the prisoner to take sure aim & kill him immediately, I ordered the officer commanding the firing party to proceed with the execution. The word of command was given, the muskets leveled, a simultaneous discharge followed and the vital spark fled forever from the body of John Connolly. Nine balls pierced his head and one his heart, and his death was instantaneous. I hope that I may never witness a like scene again.[13]

Another account of this same execution is rendered by Maj. John Warwick Daniel, AAG, general and staff of Early's Division.[14] He writes his story as a witness at Mine Run where Connolly was shot to death. He recounts the fascinating story of Connolly's desertions, but does not name him; perhaps he did not know his correct name, for he incorrectly identifies him as a member of the 7th Louisiana Infantry, whereas he was part of Company K, of the

6th Louisiana Infantry. The 5th, 6th, 7th, 8th, and 9th Louisiana Infantry made up Hays' Brigade at Port Republic, where Connolly deserted and went north. Daniel refers to him as "Nemesis," and tells of witnessing his capture at Bristow Station while delivering orders to Early's Division. At first light, as the Confederates were crossing a creek, they came upon a group of Federal soldiers asleep, whom they awakened with their bayonets. As the prisoners arose, a soldier of Connolly's company identified him as a deserter from Port Republic. Daniel states that Connolly was tried by court-martial and condemned to be shot.

Daniel goes on to explain that the prisoner was confined to the guardhouse near the Bott's Farm in Culpeper, Virginia, on November 7, 1863, when Early's Division suddenly moved out on a quick march to Rappahannock Bridge. That evening, as Hays' Brigade was crossing the river, several were captured by the Federal army. Somehow the prisoner managed to be among the captured. But a squad of Hays' men who had eluded capture met face to face with Connolly and prodded him with their bayonets back to Confederate lines where he eventually kept his rendezvous with the firing party.

Private John S. Jackman, who was a member of the famous brigade of western Kentucky regiments known as the Orphan Brigade, wrote a diary of his war experiences. He devotes a single paragraph under the date of March 25, 1864, to a description of the execution of a soldier that he identifies as "Keen":[15]

> Wind blew very hard last night, bringing up a snow storm. The ground was white again this morning with snow, but it soon melted away. The brigade has gone out to the execution of the sentence of a court martial on one Keen, of the 2nd Fla. reg't, who is to be shot for desertion. This is a murky day—I would hate to be shot on such a day—especially for desertion.

Jackman was a member of Company B of the 9th Kentucky Infantry, which was assigned to Brig. Gen. Joseph H. Lewis' Brigade at the time of this execution. Private William Keen's unit was not the 2d Florida Infantry, but rather the 3d Florida Infantry, which was part of Brig. Gen. Jesse J. Finley's Brigade. Both brigades were assigned to Maj. Gen. William B. Bate's (formerly Breckinridge's) Division of Lt. Gen. William J. Hardee's Corps, Army of Tennessee. The court-martial record indicates he was Pvt. William Keen of Company K, 3d Florida Infantry, tried February 18, 1864, for desertion, found guilty, and sentenced to be shot to death.

Executions were generally carried out by members of the brigade to which the prisoner belonged with orders coming down from army headquarters to the division commander, who was usually charged with carrying out the act. It was standard procedure for as many members of the division to witness the sentence as possible.

The typical order read very much like the one issued by Brig. Gen. Roswell Sabine Ripley, commander of the 1st Military District, South Carolina. He issued the following GO #9 at Charleston, S.C., on November 16, 1862:

   I.   In accordance with General Order #96 from Department H.Q. dated November 11, 1862, Private Bernard Donnelly of Capt. Ferguson's Co. of Artillery, P.A.C.S. will be shot to death with musketry on the front beach of Sullivan's Island at 12 o'clock M on Monday the 24th day of November 1862.

   II.   All troops on Sullivan's Island will be turned out under command of Colonel L. W. Keitt [Col. Laurence M. Keitt], commanding Sullivan's Island at 11 o'clock A.M. on the same day to witness the execution. The 30th Regt. S.C. Vols. Lt. Colonel Dantzler commanding will be armed and equipped. All other troops will appear with side arms only.

   III.   The commanding officer of Ferguson's Company to carry out the sentence of the Court Martial, providing them with nine loaded and three unloaded muskets for that purpose.

   IV.   A reserve detail of twelve men with guns similarly loaded will be made in case they are needed to complete the execution.

   V.   Captain T. H. Hurguenin is charged with the details of and execution of this order, as acting Military Provost Marshal.

                         By order of
                         Brig. Gen. R. S. Ripley.

Fortunately for Donnelly, orders from the secretary of war were received the day before, on November 23, 1862, suspending the execution. It was not unusual for orders to arrive at the last minute preventing an execution, but sometimes they arrived too late. General Samuel Cooper sent a telegram to Brig. Gen. John D. Imboden, commander of the cavalry brigade of Maj. Gen. Jubal A. Early's Army of the Valley on May 14, 1864, requesting a suspension of the sentence against Pvt. Amby Harmon, Company A, 18th Virginia Cavalry, but by the time the telegram was sent, Harmon had already been shot to death.[16]

In a few cases the reviewing authority would refer proceedings back to the court directing them to reconsider the sentence. Two death sentences were reconsidered by the court in March 1863, upon the recommendation of Gen. Braxton Bragg. Privates W. W. Brown and Thomas J. Burnett of Company K, Murray's Battalion (22d Tennessee Battalion Infantry) of Polk's Corps, Maj. Gen. Benjamin F. Cheatham's Division, Brig. Gen. Marcus J. Wright's Brigade, deserted on March 5, 1863; even though they had been gone only five days, both were convicted of desertion and sentenced to be shot to death.

Following Bragg's request, the court reduced the sentences of the two to fourteen days on bread and water diet and at the end of that term to receive 39 stripes. Bragg approved the two weeks confinement on bread and water diet, but remitted the flogging.[17]

As the war neared its end and more liberties were taken by army and corps commanders, death sentences were occasionally remitted for past heroics. In a few examples, a commander would simply remit the sentence with the citation of the soldier's bravery and return him to duty. Even though there was no authorization for such action, the president and the War Department tolerated it.

The case of Pvt. Thomas N. Faulkner of Company F, 15th N.C. Troops, provides some interesting circumstances that may have resulted in a pardon for a death sentence. Faulkner was certainly less than a sterling character with three desertions to his credit.

His most significant departure occurred on June 8, 1863, following his brigade's return to Richmond after serving in the Department of North Carolina under the field command of Maj. Gen. Daniel H. Hill. The 15th was part of Brig. Gen. John R. Cooke's Brigade.

On May 22–23, 1863, Cooke's Brigade along with Brig. Gen. Matt W. Ransom's Brigade fought a Federal force of approximate equal size at Gum Swamp and Batchelder's Creek near New Bern, N.C. On the evening of May 23, Colonel J. Richter Jones of the 58th Pennsylvania Infantry was killed at the head of his regiment.

On May 26, 1863, Maj. Gen. John G. Foster, commander of the XVIII Army Corps in the Union Department of North Carolina, eulogized Jones in GO #81, and ordered flags in the department flown at half-mast for three days.

Colonel John Richter Jones was commander of outposts in New Bern, and was something less than a hero to the North Carolinians. He was regarded as a house burner and a plunderer. Our deserter from the 15th North Carolina Infantry, Private Faulkner was credited with killing Jones.

Faulkner remained among the missing until he was brought back on April 7, 1864. His regiment was once again part of the Army of Northern Virginia, Third Corps, Maj. Gen. Henry Heth's Division, and, of course, Cooke's Brigade. Faulkner was tried on a charge of desertion in April 1864, found guilty, and sentenced to be shot.[18]

His fate following the trial is somewhat uncertain, but he was probably pardoned, for his CSR indicates that he returned to duty prior to 11/1/64, and then deserted to the enemy on 2/27/65.[19]

The fascinating question that remains unanswered is: was he pardoned for shooting Jones? If his claim to the deed was credible, he very well may have won a reprieve for it.

No amount of intervention could save some cases. Those who received no measure of clemency were the ones who were taken after going over to the enemy. Private Jasper Johnson of Company B, 19th Virginia Cavalry, was an unusual example of this group in that he was sentenced to be shot to death by both a Confederate court and a Federal court.

Johnson's CSR indicates he was absent from November 1, 1863, until February 29, 1864. Postwar history states that he was captured by Federal forces and enlisted in the United States service. He then deserted and rejoined the 19th Virginia Cavalry. After a short stay, he deserted the Confederate cavalry and determined to remain at home. He was subsequently arrested by Union soldiers and sentenced to be shot. He escaped and returned to the Confederate cavalry. The 19th Virginia was part of Brig. Gen. William L. Jackson's Brigade in the Department of Western Virginia and East Tennessee. Jackson sent Johnson to a court-martial where he was convicted of desertion to the enemy and sentenced to be shot.

Armstrong's history of the 19th Virginia Cavalry indicates that Johnson's comrades thought he was a victim of circumstances and should not be shot. They arranged for his escape, but Johnson refused to run; he stated that if the Federals caught him, he would be shot by them, so he elected to face a Confederate firing squad. He did so on March 15, 1864, at Camp Cameron in Bath County.[20]

Private Benjamin C. Gibson, a North Carolinian, outdid Johnson for divided service and lived to tell about it. He enlisted in Captain William B. Lanier's Independent Company, North Carolina Troops, on an unspecified date, and was transferred to Company H, 61st North Carolina Troops, in September 1862. He was placed in arrest in October 1862, for making an unauthorized visit home. In the process of his arrest, Gibson escaped and became a deserter.

One year later on October 29, 1863, he enlisted in Company E, 2d North Carolina Infantry (Union). At this time the 2d North Carolina was doing active recruiting in the New Bern, North Carolina area. On April 20, 1864, Gibson had the distinct misfortune to be captured by Confederate forces at Plymouth, North Carolina.

The 61st North Carolina was stationed in the Wilmington, North Carolina area shortly after its induction into Confederate service and was first in action around Plymouth in October 1862 when Gibson deserted. Later it was assigned to Brig. Gen. Thomas L. Clingman's Brigade of Brig. Gen. Robert F. Hoke's Division, Maj. Gen. Richard H. Anderson's Corps.

When Gibson was captured near Plymouth on April 20, 1864, the 61st North Carolina Infantry was stationed on James Island in Charleston harbor, so the regiment could have played no part in his capture. He did not face a court-martial until November 28, 1864. With the shifting events in the eastern theater, Hoke's Division had made several moves. Near the time of the court-martial they were in the Richmond area going into winter quarters. It is uncertain as to whether Gibson was tried under the direction of his old regiment, but such was probably the case. At any rate he was found guilty of desertion to the enemy and sentenced to be shot.

On December 20, 1864, Hoke's Division was shifted to Wilmington, North Carolina, by rail to aid in the defense of Fort Fisher. Gibson must have traveled with the 61st North Carolina Infantry under arrest, and the stars were surely working in his favor. Brigadier General Alfred H. Terry had replaced Maj. Gen. Benjamin Butler shortly after Christmas 1864, and promptly prepared to move against Fort Fisher. His initial effort was launched on January 12, 1865, with the movement of the Federal fleet.

Gibson's execution was set for Thursday, January 12, 1865, but with the Federals moving against the fort the orders to shoot him were doubtless suspended. He was subsequently allowed to rejoin Company H, 61st North Carolina Infantry and remained with them until the end of the war when the 61st surrendered on May 3, 1865. He then joined Company C, 1st North Carolina Infantry (Union), and served until June 27, 1865, when he was mustered out, thus completing two tours of duty as a Confederate and two tours as a Federal.[21]

John O. Casler, in his famous work, *Four Years in the Stonewall Brigade*, gives a vivid description of one method of the employment of stakes to support victims of a firing squad.[22] Ten North Carolinians were shot to death on September 5, 1863, for desertion and murder. Casler was serving in the Pioneer Corps of his brigade at the time, and his unit was detailed to dig the graves, make the coffins, put up the stakes, and bury the victims.

Casler explains, "We planted ten posts in the ground, about three feet high and about fifty feet apart, all in a line, boring a hole in each post near the top, and putting in a cross-piece. We dug one large grave in the edge of the woods, large enough to hold the ten coffins."

When the men were marched out, a chaplain prayed with them, then an officer took each man and conducted him to his post, placed him upon his knees with his back to the post. The man's arms were then hooked over the crosspiece and his hands tied in front of his body. The firing party consisted of 10 men for each prisoner, with a five-man firing party in reserve. The command to fire was given for all 100 men at the same time. Casler then states that a surgeon checked each prisoner and found two of them still alive, whereby the reserve firing parties for these two were brought forward and ordered to fire. When the two were pronounced dead, the division (Edward Johnson's) was marched by and then the Pioneer Corps finished their work.

In his book, Casler relates that about 30 members of the 1st and 3d North Carolina Regiments deserted in a body and took their guns with them in order to resist arrest. This type of action was not at all unusual, particularly for North Carolina Troops. Throughout the war, there was a strong element of resistance in several North Carolina counties, and no accurate record exists of the killings that took place among these opponents.

The 1st North Carolina State Troops and the 3d North Carolina State Troops were part of Brig. Gen. George H. Steuart's Brigade in Maj. Gen. Edward Johnson's Division of the Second Corps. The army was camped near Orange Court House and the deserters were headed toward North Carolina. They were unsuccessful in crossing the James River since all of the fords were heavily guarded. Adjutant Richardson Mallett, Jr., of the 46th North Carolina and a detachment from Cooke's Brigade, brought the culprits to heel and a fight ensued. Several escaped, a few were killed or wounded, but 11 members of the 3d North Carolina State Troops were captured. During the encounter, Adjutant Mallett was killed, so all the prisoners were charged with desertion and murder.

One member of the 3d North Carolina State Troops was wounded in the encounter; nevertheless, he was tried, found guilty, and sentenced to be shot. However, he was in the hospital at the time set for execution and thereby escaped the firing squad. On December 17, 1863, Private Hanson M. Futch of Company K died of smallpox while still confined to the hospital in Richmond.

The 10 that faced the muskets on that Saturday in 1863 were:

1. Bedsole, John R.—Private—Company H
2. Benson, Francis—Private—Company H
3. Bunn, Dallas—Private—Company K
4. Bunn, James Dorsey—Private—Company K
5. Clarke, Duncan R.—Private—Company H
6. Ellis, James—Private—Company H
7. Futch, John—Private—Company K
8. Kelly, Wm. H.—Private—Company H
9. Privett, Kearney—Private—Company K
10. Rainer, John N.—Private—Company K

Category 17

Hanging was seldom employed to execute Confederate soldiers. The custom of the service was to hang those persons charged with spying, but soldiers were rarely charged with this offense. On the other hand, soldiers were sometimes hanged for desertion to the enemy.

Thirty-five cases of hanging were confirmed. Three more were almost certainly carried out because of explicit general orders found. In addition, another two dozen or more are probabilities. Eleven citizens and four slaves received such sentences, but no records of their executions could be located.

Samuel W. Kenny was convicted of spying by a court-martial convened on January 23, 1863, by the Army of Tennessee. Bragg approved the finding and sentence and set Kenny's execution for Friday, February 13, 1863, in GO #22, dated February 5, 1863. Kenny was captured within the lines of the army and immediately identified as a spy. However, he was listed in the trial records as "either a citizen of the United States or a soldier of the United States." No records identifying a Samuel W. Kenny or Kenney could be found in the Union CSRs, so he is listed as "U.S. Citizen."

Two similar cases were tried by the Army of Tennessee, approximately four months later. Private John Caio and Private Joseph Ford listed as members of the 10th Ohio Infantry, with no company designation for either, were tried between April 15, 1863, and April 22, 1863, at the headquarters of Maj. Gen. Earl Van Dorn's Cavalry Corps near Spring Hill, Tennessee. Each was accused of posing as a Confederate soldier when passing through Centreville [*sic*], Tennessee on or about February 26, 1863, heading south; then on or about March 12, 1863, they were seen returning on their way north. In addition to the charge of spying, each was convicted of the crime of "depredation upon the property of private individuals."

On June 24, 1863, GO #141, Army of Tennessee, was issued listing the findings and sentence of Van Dorn's court-martial. Both men were found guilty of the two charges and sentenced to be hanged. Bragg approved the findings and sentences, and directed that the sentences be carried out on Friday following receipt of GO #141 by Van Dorn's Cavalry Corps. This would have set the execution date for July 3, 1863, unless the orders were delayed.

The 10th Ohio Infantry was assigned to the Department of the Cumberland, XIV Corps, 1st Division, 2d Brigade; the 10th Ohio Cavalry was assigned to the Department of the Cumberland, Cavalry Force, 2d Division, 2d Brigade. These designations were applicable in early 1863; therefore members of either regiment would be likely candidates for such activity. However, neither name could be located in either the 10th Ohio Volunteer Infantry or the 10th Ohio Cavalry.

Perhaps the darkest days for this mode of execution were those following the raid on New Bern, North Carolina, February 1–2, 1864. In a desperate attempt to recapture this strategic port from Union forces, Gen. Robert E. Lee sent Maj. Gen. George E. Pickett south with more than 11,000 muskets, four regiments of cavalry, and 2,300 artillerymen and other supporting units. All totaled more than 15,000 present for duty on the abstract. The plan of attack involved a reinforced brigade under Brig. Gen. Seth M. Barton, a small brigade of infantry, three guns and 300 cavalry under Col. James Dearing, and a reinforced brigade under Brig. Gen. Robert F. Hoke.

Nothing went according to plans; a coordinated three-pronged attack was ordered, but bad roads, strong Union works, and the loss of the element of surprise brought Pickett's efforts to naught. After minor engagements, he withdrew north to his base in Kinston, N.C. During the course of the attack, Hoke made a raid on the camp of the 2d N.C. Infantry (Union) and carried off approximately 45 prisoners. The 2d was organized in New Bern in November 1863, and until the raid had been recruiting enlistments from the local population.

As soon as the Confederates were safely back at their point of strategic withdrawal, an effort to determine if any of the prisoners were Confederate deserters began. This task was immediately made easier by some of the prisoners who were happy to inform on their fellow captives. Almost immediately 22 were identified as former Confederates. Most were from Col. John H. Netercutt's Battalion (8th North Carolina Battalion of Partisan Rangers).

The 8th N.C. Battalion was a home guard unit, but in 1863 the unit was merged into the 66th North Carolina Troops. Members of the battalion were given the choice of joining the 66th N.C. Infantry or being immediately conscripted into other Confederate units. Obviously, most were unhappy with such treatment and considered themselves not a part of Confederate service. The government was trying to eliminate these Partisan organizations which they considered simply served as a hiding place for men to avoid conscription.

One captive was a member of Lt. Col. John N. Whitford's Battalion (11th North Carolina Partisan Rangers) which merged into the 67th N.C. Troops, and one came from Lt. Col. Clement G. Wright's Battalion of Infantry which had merged into the 66th N.C. Troops. Two were from the 1st North Carolina Artillery, Company B (Capt. David Cogdell's Battery), and one was from the 3d North Carolina Artillery, Company H (Capt. Alexander C. Latham's Battery). One was from Company C, 27th North Carolina Infantry, and one was from Company K, 3d North Carolina Cavalry, and one was listed as an enrolled conscript.

Pickett ordered a court-martial to convene as soon as the 22 deserters were sorted out and crammed into the Lenoir County jail. The trials began immediately and as soon as the findings were approved, executions were ordered and commenced on a hastily constructed gallows behind the county jail. The first victims were the two members from Company B, 1st N.C. Artillery, Privates Joseph S. Haskett and David Jones. They were tried on February 3, 1864, found guilty, and hanged on Friday, February 5, 1864. Meanwhile, Union authorities were mounting a strong effort to save the men, claiming that they should be treated as prisoners of war. Despite the futility of such an effort, the Federals were bound to try to preserve the Union sentiment in the area.

As the trials progressed, additional convictions were obtained and a second group of 13 hapless victims were placed upon the gallows, on Monday, February 15, 1864. The troops of Hoke's Division plus local citizens were witnesses to the executions. According to the various CSRs, the remaining seven were hanged on Monday, February 22, 1864.

It is uncertain as to whether or not Pickett was on hand for all of the executions. Hoke was charged with carrying out the tasks, but Pickett would have been required to approve the proceedings of the trials and to issue the orders for the executions. General Pickett was surely having second thoughts by now about the wisdom of his enterprise, because of the vociferous outcries from the Union command all the way to Washington, and the threats to execute a like number of Confederate prisoners of war.

The Northern War Department did not forget the incident. As soon as the war officially ended, effort began to bring George E. Pickett to justice. The danger of such retribution was surely very real for him for he fled to Canada in disguise and remained there while Judge Advocate General Joseph Holt was conducting courts of inquiry into the incident and planning to arrest the general. General Ulysses S. Grant put a stop to the whole effort by declaring that such action would violate the terms of his Appomattox parole.

Grant was too powerful to oppose, and so the attempt to arrest Pickett died out, and he was eventually able to return home. Even discounting the terms of the surrender at Appomattox, Grant probably looked upon the executions ordered by Pickett as the necessary evils of war. The unlucky 22 hanged at Kinston are listed in alphabetical order. Their names are listed as they appear in the Confederate CSRs. Some variations occur in the Union CSRs, these are noted in brackets in the Union designations.

1. Amyett, Amos—Pvt.—Company H—67th N.C. Troops (Co. F—2d N.C. Infantry—Union)[23]
2. Britain, Andrew J.—Pvt.—Company A—8th N.C. Battalion P.R. (Co. F—2d N.C. Infantry—Union [Brittain])[24]
3. Brock, John J.—Pvt.—Company C—8th N.C. Battalion P.R. (Co. F—2d N.C. Infantry—Union)[25]
4. Brock, Joseph—Pvt.—Company C—27th N.C. Troops (Co. B—2d N.C. Infantry—Union)[26]
5. Bryan, Lewis C.—Pvt.—Company A—8th N.C. Battalion P.R. (Co. C—2d N.C. Infantry—Union)[27]
6. Busick, Mitchell—Pvt.—Company A—8th N.C. Battalion P.R. (Co. F—2d N.C. Infantry—Union)[28]
7. Cuthrell, Charles R.—Pvt.—Company H—3d N.C. Artillery (Co.F—2d N.C. Infantry—Union [Cuthness])[29]
8. Doyety, William H.—Pvt.—Company C—8th N.C. Battalion P.R. (Co. F—2d N.C. Infantry—Union [Dougherty])[30]
9. Freeman, John—Pvt.—Company A—8th N.C. Battalion P.R. (Co. F—2d N.C. Infantry—Union)[31]
10. Freeman, Lewis—Pvt.—Company A—8th N.C. Battalion P.R. (Co. F—2d N.C. Infantry—Union)[32]
11. Haddock, William O.—Pvt.—Company A—8th N.C. Battalion P.R. (Co. F—2d N.C. Infantry—Union)[33]
12. Haskett, Joseph S.—Pvt.—Company B—1st N.C. Artillery (Co. F—2d N.C. Infantry—Union)[34]
13. Hill, William Irving—Pvt.—Company K—3d N.C. Cavalry (Co. F—2d N.C. Infantry—Union)[35]
14. Huffman, Calvin J.—Pvt.—Company A—8th N.C. Battalion P.R. (Co. F—2d N.C. Infantry—Union)[36]
15. Irvin, William—Pvt.—Company A—8th N.C. Battalion P.R. (Co. F—2d N.C. Infantry—Union [Irving])[37]
16. Jones, David—Pvt.—Company B—1st N.C. Artillery (Co. F—2d N.C. Infantry—Union)[38]
17. Jones, Stephen H.—Pvt.—Company B—8th N.C. Battalion P.R. (Co. F—2d N.C. Infantry—Union)[39]
18. Jones, William—Pvt.—Company D—Wright's N.C. Battalion (Co. F—2d N.C. Infantry—Union)[40]
19. Kellum, Elijah—Conscript (Co. F—2d N. C. Infantry—Union)[41]
20. Stanly, John L.—Pvt.—Company A—8th N.C. Battalion P.R. (Co. F—2d N.C. Infantry—Union [Stanley, John D.])[42]
21. Summerlin, Jesse—Pvt.—Company A—8th N.C. Battalion P.R. (Co. F—2d N.C. Infantry—Union)[43]
22. Taylor, Lewis—Pvt.—Company A—8th N.C. Battalion P.R. (Co. F—2d N.C. Infantry—Union)[44]

A similar collective execution of a different nature provided eight candidates for the hangman. The Andrews Raid, which was more popularly known as the Great Locomotive Chase, ended with tragic consequences for James J. Andrews and seven of his companions. The object of the raid as conceived by Andrews and approved by Maj. Gen. Ormsby M. Mitchell was to destroy vital links in the Western and Atlantic Railroad between Chattanooga, Tennessee, and Atlanta, Georgia. The success of such an effort would have greatly improved Mitchell's chances of liberating eastern Tennessee in the spring of 1862.

On April 7, 1862, 23 volunteers were selected from Col. Joshua W. Sill's Brigade of Infantry. Sill commanded three Ohio regiments, the 2d, 21st, and 33d, along with the 10th Wisconsin.

Andrews and his followers proceeded to Marietta, Georgia, where they were to meet at 5:00 a.m. on Saturday, April 12, 1862. Two of the men did not make it to Marietta, leaving Andrews with 21 volunteers, fate played a hand in eliminating two more. The hotel clerk failed to wake them and so they missed the northbound train that Andrews and his companions boarded. This was the train pulled by the famous engine, "General."

At the first stop, Big Shanty, the train arrived at 6:00 a.m., just in time for a 20-minute meal. While the train crew and passengers were enjoying breakfast, Andrews and his 19 volunteers jumped aboard the train, uncoupled the unit after the third boxcar behind the tender, and opened the throttle on the "General" and swung out of the station at full speed.

Andrews' effort was fraught with poor planning and bad luck. He hoped to drive the next 100 miles or more burning bridges, destroying road beds, and cutting telegraph wires. But alas, none of this was accomplished. Heavy rains made the bridges impervious to fire, and rebel soldiers soon nullified any chance of the raiders doing further mischief.

Soon another train was in hot pursuit, and after a wild chase, the raiders were forced to abandon their stolen rolling stock just north of Ringgold, Georgia. The unlucky fugitives scattered into the woods where they were soon rounded up and jailed in Chattanooga, Tennessee. Meanwhile, the two who had overslept in their hotel in Marietta were captured and placed in the compound with the others. Andrews was soon identified as the leader of the raiders, and tried by court-martial near the middle of April 1862. The trial was concluded April 26, 1862, but the decision was not announced until May 31. He was transferred to Atlanta and hanged there on June 7, 1862.

Twelve of the remaining prisoners were transferred to Knoxville, Tennessee on May 31, to stand trial. Only seven of the men were tried; each accorded a separate trial, taking up approximately the first week of June. Each was charged with: "violation of Section 2nd of the 101st Article of the Rules and Articles of War," (lurking as a spy), conviction of which required a sentence of death.

General E. Kirby Smith issued GO #54, June 14, 1862, Department of East Tennessee, approving the decisions and sentences of the court and directing that the seven be hanged between June 15 and June 22. Accordingly, the seven were executed on a common scaffold in Atlanta, Georgia on June 18, 1862.

It is uncertain as to the method used to select the 12 who were sent to Knoxville to stand trial. Trials were suspended after only seven were tried because of Union activity, but it appears that the others were scheduled for courts-martial at later dates. Nine others were still in jail at Chattanooga.

Time worked in favor of all those not yet tried; eight managed to escape and six were exchanged, thus ending all prosecution. In addition to James J. Andrews, who was a civilian soldier of fortune, the others were thus identified:

1. William H. Campbell, a civilian.[45]
2. Pvt. Samuel Robertson, Company G—33d Ohio Infantry[46]
3. Sgt. Maj. Marion A. Ross, F&S—2d Ohio Infantry[47]
4. Sgt. John M. Scott—Company F—21st Ohio Infantry[48]
5. Pvt. Perry G. Shadrach—Company K—2d Ohio Infantry[49]
6. Pvt. Samuel Slavens—Company E—33d Ohio Infantry[50]
7. Pvt. George D. Wilson—Company B—2d Ohio Infantry[51]

The general practice of the courts was to sentence only enlisted men to death. Degrading punishment such as flogging or hard labor cannot be inflicted upon officers without demeaning the service, but the enforcement of the death penalty, where warranted, against commissioned officers would serve the very useful purpose of conveying a message of fairness to enlisted men.

Four officers were pardoned from execution, many others were cashiered instead of being shot, even though improper, such was the will of the president. A few fell into that undetermined class of Code #15, and one escaped while under a sentence of death.

Only three examples were found whereby death sentences were carried out. Some details were lacking, but in each case, orders to complete the execution were the last entries seen in the CSRs.

First Lieutenant William H. White was tried August 13, 1863, under charges of quitting his guard, disobedience of orders, holding correspondence with the enemy, and advising others to desert. He was a member of Company C, 4th Georgia Cavalry (Col. Isaac W.

Avery's), part of Maj. Gen. John A. Wharton's Division, Col. Charles C. Crews' Brigade. The court found him guilty and sentenced him to hang; on August 20, 1863, General Bragg issued GO #165, Army of Tennessee, directing that the sentence be carried out Saturday, August 22, 1863, between 10:00 a.m. and 2:00 p.m.

Similar information was found in the case of 2d Lt. Troy H. Spencer, Company C, 63d Virginia Infantry. He was tried September 14, 1864, under a charge of desertion, found guilty and sentenced to be shot to death. At the time of the trial, the 63d was part of Brig. Gen. Alexander W. Reynolds' Brigade, Maj. Gen. Carter L. Stevenson's Division. The last information in Spencer's CSR is the reference to GO #52, Army of Tennessee, issued by General John Bell Hood on September 23, 1864, directing that the execution be carried out on Monday, September 26, 1864, under the supervision of the commanding general of Stevenson's Division.

Captain Jabez R. Rhodes, Second Company C, 1st Confederate Regiment Georgia Infantry, was tried on August 13, 1863, under charges of: (1) making a false report, (2) conduct unbecoming an officer, (3) advising a soldier to desert, (4) disobedience of an order, and (5) drunkenness on duty. He was convicted of all of the above charges and sentenced to be shot to death. He was also charged with embezzlement, but acquitted of that crime; the third charge of advising soldiers to desert was the fatal one. The 1st Georgia Confederates were part of Brig. Gen. John King Jackson's Brigade of Maj. Gen. Benjamin F. Cheatham's Division, Polk's Corps, of the Army of Tennessee. General Bragg issued GO #174 on August 30, 1863, approving the sentence, and Captain Rhodes was shot to death on Friday, September 4, 1863.[52]

One Union officer was found in the records of courts-martial cases in the A&IGO. Captain A. C. Webster was tried on or about April 1, 1863, for "breach of parole of honor," and sentenced to be hanged. Although orders covering the trial could not be found, the trial must have been convened in Richmond. He was confined in Castle Thunder and hanged there between April 10, 1863, and April 13, 1863.

Webster is simply listed in the A&IGO ledgers as a member of the "Federal Army," but his name could not be located in Union records. Correspondence from Gen. Samuel Cooper to Brig. Gen. John Henry Winder, dated April 2, 1863, sheds no light on Webster's identity: "The Secretary of War has suspended until the 10th instant the sentence of death against Capt. A.C. Webster, of Peirpoint's [sic] army. Please direct the necessary measures in the matter."[53]

Very respectfully,
S. Cooper, A&IGO

General Cooper is surely referring to West Virginia Governor Francis Harrison Pierpont, but Webster could not be identified in the roster of either Virginia or West Virginia Union volunteer units, nor could he be found in any other Union records. He is probably not the only Union officer executed by the Confederacy, but he is the only one to appear in the court-martial records of the A&IGO.

Chapter VIII
The Numbers

The number of trials recorded in this study totaled 20,021. This certainly does not include all cases that were tried. Although it represents a reasonable summary of cases, many were lost before they found their way to the War Department in Richmond. In addition, most garrison courts-martial records were not sent to Richmond. It is hoped that the total includes most of the general courts-martial cases, but it is certain that some of these are missing. In a cursory review of available copies of general orders of the various armies and commands, more than 300 examples of general courts-martial cases were seen that were not listed in the summary of cases by the A&IGO.

The effort required to prosecute the general courts-martial cases was overwhelming at times. Had the Confederate government not resorted to the military courts to relieve the burden from army and department commanders, the daily effort by these leaders to pursue the campaigns would certainly have suffered more. It is even more baffling to consider the numbers that might have been tried. More than 100,000 desertions were recorded during the four years of war by the Confederacy. Many of these were committed by the same person two, three, or more times, and no exact record can be obtained, but the fact remains that the vast majority were never brought to trial.

Desertion was a terrible problem for the Confederacy, but the Union's troubles were similar. Although many totals are suspect, it is a certainty that at least 200,000 deserted from Union ranks. In order to arrive at a reasonably accurate percentage of the Union desertion rate, Livermore's figure of 1,556,678 enlistments was used;

this yields a desertion percentage of approximately 13%. Confederate armies recorded around 104,000 desertions from an enlistment total of 1,082,119; that percentage rounds out to 10%.[1]

Even though the South recorded a better percentage record, the numbers emphasize the distinct weakness of the Southern forces. With Northern armies recruiting nearly 475,000 more men, it quickly becomes obvious that greater numbers of desertions in the North can easily be offset. Add to that the fact that desertions in the South increased greatly during the last year of the war as her fortunes declined, plus the added burden of the North's refusal to exchange prisoners during the final year, and the desperation of the Southern cause becomes apparent.

Of the approximate 20,000 cases reviewed in this study, 4,000 or so were charged with desertion in one form or another. That is, some were simply charged with "desertion"; others were charged with "desertion and forgery" or "desertion and murder" or "desertion to the enemy," etc. In addition, a few were charged with violation of AOW #20.

Even though desertion accounted for 20% of these cases, the 4,000 total is a small percentage of the numbers who left their commands. The task of capturing deserters was a formidable one in the 1860s, especially in remote regions. No area of the Confederacy was more remote than western North Carolina. That state led all others in desertions (more than 24,000), virtually double that of Virginia and Tennessee, each of which had approximately 12,000 desertions for the second and third highest total.[2]

The Union sentiment that prevailed in the mountain region of North Carolina played a large part in influencing the desertion rate. The state furnished more than its share of fierce fighters, but many did not have their heart in the cause and paid dearly for it with the highest number of executions during the war. And for years following, the mountain area was penalized by the Democrats that returned to power after the carpetbaggers were thrown out.

The region of Union sympathizers in the Confederacy can be drawn around that vast mountainous section of the eastern part of the nation; western North Carolina, western Virginia (which later became the state of West Virginia), eastern Tennessee, and eastern Kentucky. These mountain people were by heritage independent. They were not happy with Washington dictating their lives, but neither were they happy with Richmond doing so. Their view on slavery was one of opposition; not only did they not own slaves, they were against the whole process. Not so much as abolitionists, but from an economic standpoint they were opposed to slave labor which often competed with their limited skills at hacking out a living with back-breaking labor.

Tennessee was very high in desertion rates and remained a break-away area for the Confederacy throughout the war. Many of her citizens were severely punished and most in the eastern region were suspect. Tennessee furnished almost as many men to the cause as did North Carolina, but more than 12,000 deserted the colors.

For Tennessee and Virginia the high rate of desertion seems to have been one of convenience. Most Virginia units served in Lee's army; most of the campaigning for the Army of Northern Virginia was conducted within the state. Opportunity was close at hand for the men from these units to return home rather easily. Similar circumstances prevailed for Tennessee troops. Most were part of the Army of Tennessee and the bulk of that army's maneuvers were in Tennessee, thereby placing these men within easy walking distance of home.

The cause for which the Confederacy seceded and ultimately fought was doomed from its inception because of the lack of total commitment within its own ranks. The Northern states suffered from pockets of dissension in some areas, but because an established government remained in power, the vast majority of these Northern citizens were supportive of that government. Moreover, with the large number of citizens and the ample resources, the North could function well with some degree of dissension. For the South, the only hope for success, once the fighting began, was to obtain the undying devotion of everyone to the cause.

As soon as the war opened the military had to address the issue of courts-martial. The earliest cases appear around mid-April 1861, in the Army of Pensacola. The numbers tried gradually increased as recruits continued to pour into the ranks. Green troops are prone to commit violations of the articles of war causing high numbers of prosecutions; nevertheless the total tried for the year was reasonably low at 766 for the nine-month period from April to December 1861.

Cases recorded in 1862 totaled 3,262 which were fewer than might have been expected from armies that were not yet veterans.

As regards courts-martial cases, the year of 1863 was a disaster; the numbers rose to the highest level of the war, 8,035. Considering the fact that the Confederate armies were victorious in many of the 1863 campaigns, this total is surprisingly high.

Table 8.1

Trials by Calendar Quarters—1863

Date	Total Trials
01/01/63	2,746
04/01/63	1,887

Date	Total Trials
07/01/63	863
10/01/63	2,539
	8,035

The decline in cases tried during the third quarter may be partly attributable to the extension of presidential amnesty on August 11, 1863, but the consequences of this act were not reflected in the trials this early. The chief reason is simply that the two major armies were too busy campaigning to try courts-martial cases. Trials were usually postponed until the armies were less active such as winter periods.

The two principal armies of the Confederacy, the Army of Northern Virginia and the Army of Tennessee, together accounted for nearly 50% of the cases listed. The Army of Northern Virginia's numbers totaled 7,433 and those of the Army of Tennessee 2,571 for a sum exceeding 10,000. This does not include the numbers for Longstreet's First Corps during his service in the Department of Western Virginia and East Tennessee and his Suffolk expedition in the Department of North Carolina and Southeast Virginia.

The Army of Northern Virginia would qualify for containing the most trials by virtue of its numbers and tenure. But of more importance was the composition of that army. Nearly all Virginia units served in Lee's army as did most of the North Carolina units. Troops from these two states accounted for 8,775 trials. Numbers alone are the chief cause of these many courts-martial cases. Virginia and North Carolina were the two major states contributing to Confederate enlistments. Unfortunately, exact figures for Confederate enlistments are lacking and totals by state are guesswork.

Table 8.2
Number of Cases by State

State or Special Designation	Total Trials	Percent
Alabama	1,811	9.2%
Arkansas	421	2.1%
Confederate	245	1.3%
Florida	321	1.6%
Georgia	2,135	10.8%
Kentucky	151	.8%
Louisiana	748	3.8%
Maryland	49	.2%
Mississippi	1,110	5.6%
Missouri	218	1.1%
North Carolina	3,204	16.2%

State or Special Designation	Total Trials	Percent
South Carolina	2,019	10.2%
Tennessee	736	3.7%
Texas	709	3.6%
Virginia	5,582	28.2%
Military—No State Designation	325	1.6%
Sub-Total	19,784	100.00%
C.S.A. Military	19,784	98.82%
Citizens—Confederacy	178	.89%
Citizens—U.S.A.	3	.01%
Teamsters, Storekeepers, etc.	13	.06%
Alien Enemy	3	.01%
Slaves and Free Negroes	14	.08%
No Designation	3	.01%
U.S.A. Military	23	.12%
Total Cases	20,021	100.00%

The totals of trials by state troops raise interesting questions. Why did Virginia troops account for more than 28% of trials by states? And why did Tennessee send only 736 men to face courts-martial? Virginia furnished between 14% and 15% of total troops to the cause and Tennessee accounted for 11% to 12%. Georgia's trials are approximately in line with the number of troops furnished; she provided between 11% and 12% and her trials came to 10.8%. There is only the rule of probability to account for the likelihood that cases will approximate enlistments, but the totals of Tennessee and Virginia are completely out of line with this factor.

Only three states contained units that suffered more than 100 trials by courts-martial: North Carolina, South Carolina, and Virginia. Considering that many regiments served throughout the war and had perfect or nearly perfect records; that is, no cases or only one or two, units with more than 100 were true disciplinary problems.

Table 8.3

Units That Tried 100 or More Cases

Regiment or Battalion	Cases Recorded
16th North Carolina Troops	123
22d North Carolina Troops	119
37th North Carolina Troops	101
1st S.C. Artillery	151
15th S.C. Infantry	173
18th Virginia Battn. H. Arty.	137

Regiment or Battalion	Cases Recorded
6th Virginia Cavalry	102
1st Virginia Battn. Infantry	130
14th Virginia Infantry	176
38th Virginia Infantry	109
53d Virginia Infantry	139
57th Virginia Infantry	260
25th Virginia Battn. L.D.T.	127

The 57th Virginia Infantry holds the undesirable record for number of cases tried; desertion accounted for the vast majority of charges in the 260 trials. The tantalizing question presents itself as to why the men from the 57th left the ranks in such numbers. Volunteers were recruited from Powhatan, Pittsylvania, and Botetourt Counties; Botetourt is the only western mountainous county of the three. The fact that mountainous areas accounted for a large measure of the antislavery sentiment in the South would not seem to be a significant factor for the 57th.

Two contrary issues frequently affect morale: hard campaigning and inactivity. Even though the 57th suffered greatly in two costly advances, Malvern Hill and Gettysburg, the unit did not exceed the record of several other regiments in hard fighting. The men were probably aware that they were badly used in those two hopeless assaults, but the spread of trials occurred throughout the war; that is, they were generally evenly disbursed over the four years without a preponderance occurring after Gettysburg.

Inactivity is more devastating to unit spirit than is hard fighting. During the war, disease always took a heavy toll of troops confined to a camp for long periods. With men dying from such ravages with nothing to show for it, morale soon collapses. Moreover, men quickly become bored with nothing to do. Make-work projects soon become intolerable for the veteran soldier; he recognizes them for what they are and invents ways to get around them.

The example of the 18th Virginia Battalion of Heavy Artillery is typical. The unit was not organized until June 1862, so in less than three years it compiled 137 courts-martial for five companies. The 18th spent the war in defense of Richmond and thereby saw little action until it was pressed into the infantry ranks in defense of Appomattox after the fall of Richmond.

No such lethargy can be attributed to the 57th Virginia Infantry. So without evidence of the two common enemies of morale, other causes must be tested. Was there a problem with command? Lewis A. Armistead was the colonel when the 57th was organized September 25, 1861. He remained until April 1, 1862, when he was promoted brigadier general. He commanded the brigade until his death on the third day at Gettysburg. His tenure of command of the regiment covered approximately six months, but during that time only five cases were tried. Shortly after Elisha F. Keen was promoted to colonel upon Armistead's appointment to brigade commander, the advance upon Malvern Hill was undertaken. Perhaps this had an overall effect upon morale, for Keen resigned shortly after the battle. David Dyer assumed command on July 31, 1862, and remained until January 1863, when he resigned in favor of John Bowie Magruder, who was colonel until he was lost to wounds on the third day at Gettysburg. Later in the war, Col. Clement R. Fontaine was appointed and finished the war with the 57th at Appomattox.

Brigade command was surely a factor in determining morale. During Armistead's one and one-half years in command, this brigade sent 317 men to trial. Seth M. Barton, who followed Armistead, accounted for 408 and George Hume "Maryland" Steuart 130, for an astounding total of 855 cases. In addition to the 57th Virginia Infantry, the brigade was made up of the 9th Virginia, the 14th Virginia, the 38th Virginia, and the 53d Virginia. Both the 14th and 38th had high records for trials greatly contributing to the record number of cases for the brigade.

Troop composition rather than command was likely the determining factor. Virginia troops faced courts-martial in record numbers and Maj. Gen. George E. Pickett's Division was composed of all Virginia units; that is the overriding reason why he held the record for division total trials of 1,093. But Pickett cannot entirely escape censure, he was not a favorite among his men nor highly regarded by superior officers.

A review of the trials of the 57th Virginia Infantry shows 16 men sentenced to death, but only one example whereby the death sentence was carried out; Colby Sprouse, private of Co. H, was shot to death in September 1864, for desertion.[3] Pvt. Jesse R. Clanton of Co. F was captured at Five Forks while under sentence of death; the other 14 were pardoned. Perhaps if fewer pardons were granted, more men would have remained in the ranks.

It is difficult to find any pattern whereby execution improved a unit's performance. Most units did not have multiple executions and those that did tended to occur all at the same time. For example, the record number held by the 8th North Carolina Battalion Partisan Rangers all occurred following the courts-martial at Kinston, North Carolina, in February 1864. The same is true of the 3d North Carolina State Troops when 10 members were shot for desertion and murder on September 5, 1863, and the 58th North

Carolina Troops who furnished 11 members to face firing squads on May 4, 1864.

Perhaps a pattern can be found for correcting those capital violations other than desertion. In one form or another, desertion accounted for the vast majority of executions; despite this, it seems that the threat of death did not deter literally thousands from resorting to it. However, other serious violations of the articles of war claimed relatively few lives.

The sentences handed down by the courts were often more lenient for some of these violations such as "misbehavior before the enemy." Only four persons were executed for this violation. One might say that the threat of death kept the soldiers in line, but the more likely explanation is that other motivators were responsible.

Three men were executed for mutiny, approximately 75 were found guilty of this serious charge, but most were sentenced to hard labor; three additional individuals were condemned to death, but their executions could not be verified. Given the desperate circumstances of the Confederate armies during the last year of war, this is a surprising low number of cases for this crime.

Other violations did not occur in noticeable numbers: murder, advising others to desert, striking a superior officer, giving aid and comfort to the enemy. Death was employed against only one or two violators of these charges; perhaps it was a deterrent; perhaps other factors were involved.

No record was found of a Confederate soldier executed for sleeping on post. A few were sentenced to be shot, but all were pardoned or had their sentence commuted except one case that was questionable. Private Daniel S. Cash, Co. D, 20th Virginia Battalion of Heavy Artillery, was tried on February 16, 1865, and sentenced to be shot to death for sleeping on post; Lt. Gen. Richard S. Ewell approved the orders on March 30, 1865, but the last entry in Case's CSR shows him in General Hospital #13, Richmond, on February 5, 1865.[4]

The number of soldiers charged with sleeping on post by the Confederate armies was typical; 182 were brought before general courts under the properly worded charge "sleeping on post," and an additional 90 were charged with a violation of AOW #46. AOW #46 states the nature of punishment that may be awarded for sleeping on post or for abandoning the post without proper relief. The threat of death was a necessary requirement to keep soldiers apprised of the seriousness of their responsibility, but leniency in the execution of sentences is the better option. Guard duty ranks at the top of the list of the ten most boring activities of the day; add to that the fatigue from a long march and only a special few can avoid napping. Most NCOs serving as sergeant of the guard would simply kick the sentinel awake and continue on rounds.

Of the approximate 270 who faced general courts, a large percentage were acquitted or had their sentence or findings disapproved. The most severe punishment awarded to most was hard labor, although five were drummed out of the service. This lenient approach taken by most courts seems to have been in the best interest of the service.

The most remarkable statistic is the almost total absence of the charge of rape. Only one near case was seen. Private John Duncan, Co. F, 3d Tennessee Infantry, P.A.C.S. (Vaughn's), was tried on May 26, 1863, for AWOL, assault on a citizen, and attempt to commit rape (twice). Duncan was found guilty of all charges and sentenced to 25 years at hard labor. The War Department doubtless recognized the futility of such a sentence, so on October 28, 1863, the president commuted the residue of hard labor.[5] At the time of the trial, the 3d Tennessee Infantry was in the Department of East Tennessee, Maj. Gen. Henry Heth's Division, Brig. Gen. Alexander W. Reynolds' Brigade.

The unfortunate fact that charges could not be found in 9,459 trials which represent 47% of the total number of cases, casts some doubt upon the conclusion that no other charges of rape occurred. There is, however, some evidence to support the absence of the charge. Confederate forces did little campaigning in Northern territory. The border states of Kentucky, Missouri, Maryland, and West Virginia saw considerable activity, but the major portion of conflict was restricted to the Confederate States.

Such depredations are most likely to occur in enemy territory; even the border states were sacred ground because of the special effort to bring these states into the Confederacy. There was a strong religious influence among both Northern and Southern troops and especially so among special commands such as Gen. Thomas J. Jackson's. This influence no doubt had an effect. Add to that the fact that commanders made a special effort to keep troops away from cities and towns when in garrison or on bivouac and you have two important deterrents. Regardless, it is a notable fact if no cases of rape occurred.

As would be expected, the infantry accounted for the majority of courts-martial cases. This result would occur simply from the vastly greater number of infantry units, but other factors influenced these results as well. Confederate cavalry was a special branch of the service that ostensibly recruited only qualified horsemen who were required to furnish their own mounts upon volunteering. Artillery units, except for the battalions of heavy artillery, were closely knit groups that often remained cohesive units throughout the war. Many batteries kept the same commanders from Manassas to Appomattox.

Courts-martial cases do not appear in these records for several batteries, but the record for artillerymen is not perfect. Some of the heavy artillery battalions had large numbers of cases, and many of the well-known field artillery batteries had trials totally out of proportion to their numbers.

The Barbour Light Artillery organized in Eufaula, Alabama, in April 1862, was commanded by Capt. Reuben F. Kolb. Early in the war it served in Kentucky; later it was assigned to the Army of Tennessee. It saw action with Bragg and Johnston from Chickamauga to Atlanta and with Hood during the fall and winter of 1864. It moved to North Carolina with Johnston in 1865 and surrendered in April. No trials appear in these records for Captain Kolb's battery.

A similar record was turned in by the Troup Light Artillery; that battery was formed in LaGrange, Georgia in 1861; it was soon ordered to Virginia and assigned to Col. Henry Coalter Cabell's Battalion which became part of Longstreet's First Corps. The battery fought with the Virginia army from Seven Days' to Appomattox suffering casualties in most of the major engagements. One gunner appears in the records: Pvt. William H. P. Jones was tried on unknown charges on November 26, 1863, and sentenced to confinement. The battery was commanded by Captain Henry H. Carlton and Capt. Marcellus Stanley.

Another battery of Longstreet's Corps turned in a nearly perfect record on courts-martial. The Donaldsonville Light Artillery organized in the summer of 1861 in Louisiana was quickly ordered to Virginia and placed in Maj. Charles Richardson's Battalion. It served from Williamsburg to Appomattox under the command of Capt. Victor Maurin and Capt. R. Prosper Landry. Sometime during 1864 the battery was transferred to Lt. Gen. Ambrose P. Hill's Third Corps when Richardson's Battalion was shifted to that corps. On December 1, 1864, Captain Landry was brought up on charges of neglect of duty; he was acquitted, but thus became the only member of his command to appear in the record of trials.

Stanford's Mississippi Battery also recorded only one trial. In the fall of 1861, Capt. Thomas J. Stanford was given command of a Mississippi Battery bearing his name. The unit was shifted to Tennessee and engaged in the fight at Shiloh. When the Army of Tennessee was formed, Captain Stanford's battery was assigned to that army. It went on to serve with Bragg and Johnston. During the Atlanta campaign it was in Gen. John Bell Hood's Corps as part of

Maj. John W. Eldridge's Artillery Battalion. It remained with the army under Hood, and was captured at his final battle at Nashville. During all those trying campaigns only one trial was recorded: Pvt. Richard H. Slaughter was brought up on unknown charges on January 12, 1864, found guilty, and sentenced to hard labor.

Virginia was the mother of Confederate artillery units. Many of these batteries had long lists of trials and nearly all of her artillery battalions showed record numbers. A total of more than 950 cases were found for Virginia gunners. Despite this, most of the field batteries were effective units. Southern artillerymen turned in an enviable record; as the war continued, the superiority of Northern metal prevailed and the loss of horses greatly handicapped the range and movement of Southern batteries, but the capability of Confederate gunners never flagged.

The Powhatan Light Artillery was organized in July 1861, in Powhatan County, Virginia, with Capt. Willis J. Dance in command. It served in the Richmond area and in the campaigns in Maryland. It participated in the Petersburg siege and the Appomattox battles as part of Lt. Col. Robert A. Hardaway's Battalion of the Second Corps Artillery. Only one trial appears in the records for Dance's Battery: Pvt. Anderson Cook was tried on January 24, 1865, on charges of AWOL; he was acquitted.

These are but a few examples of field artillery batteries that were well-disciplined fighting units; even though it is much easier to mold the complement of a battery (between 60–120 men) into an effective loyal company than it is to do so with a regiment, these batteries are worthy of recognition.

An outstanding example of infantry performance was seen in the 15th Georgia; it was formed in the spring of 1861 and sent to Virginia where it was assigned to the Potomac District on July 22, 1861. Later it became part of the Army of Northern Virginia under Brig. Gen. Robert A. Toombs' Brigade. It was introduced to battle in the Seven Days' campaign. When Longstreet was given command of the First Corps, the 15th was assigned to Brig. Gen. Henry L. Benning's Brigade in Maj. Gen. John Bell Hood's Division. It remained a part of Benning's Brigade until the end of the war, surrendering at Appomattox.

Despite all the hardships of the nearly four years of campaigning, only one trial appears in the record of the 15th Georgia Infantry: Pvt. William H. Davis of Co. K deserted May 6, 1864, and was brought before a court-martial on November 21, 1864; he was sentenced to hard labor with ball and chain plus pay stoppage.

One can only speculate as to what Southern commanders might have been able to accomplish had they had this kind of support from all units.

One of the most controversial Confederate trials does not appear in the list of cases tried. It came about because of General Stonewall Jackson's misreading of the Union forces at Kernstown, Virginia. On March 22–23, 1862, he advanced upon what he thought was a Union rear guard but was rather Brig. Gen. James Shields' Division of 9,000 muskets. With Col. Samuel Fulkerson's and Brig. Gen. Richard B. Garnett's Brigades he assaulted the Union right; but this force numbered less than half of that of the Union. In a short time, Garnett's Stonewall Brigade was in serious trouble. Facing the advance of superior numbers and running out of ammunition, their position became indefensible; Garnett ordered a retreat.

Even though all of Garnett's subordinate commanders agreed that he had saved the brigade, General Jackson did not see it that way; to him, Garnett had lost the day. A week later he placed Garnett under arrest and filed charges for "neglect of duty." Other pressing action prevented the court from convening in a timely manner. Not until August 6, 1862, did the court meet. But this initial session was a short one; the next day Jackson launched his forces into what was to become the battle of Cedar Mountain.

The court-martial of Garnett never reconvened. Jackson was busy with more pressing duties from that first meeting of the court until his final rendezvous with destiny at Chancellorsville, and Garnett met a similar "last post" a month later at Gettysburg on July 3, 1863. So the trial never went into the record books. It was not concluded, all entries were wiped out as if they had not occurred.

An excellent account of what is termed "The Army of Northern Virginia's Most Notorious Court Martial..." appears in *Blue & Gray* magazine.[6] Robert K. Krick explains both Jackson's position and Garnett's defense, giving an evenhanded account of the issue. The true master of the case was Gen. Robert E. Lee. He stepped in and released Garnett from arrest and assigned him to Longstreet's Corps where he drew the fateful position of command of one of General Pickett's brigades. Lee was the power behind the use of the genius of General Jackson, for he allowed the mysterious Stonewall to fight in his own way and yet salvaged the subordinates that Jackson alienated such as Garnett, A. P. Hill, and others.

In addition to the more than 20,000 trials that the Confederacy had to deal with, there were never-ending numbers of deserters to pursue. Throughout the war, approximately 104,000 unauthorized absentees kept military record keepers busy. Those sent in pursuit plus the civilian authorities employed to capture the missing, hindered the war effort. The majority were not found and never returned to the army to face trial, but an unknown number were killed by civilian or military authorities and of course do not appear in any courts-martial records. This is another uncounted aspect of the war's tragic consequences.

Pursuit of deserters was a regular endeavor throughout the war in states such as Virginia and North Carolina. That served to further divide loyalties among the Southern people. State governors tried to keep their residents united while they followed Richmond's pursuit policy. The central government was well aware of the political consequences of bringing dissenters to heel, which invariably resulted in a further erosion of the military's authority.

Politics surely played a part in the exercise of pardons and the enforcement of death sentences. The total number of executions that occurred among North Carolina troops reflects not only the deep division of Southern loyalty among North Carolinians, but also a concerted effort among commanders to bring them into line.

A total of 204 Confederate soldiers were shot to death as confirmed in this study (more than this surely met such a fate but were not verified). Twenty-five Confederate soldiers were hanged; out of the total of 229, 120 were North Carolinians. It is difficult to explain how one state could suffer 53% of the executions without factoring politics into the equation. Southern command was all too aware of the enormity of North Carolina desertions. Their efforts to curtail these crimes resulted in high numbers of executions. The two unusual incidents that accounted for 32 executions were understandable in that they were the result of prosecution of two large groups. One group was brought to trial when Pickett's forces captured the 22 unlucky deserters in blue uniforms at New Bern, North Carolina. The other group was made up of the 10 survivors of the 3d North Carolina State Troops deserters who tried to shoot their way out of a trap sprung by their pursuers.

Nevertheless, that still leaves 88 executions of North Carolina soldiers, which far exceeds the number from any other state; Virginia only counted 48, even though she sent more men to trial than any other state.

Many men appear twice in the courts-martial records; two trials during the course of the war was not an unusual statistic. However, 42 were tried three times and eight were tried four times; one man Pvt. William Finlay, Company E, 14th Alabama Infantry, faced courts-martial five times. He received sentences ranging from company punishment to hard labor. His last trial was on February 16, 1865, when he faced a charge of AWOL; he was sentenced to one month at hard labor with ball and chain, but was pardoned under GO #2, Army of the Confederate States, February 11, 1865, the president's final effort at amnesty. The most interesting fact of these cases is that 28 of the men who were tried three or more times were Virginians.

Another of the puzzling statistics involves the number of cases sent to the courts by troops from the state of Tennessee. As previously mentioned, Tennessee was one of the top states in number of desertions, documenting more than 12,000. Depending upon the accuracy of the numbers, they surpassed Virginia for the #2 spot. Why then did Tennessee troops face courts-martial only 736 times?

Part of the reason may be attributed to the fact that most Tennessee units were part of the Army of Tennessee. The army was not identified as such until November 1862, and by mid-December 1864, it was only a token force even though Gen. Joseph E. Johnston did not surrender until after Appomattox, the remnants of the Army of Tennessee made up only a small part of his command. The Army of Northern Virginia was designated June 1, 1862, and remained a formidable force until April 9, 1865, almost three years. Nevertheless, the Army of Tennessee tried 2,574 cases as opposed to 7,433 documented for the Army of Northern Virginia. That total does not include the 500 cases tried by Longstreet's Corps when it was on detached service in the Department of Western Virginia and East Tennessee.

The Army of Northern Virginia's longer tenure and greater numbers account for some of the difference, but not enough to justify the fact that the one army tried almost three times the number of cases as the other. Perhaps the commanders in Lee's army were less likely to overlook the sins of desertion and absence without official leave. Lee was a stern taskmaster who expected his army to abide by regulations. The brigade and regimental commanders were chiefly the ones who preferred charges against enlisted men who went over the hill. The preponderance of those officers in the Army of Northern Virginia had military experience from the regular army of the United States and were usually graduates of West Point or they were graduates of the Virginia Military Institute or the Citadel. These people were more likely to enforce the regulations than were volunteer officers.

Only three Tennessee regiments were originally assigned to the Army of Northern Virginia; those in Brig. Gen. James J. Archer's Brigade, the 1st, 7th, and 14th Tennessee Infantry. Although General Archer died in October 1864 shortly after returning to command of his brigade following his imprisonment, the brigade remained part of the Third Corps until the surrender at Appomattox when it was under the command of Brig. Gen. William McComb. Only 85 cases went to trial for the brigade under Archer and 2 under McComb. Such a record is enviable for a brigade that performed full service throughout the war. Approximately 36 of the trials were attributed to the three Tennessee regiments, 16 to the 1st Tennessee Infantry (Provisional Army); 12 to the 14th Tennessee Infantry, and 8 to the 7th Tennessee Infantry. Late in the war, three Tennessee units were transferred to the eastern theater: the 17th/23rd Tennessee Infantry, the 25th/44th Tennessee Infantry, and the 63rd Tennessee Infantry. These were initially engaged in Maj. Gen. Bushrod R. Johnson's Brigade at Drewry's Bluff and finished the war in Archer's old brigade.

In reviewing these cases, an interesting fact emerges: only 18 were charged with desertion; the other charges seen were a variety, from sleeping on post, to straggling, to theft, and misbehavior before the enemy. At any rate, the desertions seen were fewer than normal. Perhaps if more Tennessee troops had been assigned to the eastern theater and more Virginia troops to the western theater, the element of opportunity would have been removed for those easily disposed to desert.

An unknown factor surely played a part in determining the low number of Tennessee troops brought to trial. It is impossible to say how many of the deserters were returned to their units. Perhaps the home guard and civil authorities were not as effective in capturing deserters in Tennessee as they were in other states. Such was surely the case after the twin disasters of the Army of Tennessee at Franklin and Nashville, but prior to that the army maintained an effective control throughout the state.

A more worrisome concern is the possibility that a significant number of cases tried by the Army of Tennessee were lost. More than 300 names were found in general orders that did not appear in the A&IGO record of cases. The weakness of this discovery is the fact that all general orders were not found. Virtually all of those for the Army of Northern Virginia have been preserved, but the findings for other commands were spotty. Comparing the 300 odd cases from general orders, a few were from the Army of Northern Virginia, several were from the Army of the Peninsula, many were from the Department of the Trans-Mississippi, and the Department of Texas, and very few from the Army of Tennessee. Moreover, there are gaps in the general orders found from the Army of Tennessee.

However, another variable to the puzzle comes into play. With the creation of the military courts on October 9, 1862, the results of trials were published in general orders issued by the corps to which the court was assigned. Later in the war such orders reverted to army command. But the number of trials by military courts that were published in orders from various corps is unknown. Very few corps general orders were found, but the possibility exists that significant numbers of both orders and cases tried by the military courts never reached Richmond.

Approximately 19,700 cases were recorded in the A&IGO records. How many more were tried? That is a difficult question to answer. A few of the recorded cases were garrison courts-martial which should not have been sent to Richmond, but it is surely reasonable to assume that the Confederacy tried more than 20,000 general courts-martial, probably as many as 25,000.

The overall problem of command throughout the Army of Tennessee influenced trials. President Davis never found a star-quality commander for his western army. In addition, Gen. Braxton Bragg was never served by loyal corps commanders; furthermore, there was dissention among his division and brigade leaders. When army command was shifted from Bragg to Johnston to Hood and back to Johnston, this added to the division of loyalties among subordinates. Is it any wonder that other concerns took precedence over courts-martial?

AWOL was a first cousin to desertion. Many persons convicted of AWOL had originally been charged with desertion. The decision of the court in these cases was such that they could not prove (or be convinced) that the accused did not intend to return to his command. The key difference in conviction of one or the other charge is intent. The wording in cases of desertion generally stated "That Pvt. John Doe did desert the service . . ."; the implication is that he, Private Doe, is departing his unit once and for all.

If an accused could convince the court that he planned to return to his regiment, he had a reasonable chance of conviction under a charge of AWOL. Circumstances rather than time play a key part. Even if the accused was captured at home by the local militia and returned to his command under guard, he might plead that he was helping his desperate family get the crops in, and that he planned to return as soon as he finished the job. Any court that was convinced of the veracity of such a plea would be reluctant to sentence the prisoner to be shot for desertion.

Conversely, a substitute who is sworn in one day and receives $1,000 for his enlistment, then disappears the next day, can be assured of being charged with desertion when caught.

More than 2,400 prisoners were charged with AWOL or AWOL along with additional charges; another 255 were cited as violators of AOW #21, which sets forth the punishment to be handed out to those convicted of AWOL. Nevertheless, these numbers indicate the extent of the handicap that Confederate commanders were laboring under. Whether the charge was AWOL, desertion, violation of AOW #20, or violation of AOW #21, the important fact was that the man was not in the ranks. The effect on battle performance is obvious. The ledgers of trials from the A&IGO in some examples do not indicate a sentence. The remarks column is simply left blank in 440 examples. This is entirely different from those cases where no sentence was pronounced; these state that the sentence is "none." But the vast majority of the 440 left blank are those cases that were referred to the secretary of war. No doubt the decision for action was still pending when the entries were made into the ledger, so the sentence was left blank.

Table 8.4
Cases by Sentence

Sentence Code		Total
Sentence Undetermined		440
00	Acquitted	3,211
01	Sentence or Findings Disapproved, No Sentence, Sentence Remitted	1,372
02	Reprimanded	540
03	Fine or Pay Stoppage	983
04	Suspension From Rank & Command	457
05	Company Punishment	2,879
06	Confinement	1,240
07	Confinement on Bread & Water Diet	847
08	Reduced to the Ranks	269
09	Hard Labor	5,572
10	Flogged	209
11	Cashiered	516
12	Drummed Out of the Service (43 also flogged)	166
13	Death, remitted or pardoned by the president or other authority	655
14	Death, but sentence not carried out, accused escaped, died, etc.	101
15	Death, but evidence that sentence was carried out inconclusive	324
16	Shot to Death With Musketry	205
17	Hanged	35
	Total	20,021

Even though the accused in many trials received multiple sentences, for the sake of classification only the highest numbered sentence is recorded. Sorting out the variation would be an impossible task. A soldier sentenced to pay stoppage for one month's pay and 14 days' confinement on bread and water diet would simply appear as Code #07. Nor can the degree of the sentence be ascertained from the chart; a soldier sentenced to 15 days' hard labor appears as Code #09 the same as one sentenced to one year of hard labor with ball and chain attached to his leg. In many examples, the degree is not stated; general orders always set forth the exact sentence, but if they are not to be found, the remarks in the ledgers from A&IGO may simply say "hard labor."

The totals reflect a reasonably accurate count of sentences, but many men received two or more, so flexibility in evaluating some of the lower numbers is essential.

Chapter IX

Summary

The American Civil War is one chapter in our national history; a chapter that portrays the monumental struggle of all the people of a divided country to define the meaning of freedom. That meaning was defined in contradictory terms by both sides until there was a total failure to trust the good intentions of either to rightfully settle the issues. We, as a nation, are not unique in defining freedom in contradictory terms; the story of all struggles of liberation is framed in noble terms spelled out by each side condemning the evils of the other.

The failure to resolve these differences did not begin in 1860–61, but was, rather, a carry-over from our convention of 1787. The founding fathers knew that the issue of slavery was truly a "firebell in the night" as Thomas Jefferson defined it, but coming to terms with it was too divisive a task for them. A condemnation of slavery at the convention would have precluded some Southern states from joining the Union and would have strangled the noble concept of a new nation in its cradle. But the problem did not go away; it grew into a bigger problem that ultimately divided the country into warring camps.

The claim that the "War Between the States" was an issue for states' rights versus a central power is a valid claim. It was that, but the problem that drove such a controversy to the sword and the flame was the cause of slavery. And like all such causes, it was grounded in money; noble speeches on both sides about freedom, liberty, and justice become meaningless unless the end result is profit. By 1861, the South was simply too economically committed to slavery to let it go.

Had the war not occurred, slavery would have died a less painful death in a few more years; world opinion alone would have soon made it totally unacceptable. A shifting economy to a more industrialized work force would have soon made agricultural labor less and less in demand. But the South recognized Lincoln's election as the death knell for slavery and the people resolved to protect their property and profits by whatever means necessary.

With money in the driver's seat, reason has nowhere to ride. Voices for reason were quickly drowned out by the cries of selfish interest. This was not the first time that reason was suppressed; cool heads recognized the evils of slavery even before our War for Independence. But, despite the cries against it, it flourished; it flourished because a few were making huge profits at the business. Rum merchants, slave-ship owners, African and Arab tribes, as well as plantation owners were all lining their pockets, and no amount of preaching was going to stop them. Thus, it ever was and still is, when illicit profiteering runs out of control, all people pay the price.

The wonder of our American Civil War is that both sides furnished such overwhelming numbers to lay down their lives for a cause. A cause that transcended slavery. The majority on both sides had a higher calling; both the Northern government and the Confederacy put forward the issue of home, country, freedom, etc., but not slavery or the freedom of slaves. Both governments recognized that such things as "The Union" and the "Noble State" were more enduring reasons to go to war than the issue of emancipation. All Northern soldiers were not willing to fight to free the slaves, and all Southern soldiers were not willing to go to war to keep them on the plantations, so the politicians had to appeal to a greater calling.

The North prevailed because of her greater resources, not because of her greater calling; if the Confederacy had had more wealth, men, and materials, she would have prevailed. Our nation would then, no doubt, have been two nations, one North and one South, where slavery would have existed, but only for a limited time. Economics and world opinion would have eventually become the emancipator.

The Confederacy, however, could not withstand the overwhelming power of the North, nor could she keep the states performing at the exhausting pace necessary to sustain the war. When the end of the war did come, it came to a Southern region devastated. Recovery would take many, many years, and the scars of hatred would never heal in countless hearts. Perhaps the Confederate and Union veterans overcame their differences quicker and more completely than all others did. A bond exists between adversaries similar to that among comrades; it is nurtured from a common respect for sacrifice and a mutual admiration for commitment.

This work is the story of those Confederate soldiers who were problems for their commanders; the story of some 20,000 who were less-than-perfect soldiers. As stated and restated in previous chapters, these were only a small part of the problem cases. Those who never faced trials by courts-martial, and yet rightfully should have, far outnumber those who did. Despite these discouraging numbers, the Confederate cause endured for four bitter years. During that time, most of the white male population of military age served in the armed forces, and thousands paid with their lives. The wonder of these statistics is that so many were willing to fight so long for their beliefs.

Had the Confederate government handled the issue of military justice differently, would that have made a significant difference in the ability of commanders to fight their battles? Perhaps the presidential amnesties were failures, but the desertions may have continued at a similar pace without them. Certainly more timely return of deserters to the ranks, followed by swift courts-martial and speedy punishment of the guilty would have conveyed a hard lesson to all. But such actions were not possible. Most of the deserters could not be hastily returned to their commands, and trials had to wait for more important tasks at hand, and the "law's delay" often precluded swift justice. So the major value of military justice was lost. A deserter is not executed simply because he deserted; he is shot to death to make desertion more terrifying than remaining in the ranks; not just for him, but for all his comrades who witness the execution.

The Civil War marked the end of the execution of American soldiers for desertion. Until January 31, 1945, no American soldier was shot to death for desertion. Until that time there was no need for the extreme penalty. It was not until the Ardennes campaign in December 1944 that desertion became a major problem for American forces fighting in Europe. Desertions mounted to an unacceptable level almost overnight; drastic action was necessary. One man was selected, Private Eddie D. Slovik, doubtless because his case provided a clear example of desertion in the face of the enemy. The execution conveyed a message to the rest of the troops enduring the misery of frozen foxholes, a message that rang out loud and clear "desertion is a bad option."

When evaluating the performances of the Confederate soldiers during the Civil War, one must recognize the influence of the deteriorating circumstances on the home front as well as the desperate recruiting measures that had been imposed. The joyful parades of April 1861 had long passed away. They now had been replaced by the reality of cold nights of bivouac on an empty stomach with only a tattered blanket for cover. They had been replaced by days and days of hard marching under a hot sun with worn-out shoes or no shoes at all. They had been replaced with death and disease, hardship and heartache, and only a flimsy hope that things would get better tomorrow. But as the years went by, all things got worse, so desertion for many became an act of desperation; for others, it came as a final decision to forsake the cause that they now determined to be hopeless.

Military achievements in the war have been evaluated by eminent historians more times than can be counted, and all told, it is truly remarkable that the Southern command rolled up so many heroic victories. The reasons are manifold, but the significant fact that the Confederate soldier performed above and beyond the call of duty again and again stands foremost in any measurement of success in battle.

To separate the 20,000 or more who stood before courts-martial from the others is to overlook part of the facts. It is true that some of those tried were entirely worthless, but not all; probably not most. Many were acquitted of their charges, and many more who were found guilty were still useful soldiers. The records are full of examples of those who returned to duty and went on to serve until paroled or killed in action, or wasted by disease. It is accurate to say that the majority of those tried went on to serve worthwhile duty in the ranks.

Given the circumstances of the times, the Confederacy performed military justice within the framework of military law of the 1860s to the best extent possible. Some political decisions did not bear the expected fruit, but allowing for the many difficulties facing the struggling government in Richmond, little blame can be laid. If some of those efforts had been different, would that have prolonged the life of the Confederacy? Surely not. Even if the perfect circumstances of dealing with courts-martial had prevailed, the Confederacy would have been defeated. Perfect circumstances simply would have allowed the Southern commanders to have won another battle or two and thus to have cost more lives on both sides.

One of the tragedies of the war was the surprising performance of the Southern armies early in the war placed against the ineptitude of the Northern command. Had Union armies had the leadership they should have had, the war would have been brought to a close sooner and the suffering for all lessened.

The American Civil War was a significant agent for change in many important aspects of life in the 1860s. The obvious social, political, and economic changes that the war brought about are at the top of the list. But, in addition, it changed significantly other aspects of life that would have evolved more slowly had not the urgency of war thrust them upon the stage.

One of the most consequential revolutions occurred in the field of medicine. Surgery was drastically improved in those four years of desperate amputations. Cleanliness and sanitation became a new aspect of treatment that was heretofore nearly completely ignored. New discoveries of germs and microbes opened a whole new study in medicine. Old medications that were, at best, useless and often harmful were cast aside. Anesthesia was advanced to a new level that became both safer for the patient and more useful for the surgeon. Such mundane things as the creation of proper army field hospitals and useful ambulances to carry the wounded became standard procedure for the medical corps.

The era of modern nursing was ushered in and the beginning of our American Red Cross came about through the efforts of Clara Barton and other "busybodies" who were not willing to stand by and allow things to be done in the same old way. Hospitals were redesigned to more effectively serve the sick and wounded and to more conveniently accommodate the staff. Both sides contributed to these achievements; the Confederacy had several fine hospitals and many capable doctors and surgeons.

The nation's banking system went through a complete renovation. A national currency was created; a national banking organization was chartered; state banks were restricted in their operations which heretofore had been far too loose in many states. A more flexible system of borrowing by the government was achieved, and the foundation for modern taxation was laid.

Warfare was changed too. New tactics and weapons rushed forth upon the scene to allow armies to kill each other faster and more efficiently, and many old procedures were put into the archives. Brevets were abandoned and militias were transformed into what was to become an adjunct to the regular army—the National Guard.

The system of military justice was overhauled. The code of 1806 which was in force during the Civil War and was used by both the Union and the Confederacy was replaced by a new code in 1874. The new code consisted of 128 articles as opposed to the 101 of the old code; in addition, some of the original articles were modified.

To the extent that positive achievements resulted from the conflict, positive conclusions may be set forth. But, a balance of accounts must weigh the negatives; how does one measure the value of lives lost? How does one reconcile the suffering of the wounded? How does one evaluate the destruction of property, particularly in the Southern states that were already economically depressed when the war began? All of these negatives affected the lives of our citizens for decades. The tremendous effort of all the country to create the engines of war which have no useful purpose beyond destruction was a great waste; when the smoke cleared and the church bells rang and peace was at hand, all those arsenals were worthless.

Add to this the lasting animosity that existed between the North and South for more than 100 years, and still exists to some extent today, and the only reasonable conclusion is that there must have been a better way to resolve the differences. The emancipated slaves would surely have fared better under a more amiable solution, one devoid of bitterness and rancor which so impeded their amalgamation into society.

The Union was preserved; this was the reason for which the North fought. To the extent that such a goal was realized, the war can be classified as a victory for the North. The emancipation of the slaves in the Confederate states was a secondary outcome; as it turned out, it was a political decision by Lincoln to solidify the wavering support in the Northern states and to secure European approval for the Northern cause. It would have occurred eventually, but had circumstances differed among politicians in the North, it might have waited until the end of the war.

All of the might-have-beens have been told again and again, but it is never a waste of time to review and rethink our past actions to help solve the problems of today. All of our country's mistakes were not made in the 1860s; major problems continue to bedevil us and will continue to do so. The measure of a democratic government such as ours is to be able to face adversity and to resolve differences in a fair and honorable way. Sometimes a resort to arms is a necessary evil, but the political failure of our republic to settle those differences that divided us in the 1860s without war was the greatest failure in our nation's history.

Appendix 1
Articles of War

AN ACT FOR ESTABLISHING RULES AND ARTICLES FOR THE GOVERNMENT OF THE ARMIES OF THE CONFEDERATE STATES.[1]

Sec. 1. *The Congress of the Confederate States of America do enact,* That from and after the passage of this act the following shall be the rules and articles by which the armies of the Confederate States shall be governed:

Art. 1. Every officer now in the army of the Confederate States shall, in six months from the passing of this act, and every officer who shall hereafter be appointed, shall, before he enters on the duties of his office, subscribe these rules and regulations.

Art. 2. It is earnestly recommended to all officers and soldiers diligently to attend divine service; and all officers who shall behave indecently or irreverently at any place of divine worship shall, if commissioned officers, be brought before a general court-martial, there to be publicly and severely reprimanded by the President; if non-commissioned officers or soldiers, every person so offending shall, for his first offense, forfeit one-sixth of a dollar, to be deducted out of his next pay; for the second offence, he shall not only forfeit a like sum, but be confined twenty-four hours; and for every like offense shall suffer and pay in a like manner; which money, so forfeited, shall be applied, by the captain or senior officer of the troop or company, to the use of the sick soldiers of the company or troop to which the offender belongs.

Art. 3. Any non-commissioned officer or soldier who shall use any profane oath or execration shall incur the penalties expressed in the foregoing article; and a commissioned officer shall forfeit and pay, for each and every such offense, one dollar, to be applied as in the preceding article.

Art. 4. Every chaplain, commissioned in the army or armies of the Confederate States, who shall absent himself from the duties assigned him (excepting in cases of sickness or leave of absence), shall, on conviction thereof before a court-martial, be fined not exceeding one month's pay, besides the loss of his pay during his absence; or be discharged, as the said court-martial shall judge proper.

Art. 5. Any officer or soldier who shall use contemptuous or disrespectful words against the President of the Confederate States, against the Vice-President thereof, against the Congress of the Confederate States, or against the Chief Magistrate or Legislature of any of the Confederate States in which he may be quartered, if a commissioned officer, shall be cashiered or otherwise punished, as a court-martial shall direct; if a non-commissioned officer or soldier, he shall suffer such punishment as shall be inflicted on him by the sentence of a court-martial.

Art. 6. Any officer or soldier who shall behave himself with contempt or disrespect toward his commanding officer, shall be punished, according to the nature of his offence, by the judgement of a court-martial.

Art. 7. Any officer or soldier who shall begin, excite, cause, or join in any mutiny or sedition, in any troop or company in the service of the Confederate States, or in any party, post, detachment, or guard, shall suffer death, or such other punishment as by a court-martial shall be inflicted.

Art. 8. Any officer, non-commissioned officer, or soldier who, being present at any mutiny or sedition, does not use his utmost endeavor to suppress the same, or, coming to the knowledge of any intended mutiny, does not, without delay, give information thereof to his commanding officer, shall be punished by the sentence of a court-martial with death, or otherwise, according to the nature of his offence.

Art. 9. Any officer or soldier who shall strike his superior officer, or draw or lift up any weapon, or offer any violence against him, being in the execution of his office, on any pretense whatsoever, or shall disobey any lawful command of his superior officer, shall suffer death, or such other punishment as shall, according to the nature of his offence, be inflicted upon him by the sentence of a court-martial.

Art. 10. Every non-commissioned officer or soldier who shall enlist himself in the service of the Confederate States, shall, at the time of his so enlisting, or within six days afterward, have the articles for the government of the armies of the Confederate States read to him, and shall, by the officer who enlisted him, or by the commanding officer of the troop or company into which he was enlisted, be taken before the next justice of the peace, or chief magistrate of any city or town corporate, not being an officer of the army, or where recourse can not be had to the civil magistrate, before the judge advocate, and in his presence shall take the following oath or affirmation: "I, A. B., do solemnly swear, or affirm (as the case may be), that I will bear true allegiance to the Confederate States of America, and that I will serve them honestly and faithfully against all their enemies or opposers whatsoever; and observe and obey the orders of the President of the Confederate States, and the orders of the officers appointed over me, according to the Rules and Articles for the government of the armies of the Confederate States." Which justice, magistrate, or judge advocate is to give to the officer a certificate, signifying that the man enlisted did take the said oath or affirmation.

Art. 11. After a non-commissioned officer or soldier shall have been duly enlisted and sworn, he shall not be dismissed the service without a discharge in writing; and no discharge granted to him shall be sufficient which is not signed by a field officer of the regiment to which he belongs, or commanding officer, where no field officer of the regiment is present; and no discharge shall be given to a non-commissioned officer or soldier before his term of service has expired, but by order of the President, the Secretary of War, the commanding officer of a department, or the sentence of a general court-martial; nor shall a commissioned officer be discharged the service but by an order of the President of the Confederate States, or by sentence of a general court-martial.

Art. 12. Every colonel, or other officer commanding a regiment, troop, or company, and actually quartered with it, may give furloughs to non-commissioned officers or soldiers in such numbers, and for so long a time, as he shall judge to be most consistent with the good of the service; and a captain, or other inferior officer, commanding a troop or company, or in any garrison, fort, or barrack of the Confederate States (his field officer being absent), may give furloughs to non-commissioned officers and soldiers, for a time not exceeding twenty days in six months, but not to more than two persons to be absent at the same time, excepting some extraordinary occasion should require it.

Art. 13. At every muster, the commanding officer of each regiment, troop, or company, there present, shall give to the commissary of musters, or other officer who musters the said regiment, troop, or company, certificates signed by himself, signifying how long such officers, as shall not appear at the said muster, have been absent, and the reason of their absence. In like manner, the commanding officer of every troop or company shall give certificates, signifying the reason of the absence of the non-commissioned officers and private soldiers; which reasons and time of absence shall be inserted in the muster-rolls, opposite the names of the respective absent officers and soldiers. The certificates shall, together with the muster-rolls, be remitted by the commissary of musters, or other officer mustering, to the Department of War, as speedily as the distance of the place will admit.

Art. 14. Every officer who shall be convicted before a general court-martial of having signed a false certificate relating to the absence of either officer or private soldier, or relative to his or their pay, shall be cashiered.

Art. 15. Every officer who shall knowingly make a false muster of man or horse, and every officer or commissary of musters who shall willingly sign, direct, or allow the signing of muster-rolls wherein such false muster is contained, shall, upon proof made thereof, by two witnesses, before a general court-martial, be cashiered, and shall be thereby utterly disabled to have or hold any office or employment in the service of the Confederate States.

Art. 16. Any commissary of musters, or other officer, who shall be convicted of having taken money, or other thing, by way of gratification, on mustering any regiment, troop, or company, or on signing muster-rolls, shall be displaced from his office, and shall be thereby utterly disabled to have or hold any office or employment in the services of the Confederate States.

Art. 17. Any officer who shall presume to muster a person as a soldier who is not a soldier, shall be deemed guilty of having made a false muster, and shall suffer accordingly.

Art. 18. Every officer who shall knowingly make a false return to the Department of War, or to any of his superior officers, authorized to call for such returns, of the state of the regiment, troop, or company, or garrison, under his command; or of the arms, ammunition, clothing, or other stores thereunto belonging, shall, on conviction thereof before a court-martial, be cashiered.

Art. 19. The commanding officer of every regiment, troop, or independent company, or garrison, of the Confederate States, shall, in the beginning of every month, remit, through the proper channels to the Department of War, an exact return of the regiment, troop, independent company, or garrison under his command, specifying the names of the officers then absent from their posts, with the reasons for and the time of their absence. And any officer who shall be convicted of having, through neglect or design, omitted such returns, shall be punished, according to the nature of the crime, by the judgement of a general court-martial.

Art. 20. All officers and soldiers who have received pay, or have been duly enlisted in the service of the Confederate States, and shall be convicted of having deserted the same, shall suffer death, or such other punishment as, by the sentence of a court-martial, shall be inflicted.

Art. 21. Any non-commissioned officer or soldier who shall, without leave from his commanding officer, absent himself from his troop, company, or detachment, shall, upon being convicted thereof, be punished according to the nature of his offense, at the discretion of a court-martial.

Art. 22. No non-commissioned officer or soldier shall enlist himself in any other regiment, troop, or company, without a regular discharge from the regiment, troop, or company in which he last served, on the penalty of being reputed a deserter, and suffering accordingly. And in case any officer shall knowingly receive and entertain any such non-commissioned officer or soldier, or shall not, after his being discovered to be a deserter, immediately confine him and give notice thereof to the corps in which he last served, the said officer shall, by a court-martial, be cashiered.

Art. 23. Any officer or soldier who shall be convicted of having advised or persuaded any other officer or soldier to desert the service of the Confederate States, shall suffer death, or such other punishment as shall be inflicted upon him by the sentence of a court-martial.

Art. 24. No officer or soldier shall use any reproachful or provoking speeches or gestures to another, upon pain, if an officer, of being put in arrest; if a soldier, confined, and of asking pardon of the party offended, in the presence of his commanding officer.

Art. 25. No officer or soldier shall send a challenge to another officer or soldier to fight a duel, or accept a challenge if sent, upon pain, if a commissioned officer, of being cashiered; if a non-commissioned officer or soldier, of suffering corporal punishment, at the discretion of a court-martial.

Art. 26. If any commissioned or non-commissioned officer commanding a guard shall knowingly or willingly suffer any person whatsoever to go forth to fight a duel, he shall be punished as a challenger; and all seconds, promoters, and carriers of challenges, in order to duels, shall be deemed principals, and punished accordingly. And it shall be the duty of every officer commanding an army, regiment, company, post, or detachment, who is knowing to a challenge being given or accepted by any officer, non-commissioned officer, or soldier under his command, or has reason to believe the same to be the case, immediately to arrest and bring to trial such offenders.

Art. 27. All officers of what condition soever, have power to part and quell all quarrels, frays, and disorders, though the persons concerned should belong to another regiment, troop, or company; and either to order officers into arrest, or non-commissioned officers or soldiers into confinement, until their proper superior officers shall be acquainted therewith; and whosoever shall refuse to obey such officer (though of an inferior rank), or shall draw his sword upon him, shall be punished at the discretion of a general court-martial.

Art. 28. Any officer or soldier who shall upbraid another for refusing a challenge, shall himself be punished as a challenger; and all officers and soldiers are hereby discharged from any disgrace or opinion of disadvantage which might arise from their having refused to accept of challenges, as they will only have acted in obedience to the laws, and done their duty as good soldiers who subject themselves to discipline.

Art. 29. No sutler shall be permitted to sell any kind of liquors or victuals, or to keep their houses or shops open for the entertainment of soldiers, after nine at night, or before the beating of the reveille, or upon Sundays during divine service or sermon, on the penalty of being dismissed from all future suttling.

Art. 30. All officers commanding in the field, forts, barracks, or garrisons of the Confederate States, are hereby required to see that persons permitted to suttle shall supply the soldiers with good and wholesome provisions, or other articles, at a reasonable price, as they shall be answerable for their neglect.

Art. 31. No officer commanding in any of the garrisons, forts, or barracks of the Confederate States, shall exact exorbitant prices for houses or stalls let out to sutlers, or connive at the like exactions in others; nor by his own authority, and for his private advantage, lay any duty or imposition upon, or be interested in, the sale of any victuals, liquors, or other necessaries of life brought into the garrison, fort, or barracks for the use of the soldiers, on the penalty of being discharged from the service.

Art. 32. Every officer commanding in quarters, garrisons, or on the march, shall keep good order, and to the utmost of his power, redress all abuses or disorders which may be committed by any officer or soldier under his command; if, upon complaint made to him of officers or soldiers beating or otherwise ill-treating any person, or disturbing fairs or markets, or of committing any kind of riots, to the disquieting of the citizens of the Confederate States, he, the said commander, who shall refuse or omit to see justice done to the offender or offenders, and reparation made to the party or parties injured, as far as part of the offender's pay shall enable him or them, shall, upon proof thereof, be cashiered, or otherwise punished, as a general court-martial shall direct.

Art. 33. When any commissioned officer or soldier shall be accused of a capital crime, or of having used violence, or committed any offence against the person or property of any citizen of any of the Confederate States, such as is punishable by the known laws of the land, the commanding officer and officers of every regiment, troop, or company to which the person or persons so accused shall belong, are hereby required, upon application duly made by, or in behalf of, the party or parties injured, to use their utmost endeavors to deliver over such accused person or persons to the civil magistrate, and likewise to be aiding and assisting to the officers of justice in apprehending and securing the person or persons so accused, in order to bring him or them to trial. If any commanding officer or officers shall willfully neglect, or shall refuse, upon the application aforesaid, to deliver over such accused person or persons to the civil magistrates, or to be aiding and assisting to the officers of justice in apprehending such person or persons, the officer or officers so offending shall be cashiered.

Art. 34. If any officer shall think himself wronged by his colonel, or the commanding officer of the regiment, and shall, upon due application being made to him be refused redress, he may complain to the General commanding in the state or territory where such regiment shall be stationed, in order to obtain justice; who is hereby required to examine into said complaint, and take proper measures for redressing the wrong complained of, and transmit, as soon as possible, to the Department of War, a true state of such complaint, with the proceedings had thereon.

Art. 35. If any inferior officer or soldier shall think himself wronged by his captain or other officer, he is to complain thereof to the commanding officer of the regiment, who is hereby required to summon a regimental court-martial, for the doing justice to the complainant, from which regimental court-martial either party may, if he think himself still aggrieved, appeal to a general court-martial. But if, upon a second hearing, the appeal shall appear vexatious and groundless, the person so appealing shall be punished at the discretion of said court-martial.

Art. 36. Any commissioned officer, storekeeper, or commissary, who shall be convicted at a general court-martial of having sold, without a proper order for that purpose, embezzled, misapplied, or wilfully, or through neglect, suffered any of the provisions, forage, arms, clothing, ammunition, or other military stores belonging to the Confederate States to be spoiled or damaged, shall, at his own expense, make good the loss or damage, and shall, moreover, forfeit all his pay, and be dismissed from the service.

Art. 37. Any non-commissioned officer or soldier who shall be convicted at a regimental court-martial of having sold, or designedly or through neglect, wasted the ammunition delivered out to him to be employed in the service of the Confederate States, shall be punished at the discretion of such court.

Art. 38. Every non-commissioned officer or soldier who shall be convicted before a court-martial of having sold, lost, or spoiled, through neglect, his horse, arms, clothes, or accoutrements, shall undergo such weekly stoppages (not exceeding the half of his pay) as such court-martial shall judge sufficient for repairing the loss or damage; and shall suffer confinement, or such other corporal punishment as his crime shall deserve.

Art. 39. Every officer who shall be convicted before a court-martial of having embezzled or misapplied any money with which he may have been intrusted, for the payment of the men under his command, or for enlisting men into the service, or for other purposes, if a commissioned officer, shall be cashiered, and compelled to refund the money; if a non-commissioned officer, shall be reduced to the ranks, be put under stoppages until the money be made good, and suffer such corporal punishment as such court-martial shall direct.

Art. 40. Every Captain of a troop or company is charged with the arms, accoutrements, ammunition, clothing, or other warlike stores belonging to the troop or company under his command, which he is to be accountable for to his colonel in case of their being lost, spoiled, or damaged, not by unavoidable accidents, or on actual service.

Art. 41. All non-commissioned officers and soldier who shall be found one mile from the camp without leave, in writing, from their commanding officer, shall suffer such punishment as shall be inflicted upon them by the sentence of a court-martial.

Art. 42. No officer or soldier shall lie out of his quarters, garrison, or camp without leave from his superior officer, upon penalty of being punished according to the nature of his offence, by the sentence of a court-martial.

Art. 43. Every non-commissioned officer and soldier shall retire to his quarters or tent at the beating of the retreat; in default of which he shall be punished according to the nature of his offence.

Art. 44. No officer, non-commissioned officer, or soldier shall fail in repairing, at the time fixed, to the place of parade, of exercise, or other rendezvous appointed by his commanding officer, if not prevented by sickness or some other evident necessity, or shall go from the said place of rendezvous, without leave from his commanding officer, before he shall be regularly dismissed or relieved, on the penalty of being punished, according to the nature of his offence, by the sentence of a court-martial.

Art. 45. Any commissioned officer who shall be found drunk on his guard, party, or other duty, shall be cashiered; any non-commissioned officer or soldier so offending shall suffer such corporal punishment as shall be inflicted by the sentence of a court-martial.

Art. 46. Any sentinel who shall be found sleeping upon his post, or shall leave it before he shall be regularly relieved, shall suffer death, or such other punishment as shall be inflicted by the sentence of a court-martial.

Art. 47. No soldier belonging to any regiment, troop, or company, shall hire another to do his duty for him, or be excused from duty but in cases of sickness, disability, or leave of absence; and every such soldier found guilty of hiring his duty, as also the party so hired to do another's duty, shall be punished at the discretion of a regimental court-martial.

Art. 48. And every non-commissioned officer conniving at such hiring of duty aforesaid, shall be reduced; and every commissioned officer knowing and allowing such ill practices in the service, shall be punished by the judgement of a general court-martial.

Art. 49. Any officer belonging to the service of the Confederate States, who, by discharging of firearms, drawing of swords, beating of drums, or by any other means whatsoever, shall occasion false alarms in camp, garrison, or quarters, shall suffer death, or such other punishment as shall be ordered by the sentence of a general court-martial.

Art. 50. Any officer or soldier who shall, without urgent necessity, or without the leave of his superior officer, quit his guard, platoon, or division, shall be punished, according to the nature of his offence, by the sentence of a court-martial.

Art. 51. No officer or soldier shall do violence to any person who brings provisions or other necessaries to the camp, garrison, or quarters of the forces of the Confederate States, employed in any parts out of the said States, upon pain of death, or such other punishment as a court-martial shall direct.

Art. 52. Any officer or soldier who shall misbehave himself before the enemy, run away, or shamefully abandon any fort, post, or guard which he or they may be commanded to defend, or speak words inducing others to do the like, or shall cast away his arms and ammunition, or who shall quit his post or colors to plunder and pillage, every such offender, being duly convicted thereof, shall suffer death, or such other punishment as shall be ordered by the sentence of a general court-martial.

Art. 53. Any person belonging to the armies of the Confederate States who shall make known the watchword to any person who is not entitled to receive it according to the rules and discipline of war, or shall presume to give a parole or watchword different from what he received, shall suffer death, or such other punishment as shall be ordered by the sentence of a general court-martial.

Art. 54. All officers and soldiers are to behave themselves orderly in quarters and on their march; and whoever shall commit any waste or spoil, either in walks or trees, parks, warrens, fish ponds, houses, or gardens, cornfields, enclosures of meadows, or shall maliciously destroy any property whatsoever belonging to the inhabitants of the Confederate States, unless by order of the then commander-in-chief of the armies of the said states, shall (besides such penalties as they are liable to by law) be punished, according to the nature and degree of the offence, by the judgement of a regimental or general court-martial.

Art. 55. Whosoever, belonging to the armies of the Confederate States in foreign parts, shall force a safeguard, shall suffer death.

Art. 56. Whosoever shall relieve the enemy with money, victuals, or ammunition, or shall knowingly harbor or protect an enemy, shall suffer death, or such other punishment as shall be ordered by the sentence of a court-martial.

Art. 57. Whosoever shall be convicted of holding correspondence with, or giving intelligence to the enemy, either directly or indirectly, shall suffer death, or such other punishment as shall be ordered by the sentence of a court-martial.

Art. 58. All public stores taken in the enemy's camp, towns, forts, or magazines, whether of artillery, ammunition, clothing, forage, or provisions, shall be secured for the service of the Confederate States; for the neglect of which the commanding officer is to be answerable.

Art. 59. If any commander of any garrison, fortress, or post shall be compelled, by the officers and soldiers under his command, to give up to the enemy, or to abandon it, the commissioned officers, non-commissioned officers, or soldiers who shall be convicted of having so offended, shall suffer death, or such other punishment as shall be inflicted upon them by the sentence of a court-martial.

Art. 60. All sutlers and retainers to the camp, and all persons whatsoever, serving with the armies of the Confederate States in the field, though not enlisted soldiers, are to be subject to orders, according to the rules and discipline of war.

Art. 61. Officers having brevets or commissions of a prior date to those of the corps in which they serve, will take place on courts-martial or of inquiry, and on boards detailed for military purposes, when composed of different corps, according to the ranks given them in their brevets or former commissions; but in the regiment, corps, or company to which such officers belong, they shall do duty and take rank, both in courts and on boards as aforesaid, which shall be composed of their own corps, according to the commissions by which they are there mustered.

Art. 62. If, upon marches, guards, or in quarters, different corps shall happen to join or do duty together, the officer highest in rank, according to the commission by which he is mustered in the army, navy, marine corps, or militia, there on duty by orders from competent authority, shall command the whole, and give orders for what is needful for the service, unless otherwise directed by the President of the Confederate States, in orders of special assignment providing for the case.

Art. 63. The functions of the engineers being generally confined to the most elevated branch of military science, they are not to assume, nor are they subject to be ordered on, any duty beyond the line of their immediate profession, except by the special order of the President of the Confederate States; but they are to receive every mark of respect to which their rank in the army may entitle them respectively, and are liable to be transferred, at the discretion of the President, from one corps to another, regard being paid to rank.

Art. 64. General courts-martial may consist of any number of commissioned officers from five to thirteen, inclusively; but they shall not consist of less than thirteen, where that number can be convened without manifest injury to the service.

Art. 65. Any general officer commanding an army, or colonel commanding a force of cavalry not with and under the immediate command of the commander of an army, or other officer commanding a separate department, may appoint general courts-martial whenever necessary. But no sentence of a court-martial shall be carried into execution until after the whole proceedings shall have been laid before the officer ordering the same, or the officer commanding the troops for the time being; neither shall any sentence of a general court-martial, in the time of peace, extending to the loss of life, or the dismission of a commissioned officer, or which shall either in time of peace or war, respect a general officer, be carried into execution, until after the whole proceedings shall have been transmitted to the Secretary of War, to be laid before the President of the Confederate States for his confirmation or disapproval, and orders in the case. All other sentences may be confirmed and executed by the officer ordering the court to assemble, or the commanding officer for the time being, as the case may be.

Art. 66. Every officer commanding a regiment or corps may appoint, for his own regiment or corps, courts-martial, to consist of three commissioned officers, for the trial and punishment of offences not capital, and decide upon their sentences. For the same purpose, all officers commanding any of the garrisons, forts, barracks, or other places where the troops consist of different corps, may assemble courts-martial, to consist of three commissioned officers, and decide upon their sentences.

Art. 67. No garrison or regimental court-martial shall have the power to try capital cases or commissioned officers; neither shall they inflict a fine exceeding one month's pay, nor imprison, nor put to hard labor any non-commissioned officer or soldier for a longer time than one month.

Art. 68. Whenever it may be found convenient and necessary to the public service, the officers of the marines shall be associated with the officers of the land forces, for the purpose of holding courts-martial, and trying offenders belonging to either; and, in such cases the orders of the senior officer of either corps who may be present and duly authorized, shall be received and obeyed.

Art. 69. The judge advocate or some person deputed by him, or by the general or officer commanding the army, detachment, or garrison, shall prosecute in the name of the Confederate States, but shall so far consider himself as counsel for the prisoner, after the said prisoner shall have made his plea, as to object to any leading question to any of the witnesses, or any question to the prisoner, the answer to which might tend to criminate himself, and administer to each member of the court, before they proceed upon any trial, the following oath, which shall also be taken by all members of the regimental and garrison courts-martial.

"You, A.B., do swear that you will well and truly try and determine, according to evidence, the matter now before you, between the Confederate States of America and the prisoner to be tried, and that you will duly administer justice, according to the provisions of 'An act establishing Rules and Articles for the government of the armies of the Confederate States,' without partiality, favor, or affection; and if any doubt should arise, not explained by said Articles, according to your conscience, the best of your understanding, and the custom of war in like cases; and you do further swear that you will not divulge the sentence of the court until it shall be published by the proper authority; neither will you disclose or discover the vote or opinion of any particular member of the court-martial, unless required to give evidence thereof, as a witness, by a court of justice, in a due course of law. So help you God."

And so soon as the said oath shall have been administered to the respective members, the president of the court shall administer to the judge advocate, or person officiating as such, an oath in the following words:

"You, A.B., do swear that you will not disclose or discover the vote or opinion of any particular member of the court-martial, unless required to give evidence thereof, as a witness, by a court of justice, in due course of law; nor divulge the sentence of the court to any but the proper authority, until it shall be duly disclosed by the same. So help you God."

Art. 70. When a prisoner, arraigned before a general court-martial, shall from obstinacy and deliberate design, stand mute, or answer foreign to the purpose, the court may proceed to trial and judgement as if the prisoner had regularly pleaded not guilty.

Art. 71. When a member shall be challenged by a prisoner, he must state his cause of challenge, of which the court shall, after due deliberation, determine the relevancy or validity, and decide accordingly; and no challenge to more than one member at a time shall be received by the court.

Art. 72. All the members of a court-martial are to behave with decency and calmness; and in giving their votes are to begin with the youngest in commission.

Art. 73. All persons who give evidence before a court-martial are to be examined on oath or affirmation, in the following form:

"You swear, or affirm (as the case may be) the evidence you shall give in the cause, now in hearing shall be the truth, the whole truth, and nothing but the truth. So help you God."

Art. 74. On the trials of cases not capital, before courts-martial, the deposition of witnesses, not in the line or staff of the army, may be taken before some justice of the peace, and read in evidence; provided the prosecutor and person accused are present at the taking the same, or are duly notified thereof.

Art. 75. No officer shall be tried but by a general court-martial, nor by officers of an inferior rank, if it can be avoided. Nor shall any proceedings of trials be carried on, excepting between the hours of eight in the morning and three in the afternoon; excepting in cases which, in the opinion of the officer appointing the court-martial, require immediate example.

Art. 76. No person whatsoever shall use any menacing words, signs, or gestures, in presence of a court-martial, or shall cause any disorder or riot, or disturb their proceedings, on the penalty of being punished at the discretion of the said court-martial.

Art. 77. Whenever any officer shall be charged with a crime, he shall be arrested and confined in his barracks, quarters, or tent, and deprived of his sword by the commanding officer. And any officer who shall leave his confinement before he shall be set at liberty by the commanding officer, or by a superior officer shall be cashiered.

Art. 78. Non-commissioned officers and soldiers, charged with crimes, shall be confined until tried by a court-martial, or released by proper authority.

Art. 79. No officer or soldier who shall be put in arrest shall continue in confinement more than eight days, or until such time as a court-martial can be assembled.

Art. 80. No officer commanding a guard, or provost marshal, shall refuse to receive or keep any prisoner committed to his charge by an officer belonging to the forces of the Confederate States; provided the officer committing shall, at the same time, deliver an account in writing, signed by himself, of the crime of which the said prisoner is charged.

Art. 81. No officer commanding a guard, or provost marshal, shall presume to release any person committed to his charge without proper authority for so doing, nor shall he suffer any person to escape, on the penalty of being punished for it by the sentence of a court-martial.

Art. 82. Every officer or provost marshal, to whose charge prisoners shall be committed, shall, within twenty-four hours after such commitment, or as soon as he shall be relieved from his guard, make report in writing to the commanding officer, of their names, their crimes, and the names of the officers who committed them, on the penalty of being punished for disobedience or neglect, at the discretion of a court-martial.

Art. 83. Any commissioned officer convicted before a general court-martial of conduct unbecoming an officer and a gentleman, shall be dismissed the service.

Art. 84. In cases where a court-martial may think it proper to sentence a commissioned officer to be suspended from command, they shall have power also to suspend his pay and emoluments for the same time, according to the nature and heinousness of the offence.

Art. 85. In all cases where a commissioned officer is cashiered for cowardice or fraud, it shall be added in the sentence that the crime, name, and place of abode, and punishment of the delinquent, be published in the newspapers in and about the camp, and of the particular State from which the offender came, or where he usually resides; after which it shall be deemed scandalous for an officer to associate with him.

Art. 86. The commanding officer of any post or detachment, in which there shall not be a number of officers adequate to form a general court-martial, shall, in cases which require the cognizance of such a court, report to the commanding officer of the department, who shall order a court to be assembled at the nearest post or department, and the party accused, with necessary witnesses, to be transported to the place where the said court shall be assembled.

Art. 87. No person shall be sentenced to suffer death but by the concurrence of two-thirds of the members of a general court-martial, nor except in the cases herein expressly mentioned; and no officer, non-commissioned officer, soldier, or follower of the army, shall be tried a second time for the same offence.

Art. 88. No person shall be liable to be tried and punished by a general court-martial for any offence which shall appear to have been committed more than two years before the issuing of the order for such trial, unless the person, by reason of having absented himself or some other manifest impediment, shall not have been amenable to justice within that period.

Art. 89. Every officer authorized to order a general court-martial shall have power to pardon or mitigate any punishment ordered by such court, except the sentence of death, or of cashiering an officer; which, in the case where he has authority (by Article 65) to carry them into execution, he may suspend, until the pleasure of the President of the Confederate States can be known; which suspension, together with copies of the proceedings of the court-martial, the said officer shall immediately transmit to the President for his determination. And the colonel or commanding officer of the regiment or garrison where any regimental or garrison court-martial shall be held, may pardon or mitigate any punishment ordered by such court to be inflicted.

Art. 90. Every judge advocate, or person officiating as such, at any general court-martial, shall transmit, with as much expedition as the opportunity of time and distance of place can admit, the original proceedings and sentence of such court-martial to the Secretary of War; which said original proceedings and sentence shall be carefully kept and preserved in the office of said Secretary, to the end that the persons entitled thereto may be enabled, upon application to the said officer, to obtain copies thereof.

The party tried by any general court-martial shall, upon demand thereof, made by himself, or by any person or persons in his behalf, be entitled to a copy of the sentence and proceedings of such court-martial.

Art. 91. In cases where the general, or commanding officer may order a court of inquiry to examine into the nature of any transaction, accusation, or imputation against any officer or soldier, the said court shall consist of one or more officers, not exceeding three, and a judge advocate, or other suitable person, as a recorder, to reduce the proceedings and evidence to writing; all of whom shall be sworn to the faithful performance of their duty. This court shall have the same power to summon witnesses as a court-martial, and to examine them on oath. But they shall not give their opinion on the merits of the case, excepting they shall be thereto specially required. The parties accused shall also be permitted to cross-examine and interrogate the witnesses, so as to investigate fully the circumstances in the question.

Art. 92. The proceedings of a court of inquiry must be authenticated by the signature of the recorder and the president, and delivered to the commanding officer, and the said proceedings may be admitted as evidence by a court-martial, in cases not capital, or extending to the dismission of an officer, provided, that the circumstances are such that oral testimony cannot be obtained. But as courts of inquiry may be perverted to dishonorable purposes, and may be considered as engines of destruction to military merit, in the hands of weak and envious commandants, they are hereby prohibited, unless directed by the President of the Confederate States, or demanded by the accused.

Art. 93. The judge advocate or recorder shall administer to the members the following oath:

"You shall well and truly examine and inquire, according to your evidence, into the matter now before you, without partiality, favor, affection, prejudice, or hope of reward. So help you God."

After which the president shall administer to the judge advocate or recorder the following oath:

"You, A.B., do swear that you will, according to your best abilities, accurately and impartially record the proceedings of the court, and the evidence to be given in the case in hearing. So help you God."

The witnesses shall take the same oath as witnesses sworn before a court-martial.

Art. 94. When any commissioned officer shall die or be killed in the service of the Confederate States, the major of the regiment, or the officer doing the major's duty in his absence, or in any post or garrison the second officer in command, or the assistant military agent, shall immediately secure all his effects or equipage, then in camp or quarters, and shall make an inventory thereof, and forthwith transmit the same to the office of the Department of War, to the end that his executors or administrators may receive the same.

Art. 95. When any non-commissioned officer or soldier shall die, or be killed in the service of the Confederate States, the then commanding officer of the troop or company shall, in the presence of two other commissioned officers, take an account of what effects he died possessed of, above his arms and accoutrements, and transmit the same to the office of the Department of War, which said effects are to be accounted for and paid to the representatives of such deceased non-commissioned officer or solider. And in case any of the officers, so authorized to take care of the effects of such deceased non-commissioned officers and soldiers should, before they have accounted to their representatives for the same, have occasion to leave the regiment or post, by preferment or otherwise, they shall, before they be permitted to quit the same, deposit it in the hands of the commanding officer, or of the assistant military agent, all the effects of such deceased non-commissioned officers and soldiers, in order that the same may be secured for, and paid to their respective representatives.

Art. 96. All officers, conductors, gunners, matrosses, drivers, or other persons whatsoever, receiving pay or hire in the service of the artillery, or corps of engineers of the Confederate States, shall be governed by the aforesaid rules and articles, and shall be subject to be tried by courts-martial, in like manner with the officers and soldiers of the other troops in the service of the Confederate States.

Art. 97. The officers and soldiers of any troops, whether militia or others, being mustered and in pay of the Confederate States, shall, at all times and in all places, when joined, or acting in conjunction with the regular forces of the Confederate States, be governed by these Rules and Articles of War, and shall be subject to be tried by courts-martial, in like manner with the officers and soldiers in the regular forces; save only that such courts-martial shall be composed entirely of militia officers.

Art. 98. All officers serving by commission from the authority of any particular State shall, on all detachments, courts-martial, or other duty, wherein they may be employed in conjunction with the regular forces of the Confederate States, take rank next after all officers of the like grade in said regular forces, notwithstanding the commissions of such militia or state officers may be older than the commissions of the officers of the regular forces of the Confederate States.

Art. 99. All crimes not capital, and all disorders and neglects, which officers and soldiers may be guilty of, to the prejudice of good order and military discipline, though not mentioned in the foregoing Articles of War, are to be taken cognizance of by a general or regimental court-martial, according to the nature and degree of the offence, and be punished at their discretion.

Art. 100. The President of the Confederate States shall have power to prescribe the uniform of the army.

Art. 101. The foregoing articles are to be read and published, once every six months, to every garrison, regiment, troop, or company, mustered, or to be mustered, in the service of the Confederate States, and are to be duly observed and obeyed by all officers and soldiers who are, or shall be, in said service.

Sec. 2. *And it be further enacted,* That in time of war, all persons not citizens of, or owing allegiance to the Confederate States of America, who shall be found lurking as spies in and about the fortifications or encampments of the armies of the Confederate States, or any of them, shall suffer death, according to the law and usage of nations, by sentence of a general court-martial.

Appendix 2

An Act to Organize Military Courts

An ACT to organize military courts to attend the Army of the Confederate States in the field, and to define the powers of said courts.

The Congress of the Confederate States of America do enact, That courts shall be organized, to be known as military courts, one to attend each army corps in the field, under the direction of the President. Each court shall consist of three members, two of whom shall constitute a quorum, and each member shall be entitled to the rank and pay of a colonel of cavalry, shall be appointed by the President, by and with the advice and consent of the Senate, and shall hold his office during the war, unless the court shall be sooner abolished by Congress. For each court there shall be one judge-advocate, to be appointed by the President, by and with the advice and consent of the Senate, with the rank and pay of a captain of cavalry, whose duties shall be as prescribed by the Rules and Articles of War, except as enlarged and modified by the purposes and provisions of this act, and who shall also hold his office during the war, unless the court shall be sooner abolished by the Congress; and in case of the absence or disability of the judge-advocate, upon the application of the court, the commander of the army corps to which such court is attached may appoint or detail an officer to perform the duties of judge-advocate during such absence or disability, or until the vacancy, if any, shall be filled by the President.

Sec. 2. Each court shall have the right to appoint a provost-marshal, to attend its sittings and execute the orders of the court, with the rank and pay of a captain of cavalry; and also a clerk, who shall have a salary of one hundred and twenty-five dollars per month, who shall keep the record of the proceedings of the court, and shall reduce to writing the substance of the evidence in each case, and file the same in court. The provost-marshal and the clerk shall hold their offices during the pleasure of the court. Each member and officer of the court shall take an oath well and truly to discharge the duties of his office to the best of his skill and ability, without fear, favor or reward, and to support the Constitution of the Confederate States. Each member of the court, the judge-advocate and the clerk, shall have the power to administer oaths.

Sec. 3. Each court shall have power to adopt rules for conducting business and for the trial of causes, and to enforce the rules adopted, and to punish for contempt, and to regulate the taking of evidence, and to secure the attendance of witnesses, and to enforce and execute its orders, sentences and judgements, as in cases of courts-martial.

Sec. 4. The jurisdiction of each court shall extend to all offenses now cognizable by courts-martial under the Rules and Articles of War and the customs of war, and also to all offenses defined as crimes by the laws of the Confederate States or of the several States, and when beyond the territory of the Confederate States, to all cases of murder, manslaughter, arson, rape, robbery and larceny, as defined by the common law, when committed by any private or officer in the Army of the Confederate States against any other private or officer in the Army, or against the property or person of any citizen or other person not in the Army: *Provided*, Said courts shall not have jurisdiction of offenders above the grade of colonel. For offenses cognizable by courts-martial the court shall, on conviction, inflict the penalty prescribed by the Rules and Articles of War, and in the manner and mode therein mentioned; and for offenses not punishable by the Rules and Articles of War, but punishable by the laws of the Confederate States; said court shall inflict the penalties prescribed by the laws of the Confederate States; and for offenses against which penalties are not prescribed by the Rules and Articles of War, nor by the laws of the Confederate States, but for which penalties are prescribed by the laws of a State, said court shall inflict the punishment prescribed by the laws of the State in which the offense was committed: *Provided*, That in cases in which, by the laws of the Confederate States, or of the State, the punishment is by fine or by imprisonment, or by both, the court may, in its discretion, inflict any other punishment less than death; and for the offenses defines as murder, manslaughter, arson, rape, robbery and larceny, by the common law, when committed beyond the territorial limits of the Confederate States, the punishment shall be in the discretion of the court. That when an officer under the grade of brigadier-general, or private, shall be put under arrest for any offense cognizable by the court herein provided for, notice of his arrest and of the offense with which he shall be charged shall be given to the judge-advocate by the officer ordering said arrest, and he shall be entitled to as speedy a trial as the business before said court will allow.

Sec. 5. Said courts shall attend the Army, shall have appropriate quarters within the lines of the Army, shall be always open for the transaction of business, and the final decisions and sentences of said courts in convictions shall be subject to review, mitigation and suspension, as now provided by the Rules and Articles of War in cases of courts-martial,

Sec. 6. That during the recess of the Senate the President may appoint the members of the courts and the judges-advocate provided for in the previous sections, subject to the confirmation of the Senate at its session next ensuing said appointments.

Approved October 9, 1862.[1]

Appendix 3
British Articles of War of 1765

BRITISH ARTICLES OF WAR OF 1765, IN FORCE AT THE BEGINNING OF OUR REVOLUTIONARY WAR.[1]

Rules and Articles for the better government of our Horse and Foot Guards, and all other Our Forces in our Kingdoms of Great Britain and Ireland, Dominions beyond the Seas, and Foreign Parts.

Section I.—Divine Worship.

Art. I.

All Officers and Soldiers, not having just Impediment, shall diligently frequent Divine Service and Sermon, in the Places appointed for the assembling of the Regiment, Troop, or Company, to which they belong; such as wilfully absent themselves, or, being present, behave indecently or irreverently, shall, if Commissioned Officers, be brought before a Court-Martial, there to be publickly and severely reprimanded by the President; if Non-commissioned Officers, or Soldiers, every Person so offending shall, for his First Offence, forfeit Twelve Pence, to be deducted out of his next pay; for the Second Offence he shall not only forfeit Twelve Pence, but be laid in Irons for Twelve Hours; and for every like Offence, shall suffer and pay in like Manner: Which Money so forfeited shall be applied to the use of the sick Soldiers of the Troop or Company to which the Offender belongs.

Art. II.

Whatsoever Officer or Soldier shall use any unlawful Oath or Execration, shall incur the Penalties expressed in the First Article.

Art. III.

Whatsoever Officer or Soldier shall presume to speak against any known Article of the Christian Faith, shall be delivered over to the Civil Magistrate, to be proceeded against according to Law.

Art. IV.

Whatsoever Officer or Soldier shall profane any Place dedicated to Divine Worship, or shall offer Violence to a Chaplain of the Army, or to any other Minister of God's Word; he shall be liable to such Penalty or corporal Punishment as shall be inflicted on him by a Court-martial.

Art. V.

No Chaplain who is commissioned to a Regiment, Company, Troop, or Garrison, shall absent himself from the said Regiment, Company, Troop, or Garrison (excepting in case of Sickness or Leave of Absence) upon Pain of being brought to a Court-Martial, and punished as their Judgement and the Circumstances of the Offence may require.

Art. VI.

Whatsoever Chaplain to a Regiment, Troop, or Garrison, shall be guilty of Drunkenness, or other scandalous or vicious Behaviour, derogating from the Sacred Character with which he is invested, shall upon due Proofs before a Court-martial, be discharged from his said Office.

Section II.—Mutiny.
Art. I.

Whatsoever Officer or Soldier shall presume to use traiterous or disrespectful Words against the Sacred Person of his Majesty, or any of the Royal Family; if a commissioned Officer, he shall be cashiered; if a Non-commissioned Officer or Soldier, he shall suffer such Punishment as shall be inflicted upon him by the Sentence of a Court-martial.

Art. II.

Any Officer or Soldier who shall behave himself with Contempt or Disrespect towards the General, or other Commander in Chief of Our Forces, or shall speak Words tending to his Hurt or Dishonour, shall be punished according to the Nature of his Offence, by the Judgement of a Court-martial.

Art. III.

Any Officer or Soldier who shall begin, excite, cause, or join in, any Mutiny or Sedition, in the Troop, Company or Regiment, to which he belongs, or in any other Troop or Company in Our Service, or in any Party, Post, Detachment, or Guard, on any Pretence whatsoever, shall suffer Death, or such other Punishment as by a Court-martial shall be inflicted.

Art. IV.

Any Officer, Non-commissioned Officer, or Soldier, who being present at any Mutiny or Sedition, does not use his utmost Endeavour to suppress the same, or coming to the knowledge of any Mutiny or intended Mutiny, does not without Delay give Information thereof to his Commanding Officer, shall be punished by a Court-martial with Death, or otherwise according to the Nature of the Offence.

Art. V.

Any Officer or Soldier, who shall strike his superior Officer, or draw, or offer to draw, or shall lift up any Weapon, or offer any Violence against him, being in the Execution of his Office, on any Pretence whatsoever, or shall disobey any lawful Command of his superior Officer, shall suffer Death, or such other Punishment as shall, according to the Nature of his Offence, be inflicted upon him by the Sentence of a Court-martial.

Section III.—Of Inlisting Soldiers.
Art. I.

Every Non-commissioned Officer and Soldier, who shall inlist himself in Our Service, shall, at the Time of his so Inlisting, or within Four Days afterwards, have the Articles against Mutiny and Desertion read to him, and shall, by the Officer who inlisted him or by the Commanding Officer of the Troop or Company into which he was inlisted, be taken before the next Justice of the Peace, or Chief Magistrate of any City or Town Corporate (not being an officer of the Army) or in Foreign Parts, where Recourse cannot be had to the Civil Magistrate, before the Judge Advocate, and in his presence shall take the following Oath:

I Swear to be true to our Sovereign Lord King GEORGE, and to serve him honestly and faithfully, in Defence of his Person, Crown, and Dignity, against all His Enemies or Opposers whatsoever: And to observe and obey His Majesty's Orders, and the Orders of the Generals and Officers set over me by his Majesty.

Which Justice or Magistrate is to give the Officer a Certificate signifying that the Man inlisted did take the said Oath, and that the Articles of War were read to him, according to the Act of Parliament.

Art. II.

After a Non-commissioned Officer or Soldier shall have been duly inlisted and sworn, he shall not be dismissed Our Service without a Discharge in Writing; and no Discharge granted to him shall be Allowed of as sufficient, which is not signed by a Field Officer of the Regiment into which he was inlisted; or Commanding Officer, where no Field Officer of the Regiment is in Great Britain.

Section IV.—Musters.

Art. I.

Every Officer commanding a Regiment, Troop, or Company, shall upon the Notice given to him by the Commissary of the Musters, or from One of his Deputies, assemble the Regiment, Troop, Or Company under his Command, in the next convenient place for their being mustered.

Art. II.

Every Colonel or other Field Officer Commanding the Regiment, Troop, or Company, and actually residing with it, may give Furloughs to Non-commissioned Officers and Soldiers, in such Numbers, and for so long a Time, as he shall judge to be most consistent with the good of Our Service; but no Non-commissioned Officer or Soldier shall by Leave of his Captain, or inferior Officer commanding the Troop or Company (his Field Officer not being present) be absent above Twenty Days in Six Months, nor shall more than Two private Men be absent at the same Time from their Troop or Company, excepting some extraordinary Occasion shall require it, of which Occasion the Field Officer present with, and commanding the Regiment, is to be the Judge.

Art. III.

At every Muster the Commanding Officer of each Regiment, Troop, or Company there present, shall give to the Commissary Certificates signed by himself, signifying how long such Officers who shall not appear at the said Muster have been absent, and the Reason of their Absence; in like Manner the Commanding Officer of every Troop or Company shall give Certificates, signifying the Reasons of the Absence of the Non-commissioned Officers and private Soldiers; which Reasons and Time shall be inserted in the Muster-rolls opposite to the Names of the respective absent Officers and Soldiers: The said Certificates shall, together with the Muster-rolls, be remitted to Our Commissary's Office within Twenty Days after such Muster being taken; on the Failure thereof, the Commissary so offending shall be discharged from Our Service.

Art. IV.

Every Officer who shall be convicted before a General Court-martial of having signed a false Certificate, relating to the Absence of either Officer or private Soldier, shall be cashiered.

Art. V.

Every Officer who shall knowingly make a false Muster of Man or Horse, and every Officer or Commissary who shall willingly sign, direct, or allow the signing of the Muster-rolls, wherein such false Muster is contained, shall, upon Proof made thereof by Two Witnesses before a General Court-Martial, be cashiered, and suffer such other Penalty as by the Act of Parliament is for that Purpose inflicted.

Art. VI.

Any Commissary who shall be convicted of having taken Money by way of Gratification on the mustering any Regiment, Troop, or Company, or on the signing the Muster-rolls, shall be displaced from his office, and suffer such other Penalty as by the Act of Parliament is inflicted.

Art. VII.

Any Officer who shall presume to muster any Person as a Soldier, who is at other Times accustomed to wear a Livery, or who does not actually do his duty as a Soldier, shall be deemed guilty of having made a false Muster, and shall suffer accordingly.

Section V.—Returns.

Art. I.

Every Officer who shall knowingly make a false Return to Us, to the Commander in Chief of Our Forces, or to any of his superior Officers authorized to call for such Returns, of the State of the Regiment, Troop, or Company, or Garrison, under his Command, or of Arms, Ammunition, Clothing, or other Stores thereunto belonging, shall by a Court-martial be cashiered.

Art. II.

The Commanding Officer of every Regiment, Troop, or Independent Company, or Garrison in South Britain, shall in the Beginning of every Month, remit to the Commander in Chief of Our Forces, and to Our Secretary at War, an exact Return of the State of the Regiment, Troop, Independent Company, or Garrison under his Command, specifying the Names of the Officers not then residing at their Posts, and the Reason for, and Time of, their Absence: Whoever shall be convicted of having, through Neglect or

Design, omitted the sending such Returns, shall be punished according to the Nature of his Crime by the Judgement of a General Court-Martial.

Art. III.

Returns shall be made in like Manner of the State of Our Forces in Our Kingdom of Ireland, to the Chief Governor or Governors thereof, as likewise of Our Forces in North Britain, to the Officer there commanding in Chief; which Returns shall from time to time be remitted to Us, as it shall be best for Our Service.

Art. IV.

It is Our Pleasure, That exact Returns of the State of our Garrisons at Gibraltar and Port Mahon, and of Our Regiments, Garrisons, and Independent Companies in America, be by their respective Governors or Commanders there residing, by all convenient Opportunities, remitted to Our Secretary at War, for their being laid before Us.

Section VI.—Desertion.
Art. I.

All Officers and Soldiers, who having received Pay, or having been duly inlisted in Our Service, shall be convicted of having deserted the same, shall suffer Death, or such other Punishment as by a Court-martial shall be inflicted.

Art. II.

Any Non-commissioned Officer or Soldier, who shall, without Leave from his Commanding Officer, absent himself from his Troop or Company, or from any Detachment with which he shall, upon being convicted thereof, be punished according to the Nature of his Offence at the Discretion of a Court-martial.

Art. III.

No Non-commissioned Officer or Soldier shall inlist himself in any other Regiment, Troop, or Company, without a regular Discharge from the Regiment, Troop, or Company, in which he last served, on the Penalty of being reputed a Deserter, and suffering accordingly: And in case any officer shall knowingly receive and entertain such Non-commissioned Officer or Soldier, or shall not, after his being discovered to be a Deserter, immediately confine him, and give Notice thereof to the Corps in which he last served, he the said Officer so offending shall by a Court-Martial be cashiered.

Art. IV.

Whatsoever Officer or Soldier shall be convicted of having advised or persuaded any other Officer or Soldier to desert Our Service, shall suffer such Punishment as shall be inflicted upon him by the Sentence of a Court-martial.

Section VII.—Quarrels and Sending Challenges.

Art. I.

No Officer or Soldier shall use any reproachful or provoking Speeches or Gestures to another, upon Pain, if an Officer, of being put in Arrest: if a Soldier, imprisoned, and of asking Pardon of the Party offended, in the Presence of his Commanding Officer.

Art. II.

No Officer or Soldier shall presume to send a Challenge to any other Officer or Soldier, to fight a duel, upon Pain, if a Commissioned Officer, of being cashiered; if a Non-commissioned Officer, or Soldier, of suffering corporal punishment, at the Discretion of a Court-martial.

Art. III.

If any Commissioned or Non-commissioned Officer commanding a Guard shall knowingly and willingly suffer any Person whatsoever to go forth to fight a Duel, he shall be punished as a challenger: And likewise all Seconds, Promoters, and Carriers of Challenges, in order to Duels, shall be deemed as Principals, and be punished accordingly.

Art. IV.

All Officers, of what Condition soever, have power to part and quell all Quarrels, Frays, and Disorders, though the Persons concerned should belong to another Regiment, Troop, or Company; and either to order Officers into Arrest, or Non-commissioned Officers or Soldiers to Prison, till their proper superior Officers shall be acquainted therewith; and whomsoever shall refuse to obey such Officer (though of an inferior Rank) or shall draw his Sword upon him, shall be punished at the discretion of a General Court-martial.

Art. V.

Whatsoever Officer or Soldier shall upbraid another for refusing a Challenge, shall himself be punished as a Challenger; and We hereby acquit and discharge all Officers and Soldiers of any Disgrace, or Opinion of Disadvantage, which might arise from their having refused to accept of Challenges, as they will have only acted in Obedience to Our Orders, and done their Duty as good Soldiers, who subject themselves to Discipline.

Section VIII.—Suttling.

Art. I.

No Suttler shall be permitted to sell any Kind of Liquors or Victuals, or to keep their Houses or Shops open, for the Entertainment of Soldiers, after Nine at Night, or before the Beating of the Reveilles, or upon Sundays, during Divine Service or Sermon, on the Penalty of being dismissed from all future Suttling.

Art. II.

All Officers, Soldiers, and Suttlers, shall have full Liberty to bring into any of Our Forts or Garrisons, any Quantity or Species of Provisions, eatable or drinkable, except where any Contract or Contracts are or shall be entered into by Us, or by Our Order, for furnishing such Provisions, and with respect only to the Species of Provisions so contracted for.

Art. III.

All Governors, Lieutenant Governors, and Officers commanding in Our Forts, Barracks, or Garrisons, are hereby required to see, that the Persons permitted to Suttle shall supply the Soldiers with good and wholesome Provisions at the Market Price, as they shall be answerable to Us for their Neglect.

Art. IV.

No Governors, or Officers commanding in any of Our Garrisons, Forts, or Barracks, shall either themselves exact exhorbitant Prices for Houses or Stalls let out to Suttlers, or shall connive at the like Exactions in others; nor by their own Authority, and for their private Advantage, shall they lay any Duty or Imposition upon, or be interested in the Sale of such Victuals, Liquors, or other Necessaries of Life, which are brought into the Garrison, Fort, or Barracks, for the use of the Soldiers, on the Penalty of being discharged from Our Service.

Section IX.—Quarters.

Art. I.

No Officer shall demand Billets for Quartering more than his effective Men; nor shall he quarter any Wives, Children, Men or Women Servants, in the Houses assigned for the Quartering of Officers or Soldiers, without the Consent of the Owners; nor shall he take Money for the freeing of Landlords from the Quartering of Officers or Soldiers: If a Commissioned Officer so offending, he shall be cashiered; if a Non-commissioned Officer, he shall be reduced to private Centinel, and suffer such corporal Punishment as shall be inflicted upon him by the Sentence of a Court-martial.

Art. II.

Every Officer commanding a Regiment, Troop, or Company, or Party, whether in settled Quarters, or upon a March, shall take Care that his own Quarters, as also the Quarters of every Officer and Soldier under his Command, be regularly cleared at the End of every Week, according to the Rules specified by the Act of Parliament now in Force; but in case any such Regiment, Troop, or Company or Party be ordered to march before Money may be come to the Hands of the Commanding Officer aforesaid, he is hereby required to see that the Accounts with all Persons who shall have Money due to them for the Quartering of Officers and Soldiers, be exactly stated; specifying what Sum is then justly due to him, as likewise the Regiment, Troop, or Company to which the Officers and Soldiers so indebted to him belong, and is, by the first Opportunity, to remit Duplicates of the said Certificates to Our Paymaster General: Any Commanding Officer who shall refuse or neglect the making up such Accounts, and certifying the same as is above directed, shall be cashiered.

Art. III.

The Commanding Officer of every Regiment, Troop, or Company, or Detachment, shall, upon their first coming to any City, Town, or Village, where they are to remain in Quarters, cause publick Proclamation to be made, signifying, That if the Landlords or other Inhabitants suffer the Non-commissioned Officers or Soldiers to contract Debts beyond what their daily Subsistence will answer, that such Debts will not be discharged; he the said Commanding Officer shall, for refusing or neglecting so to do, be suspended for Three Months; during which Time his whole Pay shall be applied to the discharging such Debts as shall have been contracted by the Non-commissioned Officers or Soldiers under his Command, beyond the Amount of their daily Subsistence: If there be any Overplus remaining, it may be returned to him.

Art. IV.

If, after publick Proclamation to be made, the Inhabitants shall notwithstanding suffer the Non-commissioned Officers and Soldiers to contract Debts beyond what the Money issued out, or to be issued out for their daily Subsistence will answer, it will be at their own Peril, the Officers not being obliged to discharge the said Debts.

Art. V.

Every Officer commanding in Quarters, Garrisons, or on a March, shall keep good Order, and to the utmost of his Power redress all such abuses or disorders which may be committed by any Officer or Soldier under his Command; if, upon Complaint made to him of Officers or Soldiers beating, or otherwise ill-treating of their Landlords, or of extorting more from them than they are obliged to furnish by Law; of disturbing Fairs or Markets, or of committing any Kind of Riots, to the disquieting of Our People; he the said commander who shall refuse or omit to see Justice done on the Offender or Offenders, and Reparation made to the Party or Parties injured, as far as Part of the Offender's Pay shall enable him or them, shall, upon Proof thereof, be punished by a General Court-martial, as if he himself had committed the Crimes or Disorders complained of.

Section X.—Carriages.

The Commanding Officer of every Regiment, Troop, Company or Detachment, which shall be ordered to march, is to apply to the proper Magistrate for the necessary Carriages, and is to pay for them as is directed by the Act of Parliament; taking Care not himself to abuse, nor to suffer any Persons under his Command to beat or abuse the Waggoners, or other Persons attending such Carriages; nor to suffer more than Thirty hundred Weight to be loaded on any Wain or Waggon so furnished, or in Proportion on Carts or Carrs; not to permit Soldiers (except such as are sick or lame) or Women to ride upon the said Carriages; Whatsoever Officer shall offend herein, or, in case of Failure of Money, shall refuse to Grant Certificates, specifying the Sums due for the Use of such Carriages, and the Name of the Regiment, Troop, or Company in whose Service they were employed, shall be cashiered, or be otherwise punished according to the Degree of his Offence by a General Court-martial.

Section XI.—Of Crimes Punishable by Law.

Art. I.

Whenever any Officer or Soldier shall be accused of a capital Crime, or of having used Violence, or committed any Offence against the Persons or Property of Our Subjects, such as is punishable by the known Laws of the Land, the Commanding Officer and Officers of every Regiment, Troop, or Party, to which the Person or Persons so accused shall belong, are hereby required, upon Application duly made by or in behalf of the Party or Parties injured, to use his utmost Endeavours to deliver over such accused Person or Persons to the Civil Magistrate; and likewise to be aiding and assisting to the Officers of Justice, in apprehending and securing the Person or

Persons so accused, in order to bring them to Trial. If any Commanding Officer or Officers shall willfully neglect or shall refuse, upon the Application aforesaid, to deliver over such accused Person or Persons to the Civil Magistrates, or to be aiding and assisting to the Officers of Justice in apprehending such Person or Persons, the Officer or Officers so offending shall be cashiered.

Art. II.

No Officer shall protect any Person from his Creditors on the Pretence of his being a Soldier, nor any Non-commissioned Officer or Soldier who does not actually do all Duties as such, and no further than is allowed by the present Act of Parliament, and according to the true Intent and Meaning of the said Act: Any Officer offending herein, being convicted thereof before a Court-martial, shall be cashiered.

Section XII.—Of Redressing Wrongs.
Art. I.

If any Officer shall think himself to be wronged by his Colonel, or the Commanding Officer of the Regiment, and shall, upon due Application made to him, be refused to be redressed, he may complain to the General, commanding in Chief, of Our Forces, in order to obtain Justice; who is hereby required to examine into the said Complaint; and either by himself, or by Our Secretary at War, to make his Report to Us thereupon, in order to receive Our further Directions.

Art. II.

If any inferior Officer or Soldier shall think himself wronged by his Captain, or other Officer commanding the Troop or Company to which he belongs, he is to complain thereof to the Commanding Officer of the Regiment, who is hereby required to summon a Regimental Court-martial, for the doing Justice to the Complainant; from which Regimental Court-martial either Party may, if he thinks himself still aggrieved, appeal to a General Court-martial: But if, upon a Second Hearing, the Appeal shall appear to be vexatious and groundless, the Person so appealing shall be punished at the Discretion of the said General Court-martial.

Section XIII.—Of Stores, Ammunition, &c.
Art. I.

Whatsoever Commissioned Officer, Store-keeper, or Commissary shall be convicted at a General Court-martial of having sold (without a proper Order for that Purpose) embezzled, misapplied, or wilfully, or through neglect, suffered any of Our Provisions, Forage,

Arms, Clothing, Ammunition, or other Military Stores, to be spoiled or damaged, the said Officer, Storekeeper, or Commissary so offending, shall, at his own Charge, make good the Loss or Damage, and be dismissed from Our service, and suffer such other Penalty as by the Acts of Parliament is inflicted.

Art. II.

Whatsoever Non-commissioned Officer or Soldier shall be convicted at a Regimental Court-martial of having sold, or designedly, or through Neglect, wasted the Ammunition delivered out to him to be employed in Our Service, shall, if a Non-commissioned Officer, be reduced to a private Centinel, and shall besides suffer corporal Punishment, in the same Manner as a private Centinel so offending, at the Discretion of a Regimental Court-martial.

Art. III.

Every Non-commissioned Officer or Soldier who shall be Convicted at a Court-martial of having sold, lost, or spoiled, through Neglect, his Horse, Arms, Clothes, or Accoutrements, shall undergo such Weekly Stoppages (not exceeding the Half of his Pay) as a Court-martial shall judge sufficient for repairing the Loss or Damage; and shall suffer Imprisonment, or such other corporal Punishment, as his crime shall deserve.

Art. IV.

Every Non-commissioned Officer who shall be convicted at a General or Regimental Court-martial, of having embezzled or misapplied any Money, with which he may have been intrusted for the Payment of the Men under his Command, or for inlisting Men into Our Service, shall be reduced to serve in the Ranks as a private Soldier, be put under Stoppages until the Money be made good, and suffer such corporal Punishment (not extending to Life or Limb) as the Court-martial shall think fit.

Art. V.

Every Captain of a Troop or Company, is charged with the Arms, Accoutrements, Clothing, or other warlike Stores belonging to the Troop or Company under his Command, which he is to be accountable for to his Colonel, in case of their being lost, spoiled, or damaged, not by unavoidable Accidents, or on actual Service.

Section XIV.—Of Duties in Quarters, in Garrison, or in the Field.

Art. I.

All Non-commissioned Officers and Soldiers, who shall be found One Mile from the Camp, without Leave in Writing from their

Commanding Officer, shall suffer such Punishment as shall be inflicted upon them by the sentence of a Court-martial.

Art. II.

No Officer or Soldier shall lie out of his Quarters, Garrison, or Camp without Leave from his superior Officer, upon Penalty of being punished according to the Nature of his Offence by the Sentence of a Court-Martial.

Art. III.

Every Non-commissioned Officer and Soldier shall retire to his Quarters or Tent at the Beating of the Retreat; in Default of which, he shall be punished according to the Nature of his Offence, by the Commanding Officer.

Art. IV.

No Officer, Non-commissioned Officer, or Soldier shall fail of repairing, at the time fixed, to the Place of Parade of Exercise, or other Rendezvous appointed by his Commanding Officer, if not prevented by Sickness, or some other evident Necessity; or shall go from the said Place of Rendezvous, or from his Guard, without Leave from his Commanding Officer, before he shall be regularly dismissed or relieved, on the Penalty of being punished according to the Nature of his Offence, by the Sentence of a Court-martial.

Art. V.

Whatever Commissioned Officer shall be found drunk on his Guard, Party, or other Duty, under Arms, shall be cashiered for it; any Non-commissioned Officer or Soldier so offending shall suffer such corporal Punishment as shall be inflicted by the Sentence of a Court-martial.

Art. VI.

Whatever Centinel shall be found sleeping upon his Post, or shall leave it before he shall be regularly relieved, shall suffer Death, or such other Punishment as shall be inflicted by the Sentence of a Court-martial.

Art. VII.

No Soldier belonging to any of Our Troops or Regiments of Horse or Foot Guards, or to any other Regiment of Horse, Foot, or Dragoons in Our Service, shall hire another to do his Duty for him, or be excused from Duty, but in case of sickness, Disability, or Leave of Absence; and every such soldier found guilty of hiring his Duty, as also the party so hired to do another's Duty, shall be punished at the next Regimental Court-martial.

Art. VIII.

And every Non-commissioned Officer conniving at such Hiring of Duty as aforesaid, shall be reduced for it; and every Commissioned Officer, knowing and allowing of such ill Practices in Our Service, shall be punished by the Judgment of a General Court-martial.

Art. IX.

Any Person belonging to Our Forces employed in Foreign Parts who, by discharging of Fire Arms, drawing of Swords, beating of Drums, or by any other Means whatsoever, shall occasion false Alarm in Camp, Garrison, or Quarters, shall suffer Death, or such other Punishment as shall be ordered by the Sentence of a General Court-martial.

And whosoever shall be found guilty of the said Offence in *Great Britain* or *Ireland*, shall be punished at the Discretion of a General Court-martial.

Art. X.

Any Officer or Soldier who shall, without urgent Necessity, or without the Leave of his superior Officer, quit his Platoon or division, shall be punished according to the nature of his Offence by the Sentence of a Court-martial.

Art. XI.

No Officer or Soldier shall do violence to any Person who brings Provisions or other Necessaries to the Camp, Garrison, or Quarters of Our Forces employed in Foreign Parts, on Pain of Death.

Art. XII.

Whatsoever Officer or Soldier shall misbehave himself before the Enemy, or shamefully abandon any Post committed to his Charge, or shall speak Words inducing others to do the like, shall suffer Death.

Art. XIII.

Whatsoever Officer or Soldier shall misbehave himself before the Enemy, and run away, or shamefully abandon any Fort, Post, or Guard, which he or they shall be commanded to defend, or speak Words inducing others to do the like; or who, after Victory, shall quit his Commanding Officer, or Post, to plunder and pillage; every such Offender being duly convicted thereof, shall be reputed a Disobeyer of Military Orders; and shall suffer Death, or such other Punishment as by a General Court-martial shall be inflicted upon him.

Art. XIV.

Any Person belonging to Our Forces employed in Foreign Parts, who shall cast away his Arms and Ammunition, shall suffer Death, or such other Punishment as shall be ordered by the Sentence of a General Court-martial.

And whosoever shall be found guilty of the said Offence in *Great Britain* or *Ireland*, shall be punished at the discretion of a General Court-martial.

Art. XV.

Any Person belonging to Our Forces employed in Foreign Parts, who shall make known the Watch Word to any Person who is not entitled to receive it according to the Rules and Discipline of War, or shall presume to give a Parole or Watch Word different from what he received, shall suffer Death, or such other Punishment as shall be ordered by the Sentence of a General Court-martial.

And whosoever shall be found guilty of the said Offence in *Great Britain* or *Ireland*, shall be punished at the Discretion of a General Court-Martial.

Art. XVI.

All Officers and Soldiers are to behave themselves orderly in Quarters, and on their March; and whosoever shall commit any Waste or Spoil, either in Walks of Trees, Parks, Warrens, Fish-ponds, Houses, or Gardens, Cornfields, Enclosures, or Meadows, or shall maliciously destroy any Property whatsoever belonging to any of Our subjects, unless by Order of the then Commander in Chief of Our Forces to annoy Rebels, or other Enemies in Arms against Us, he or they that shall be found guilty of offending herein, shall (besides such Penalties as they are liable to by Law) be punished according to the Nature and Degree of the Offence, by the Judgment of a Regimental or General Court-martial.

Art. XVII.

Whosoever of Our Forces employed in Foreign Parts shall force a Safeguard, shall suffer Death.

Art. XVIII.

Whosoever shall relieve the Enemy with Money, Victuals, or Ammunition, or shall knowingly harbour or protect an Enemy, shall suffer Death, or such other Punishment as by a Court-martial shall be inflicted.

Art. XIX.

Whosoever shall be convicted of holding Correspondence with, or giving Intelligence to, the Enemy, either directly or indirectly, shall suffer Death, or such other Punishment as by a Court-martial shall be inflicted.

Art. XX.

All Public Stores taken in the Enemies Camp, Towns, Forts, or Magazines, whether of Artillery, Ammunition, Clothing, Forage, or Provisions, shall be secured for Our Service; for the Neglect of which Our Commanders in Chief are to be answerable.

Art. XXI.

If any Officer or Soldier shall leave his Post or Colours to go in Search of Plunder, he shall, upon being convicted thereof before a General Court-martial suffer Death, or such other Punishment as by a Court-martial shall be inflicted.

Art. XXII.

If any Governor or Commandant of any Garrison, Fortress, or Post, shall be compelled by the Officers or Soldiers under his Command to give up to the enemy, or to abandon it, the Commissioned Officers, Non-commissioned Officers, or Soldiers, who shall be convicted of having so offended, shall suffer Death, or such other punishment as may be inflicted upon them by the sentence of a Court-martial.

Art. XXIII.

All Suttlers and Retainers to a Camp, and all persons whatsoever serving with Our Armies in the Field, though no inlisted Soldiers, are to be subject to orders, according to the Rules and Discipline of War.

Art. XXIV.

Officers having Brevetts, or Commissions of a prior Date to those of the Regiment in which they now serve, may take Place in Courts-martial and on Detachments, when composed of different Corps, according to the Ranks given them in their Brevetts, or dates of their former Commissions; But in the Regiment, Troop, or Company, to which such Brevett Officers, and those who have Commissions of a prior Date, do belong, they shall do Duty, and take Rank both on Courts-martial and on Detachments, which shall be composed only of their own Corps, according to the Commissions by which they are mustered in the said Corps.

Art. XXV.

If upon Marches, Guards, or in Quarters, any of our Troops of Horse Guards, Grenadier Guards, or Regiment of Horse Guards, shall happen to join or do Duty together, the eldest Officer by

Commission there, on Duty or in Quarters, shall command the Whole, and give out Orders for what is needful to Our Service; Regard being always had to the several Ranks of those Corps, and the Posts they usually occupy.

Art. XXVI.

And in like Manner also, if any Regiments, Troop, or Detachments of Our Horse or Foot Guards shall happen to march with, or be encamped or quartered with any Bodies or Detachments of Our other Troops, the eldest Officer, without Respect to Corps, shall take upon him the Command of the Whole, and give the necessary Orders to Our Service.

Art. XXVII.

When Our Regiments of Foot Guards, or Detachments from Our said Regiments, shall do Duty together, unmixed with other Corps, they shall be considered as One Corps; and the Officers shall take Rank and do Duty according to the Commissions by which they are mustered.

Section XV.—Administration of Justice.
Art. I.

A General Court-martial in Our Kingdoms of *Great Britain* or *Ireland*, shall not consist of less than Thirteen Commissioned Officers, and the President of such Court-martial shall not be the Commander in Chief, or Governor of the Garrison, where the Offender shall be tried, nor be under the Degree of a Field Officer.

Art. II.

A General Court-martial, held in Our Garrison of *Gibraltar*, Island of *Minorca*, or in any other Place beyond the Seas, shall not consist of less than Thirteen Commissioned Officers; nor shall the President of such General Court-martial be the Commander in Chief, or Governor of the Garrison, where the Offender shall be tried, nor under the Degree of a Field Officer, unless where a Field Officer cannot be had, in which Case the Officer next in Seniority to the Commander, not being under the Degree of Captain, shall preside at such Court-martial.

Art. III.

Whereas these Our Rules and Articles are to be observed by, and do in all Respects regard Our Troops and Regiments of Horse and Foot Guards, as well as Our other Forces; and that several Disputes have arisen, and may arise, between the Officers of Our Horse and Foot Guards, in relation to their holding of Courts-martial, and also among the Officers of Our Troops of Horse Guards, Grenadier Guards, and Regiment of Horse Guards, on that and other Points of Duty; we do therefore herein declare it to be Our Will and Pleasure, That when any Officer or Soldier belonging to Our said Troops of Horse Guards, Grenadier Guards, or Regiment of Horse Guards, shall happen to be brought before a General Court-martial, for Differences arising purely among themselves, or for Crimes relating to Discipline, or Breach of Orders, such Courts-martial shall be composed of Officers serving in any or all of those Corps of Horse Guards (as they may then happen to lie for their being most conveniently assembled) where the Officers are to take Post according to the Dates and Degrees of Rank granted them in their respective Commissions, without Regard, to the Seniority of Corps, or other formerly pretended Privileges.

Art. IV.

In like Manner also, the Officers of Our Three Regiments of Foot Guards, when appointed to hold Courts-martial for Differences or Crimes as aforesaid, shall of themselves compose Courts-martial, and take Rank according to their Commissions; but for all Disputes or Differences which may happen between Officers or Soldiers belonging to Our said Corps of Horse Guards, and other Officers and Soldiers belonging to Our Regiments of Foot Guards, or between any Officers or Soldiers belonging to either of those Corps of Horse or Foot Guards, and Officers and Soldiers of Our other Troops, the Courts-martial to be appointed in such Cases shall be equally composed of Officers belonging to the Corps in which the Parties complaining and complained of do then serve; and the President to be ordered by Turns, beginning first by an Officer of One of Our Troops of Horse Guards; and so on in Course out of the other Corps.

Art. V.

The Members both of General and Regimental Courts-martial shall, when belonging to different Corps, take the same Rank which they hold in the Army; but when Courts-martial shall be composed of Officers of One Corps, they shall take their Ranks according to the Dates of the Commissions by which they are mustered in the said Corps.

Art. VI.

The Judge Advocate General, or some Person deputed by him, shall prosecute in His Majesty's Name; and in all Trials of Offenders by General Courts-martial, administer to each Member the following oaths:

You shall well and truly try and determine, according to your Evidence, the Matter now before you, between our Sovereign Lord the King's Majesty, and the Prisoner to be tried.

I, A.B. do swear, That I will duly administer Justice according to the Rules and Articles for the better Government of His Majesty's Forces, and according to an Act of Parliament now in Force for the Punishment of Mutiny and Desertion, and other Crimes therein mentioned, without Partiality, Favour, or Affection; and if any doubt shall arise, which is not explained by the said Articles or Act of Parliament, according to my Conscience, the best of my Understanding, and the Custom of War in the like Cases. And I do further swear, That I will not divulge the Sentence of the Court, until it shall be approved by His Majesty, the General, or Commander in Chief; neither will I, upon any account, at any Time whatsoever, disclose or discover the Vote or Opinion of any particular Member of the Court-martial, unless required to give Evidence thereof, as a witness, by a Court of Justice, in a due Course of Law.

And as soon as the said Oath shall have been administered to the respective Members, the President of the Court shall administer to the Judge Advocate, or Person officiating as such, an Oath in the following words:

I A.B. do swear, That I will not upon any account, at any Time whatsoever, disclose or discover the Vote or Opinion of any particular Member of the Court-martial, unless required to give Evidence thereof, as a Witness, by a Court of Justice in a due Course of Law.

Art. VII.

All the Members of a Court-martial are to behave with Decency; and in the giving of their Votes are to begin with the youngest.

Art. VIII.

All Persons who give Evidence before a General Court-martial, are to be examined upon Oath; nor shall any sentence of Death be given against any offender by any General Court-martial, unless Nine Officers present shall concur therein; And if there be more than Thirteen, then the Judgement shall pass by the Concurrence of Two-thirds of the Officers present.

Art. IX.

No Field Officer shall be tried by any Person under the Degree of a Captain; nor shall any Proceedings or Trials be carried on excepting between the Hours of Eight in the Morning, and of Three in the Afternoon, except in Cases which require an immediate Example.

Art. X.

No sentence of a General Court-martial shall be put in Execution, till after a Report shall be made of the whole Proceedings to Us, or to Our General or Commander in Chief, and Our or his Directions shall be signified thereupon; excepting in *Ireland*, where the Report is to be made to the Lord Lieutenant, and to Our Chief Governor or Governors of that Kingdom, and his or their Directions be received thereupon.

Art. XI.

For the more equitable Decision of Disputes which may arise between Officers and Soldiers belonging to different Corps, whether they be of Our Troops, or Regiment of Horse Guards, Our Three Regiments of Foot Guards, or Our other Regiments of Horse or Foot, We direct, That the Court-martial shall be equally composed of Officers belonging to the Corps in which the parties in question do then serve; and that the Presidents shall be taken in Turns, beginning with that Corps which shall be eldest in Rank.

Art. XII.

The Commissioned Officers of every Regiment may, by the Appointment of their Colonel or Commanding Officer, hold Regimental Courts-martial for the enquiring into such Disputes, or Criminal Matters, as may come before them, and for the inflicting corporal Punishment for small Offences, and shall give Judgement by the Majority of Voices; but no Sentence shall be executed till the Commanding Officer (not being a Member of the Court-martial) or the Governor of the Garrison shall have confirmed the same.

Art. XIII.

No Regimental court-martial shall consist of less than Five Officers, excepting in Cases where that Number cannot be conveniently assembled, when Three may be sufficient; who are likewise to determine upon the Sentence by the Majority of Voices; which Sentence is to be confirmed by the Commanding Officer, not being a Member of the Court-martial.

Art. XIV.

Every Officer commanding in any of Our Forts, Castles, or Barracks, or elsewhere, where the Corps under his Command consists of Detachments from different Regiments, or of Independent Companies, may assemble Courts-martial for the Trial of Offenders in the same manner as if they were Regimental, whose Sentence is not to be executed till it shall be confirmed by the said Commanding Officer,

Art. XV.

No Commissioned Officer shall be cashiered or dismissed from Our Service, excepting by an Order from Us, or by the Sentence of a General Court-martial, approved by Us, or by such General or Commander in Chief, who shall by Our Authority appoint the same to be held; but Non-commissioned Officers may be discharged as private Soldiers, and, by the Order of the Colonel of the Regiment, or by the Sentence of a Regimental Court-martial, be reduced to private Centinels.

Art. XVI.

No Person whatever shall use menacing Words, Signs, or Gestures, in the Presence of a Court-martial then sitting, or shall cause any Disorder or Riot, so as to disturb their Proceedings, on the Penalty of being punished at the Discretion of the said Court-martial.

Art. XVII.

To the end that Offenders may be brought to Justice, We hereby direct, That whenever any Officer or Soldier shall commit a Crime deserving Punishment, he shall, by his commanding Officer, if an Officer, be put in Arrest; if a Non-commissioned Officer or Soldier, be imprisoned till he shall be either tried by a Court-martial, or shall be lawfully discharged by a proper Authority.

Art. XVIII.

No Officer or Soldier who shall be put in Arrest or Imprisonment shall continue in his Confinement more than Eight Days, or till such time as a Court-martial can be conveniently assembled.

Art. XIX.

No Officer commanding a Guard, or Provost-martial, shall refuse to receive, or keep any Prisoner committed to his Charge, by any Officer belonging to Our Forces; which Officer shall at the same Time, deliver an Account in Writing signed by himself, of the Crime with which the said Prisoner is charged.

Art. XX.

No Officer commanding a Guard, or Provost-martial, shall presume to release any Prisoner committed to his Charge, without proper Authority for so doing; nor shall he suffer any Prisoner to escape on the Penalty of being punished for it by the Sentence of a Court-martial.

Art. XXI.

Every officer or Provost-martial to whose charge Prisoners shall be committed, is hereby required within Twenty-four Hours after such Commitment, or as soon as he shall be relieved from his Guard, to give in Writing to the Colonel of the Regiment to whom the Prisoner belongs (where the Prisoner is confined upon the Guard belonging to the said Regiment, and that his Offence only relates to the Neglect of Duty in his own Corps) or to the Commander in Chief, their Names, their Crimes, and the Names of the Officer who committed them, on the Penalty of his being punished for his Disobedience or Neglect, at the Discretion of a Court-martial.

Art. XXII.

And if any Officer under Arrest shall leave his Confinement, before he is set at Liberty by the Officer who confined him, or by a superior Power, he shall be cashiered for it.

Art. XXIII.

Whatsoever Commissioned Officer shall be convicted before a General Court-martial, of behaving in a scandalous infamous Manner, such as is unbecoming the Character of an Officer and a Gentleman, shall be discharged from Our Service.

Section XVI.—Entry of Commissions.

All Commissions granted by Us, or by any of Our Generals having Authority from Us, shall be entered in the Books of Our Secretary at War, and Commissary General, otherwise they will not be allowed of at the Musters.

Section XVII.—Concerning the Effects of Deceased Officers and Soldiers.

Art. I.

When any Commissioned Officer shall happen to die, or be killed in Our Service, the Major of the Regiment, or the Officer doing the Major's Duty in his Absence, shall immediately secure all his Effects or Equipage then in Camp or Quarters; and shall before the next Regimental Court-martial make an Inventory thereof, and forthwith transmit the same to the Office of Our Secretary at War, to the end that his Executors may, after Payment of his Debts in Quarters, and Interment, receive the Overplus, if any be, to his or their Use.

Art. II.

When any Non-commissioned Officer or Private Soldier shall happen to die, or to be killed in Our Service, the then Commanding Officer of the Troop or Company shall, in the Presence of two other Commissioned Officers, take an Account of whatever Effects he dies possessed of, above his Regimental Clothing, Arms, and Accoutrements, and transmit the same to the Office of Our Secretary at War; which said Effects are to accounted for, and paid to the Representative of such deceased Non-commissioned Officer or Soldier. And in case of the Officers, so authorized to take care of the Effects of dead Officers and Soldiers, should, before they shall have accounted to their Representatives for the same, have Occasion to leave the Regiment, by Preferment or otherwise, they shall, before they be permitted to quit the same, deposit in the Hands of the Commanding Officer, or of the Agent of the Regiment, all the effects of such deceased Non-commissioned Officers and Soldiers, in order that the same may be secured for and paid to, their respective Representatives.

Section XVIII.—Artillery.
Art. I.

All Officers, Conductors, Gunners, Matrosses, Drivers, or any other Persons whatsoever receiving Pay or Hire in the Service of Our Artillery, shall be governed by the aforesaid Rules and Articles, and shall be subject to be tried by Courts-martial, in like Manner with the Officers and Soldiers of Our other Troops.

Art. II.

For Differences arising amongst themselves or in Matters relating solely to their own Corps, the Courts-martial may be composed of their own Officers; but where a Number sufficient of such Officers cannot be assembled or in Matters wherein other Corps are interested, the Officers of Artillery shall sit in Courts-martial with the Officers of Our other Corps, taking their Rank according to the Dates of their respective Commissions, and no otherwise.

Section XIX.—American Troops.
Art. I.

The Officers and Soldiers of any Troops which are or shall be raised in America, being mustered and in Pay, shall, at all Times, and in all Places, when joined, or acting in Conjunction with Our *British* Forces, be governed by these Rules or Articles of War, and shall be subject to be tried by Courts-martial in like Manner with the Officers and Soldiers of Our *British* Troops.

Art. II.

Whereas, notwithstanding the Regulations which We were pleased to make for setting the Rank of Provincial and Field Officers in *North America*, Difficulties have arisen with regard to the Rank of the said Officers when acting in Conjunction with Our Regular Forces; and We being willing to give due Encouragement to

Officers serving in Our Provincial Troops, it is Our Will and Pleasure, That, for the future, all General Officers and Colonels serving
by Commission from any of the Governors, Lieutenant or Deputy
Governors, or Presidents of the Council for the time being of Our
Provinces and Colonies in *North America*, shall, on all Detachments,
Courts-martial, or other Duty, wherein they may be employed in
Conjunction with Our Regular Forces, take Rank next after all Colonels serving by Commissions signed by Us, though the Commissions of such Provincial Generals and Colonels should be of elder
Date: And, in like Manner, that Lieutenant Colonels, Majors, Cap-
tains, and other inferior Officers serving by Commission from Gov-
ernors, Lieutenant or Deputy Governors, or Presidents of the Council
for the time being of Our said Provinces and Colonies in *North
America*, shall, on all Detachments, Courts-martial, or other Duty,
wherein they may be employed in Conjunction with Our Regular
Forces have Rank next after all Officers of the like Rank serving by
Commissions signed by Us, or by Our General Commanding in
Chief in *North America*, though the Commissions of such Lieutenant Colonels, Majors, Captains, and other inferior Officers, should
be of elder Date to those of the like Rank signed by Us, or Our said
General.

Section XX.—Relating to the aforegoing Articles.
Art. I.

The aforegoing Articles are to be read and published Once in
every Two Months at the Head of every Regiment, Troop, or Company, mustered or to be mustered in Our Service; and are to be
duly observed and exactly obeyed by all Officers and Soldiers who
are or shall be in Our Service, excepting in what relates to the Payment of Soldiers Quarters, and to Carriages, which is, in Our Kingdom of *Ireland*, to be regulated by the Lord Lieutenant or Chief
Governor or Governors thereof, and in Our Islands, Provinces, and
Garrisons beyond the Seas, by the respective Governors of the same,
according as the different Circumstances of the said Islands, Provinces, or Garrisons may require.

Art. II.

Notwithstanding its being directed in the Eleventh Section of
these Our Rules and Articles, that every Commanding Officer is
required to deliver up to the Civil Magistrate all such Persons under his Command who shall be accused of any Crimes which are
punishable by the known Laws of the Land; yet in Our Garrison of
Gibraltar, Island of *Minorca*, Forts of *Placentia* and *Annapolis Royal*,
where Our Forces now are, or in any other Place beyond the Seas,

to which any of Our Troops are or may hereafter commanded, and where there is no Form of Our Civil Judicature in Force, the Generals or Governors, or Commanders respectively, are to appoint General Courts-martial to be held, who are to try all persons guilty of Wilful Murder, Theft, Robbery, Rapes, Coining or Clapping the Coin of *Great Britain*, or of any Foreign Coin current in the Country or Garrison, and all other Capital Crimes, or other Offences, and punish Offenders with Death, or otherwise, as the Nature of their Crimes shall deserve.

Art. III.

All Crimes not Capital, and all Disorders or Neglects, which Officers and Soldiers may be guilty of, to the Prejudice of good Order and Military Discipline, though not mentioned in the above Articles of War, are to be taken Cognizance of by a Court-martial, and be punished at their Discretion.

George R.

Notes

ABBREVIATIONS

A&IGO	Adjutant & Inspector General's Office
AHC	Arkansas History Commission, Little Rock, Arkansas
ANV	Army of Northern Virginia
AOP	Army of the Potomac
AOT	Army of Tennessee
AOW	Article of War
BPL	Birmingham Public Library, Birmingham, Alabama
CSR	Compiled Service Records
GO	General Order
MDAH	Mississippi Dept. of Archives and History, Jackson, Mississippi
NA	National Archives, Washington, D.C.
NCDAH	North Carolina Dept. of Archives and History, Raleigh, North Carolina
OR	U.S. War Department, *The War of the Rebellion: A Compilation of the Official Records of the Union and Confederate Armies,* 128 vols., Washington, D.C., 1880–1901
SO	Special Order
UV	University of Virginia, Charlottesville, Virginia
WVAHL	West Virginia Archives and History Library, Charleston, West Virginia

CHAPTER I

1. "ACT FOR THE ESTABLISHMENT AND ORGANIZATION OF THE ARMY OF THE CONFEDERATE STATES OF AMERICA," March 4, 1861, Journal of the Congress of the Confederate States of America 1861–1865, pp. 101–6.

2. Article 10 was amended by Congress on August 3, 1861, sec. 2, chap. 42, to allow any commissioned officer of the army to administer the oath of allegiance.

   Article 20 was amended by an act of Congress dated May 29, 1830, to establish that no officer or soldier in the army of the United States shall be subject to the punishment of death, for desertion in time of peace.

Article 65 was amended by an act of Congress dated May 29, 1830, to establish that when a general officer commanding an army or a colonel commanding a separate department shall be the accuser or prosecutor of an officer of the army of the United States the general court-martial for the trial shall be appointed by the president of the United States.

Article 87—so much of the article as authorizes the infliction of corporal punishment by stripes or lashes—was specially repealed by an act of Congress, May 16, 1812. By act of March 2, 1833, the repealing act was repealed so far as it applied to the crime of desertion, which, of course, revived the punishment by lashes for that offense. Flogging was totally abolished by sec. 3, chap. 54, dated August 5, 1861.

3. CSA, AOW #64 and #65.
4. Charles Henry Lee, *The Judge Advocate's Vade Mecum*, pp. 103–4.
5. *Regulations for the Army of the Confederate States*, art. 41, par. 1021–24.
6. CSA, AOW #35.
7. Driver, *52nd Virginia Infantry*, p. 139.
8. An Act of the Congress of the Confederate States of America, ser. 4, vol. 2, par. 19, October 9, 1862.
9. On February 17, 1864, The Act to Establish Military Courts was amended: sec. 3, "That the fourth section of the act of which this is amendatory be and the same is hereby so amended as to extend the jurisdiction of the military courts to all offenders below the grade of Lieutenant General." Published in GO #29 A&IGO, March 5,1864, par. 12.
10. GO #29, A&IGO, March 5, 1864, par. 12.
11. On March 29, 1862, the Confederate Congress enacted a Conscription Law that made every white male between the ages of 18 and 35 liable for service in the army, and extended the length of service of those already in the army to the duration of the war.

A subsequent act in 1864 set the age range at 17 to 50 years.
12. GO #109, A&IGO, August 11, 1863.

I. A general pardon is given to all officers and men within the Confederacy, now absent without leave from the army, who shall (within twenty days from the publication of the address of the president in the state in which the absentees may then be) return to their posts of duty.

II. All men who have been accused or convicted, and undergoing sentence for absence without leave, or desertion, except only those who have been twice convicted of desertion, will be returned to their respective commands for duty.

By Order S. Cooper
Adjutant and Inspector General

CHAPTER II

1. 1 Journals of Congress 90, June 30,1775.
2. 1 Journals of Congress 435, 482, September 20, 1776.
3. Act of Congress, sec. 1, April 10, 1806.
4. British Articles of War of 1765: Rules and Articles for the Better Government of our Horse and Foot Guards, and all Other our forces in our Kingdoms of Great Britain and Ireland, Dominions Beyond the Seas, and Foreign Parts.
5. NA, Office of the Judge Advocate General (Army), record group 153, microfilm roll 2, target 1, volume 3, 1851–1863, HH–KK.
6. Macomb's work provided a much-needed guide to the procedure of courts-martial in the United States Army of the 1840s; however, its weakness lies in its lack of interpretation of the articles of war.

7. DeHart's work was first published in 1846 with a reprint following in 1859 as a timely benefit for all those officers of the Civil War who were able to obtain a copy. Although DeHart becomes overly wordy at times, his analyses are comprehensive and provide the reader with a thorough evaluation of the strength and weaknesses of the articles of war.

8. Lee, *Vade Mecum.*

9. GO #57, ANV, April 18,1863, par. 19.

10. GO #3, Headquarters Richmond, January 13, 1863, case 20.

11. Lee, *Vade Mecum*, sec. 70, p. 74.

12. GO #61, Dept. Trans-Mississippi, August 5, 1864.

13. CSA, AOW #88.

14. GO #3, Headquarters Richmond, January 13, 1863, case 9.

15. GO #17, Dept. S.C., Ga., & Fla., January 28, 1863.

16. SO #89, A&IGO, April 11, 1863, par. 15.

17. Winthrop, *Military Law and Precedents*, p. 518.

18. CSA, AOW #75.

19. GO #139, A&IGO, October 28, 1863, par. 4.

CHAPTER III

1. Lee, *Vade Mecum*, sec. 170, p. 134.

2. DeHart, p. 100.

3. GO #8, ANV, January 23, 1863.

4. Kipling's Verse, Doubleday, 1952, p. 432.

5. GO #98, ANV, August 14, 1862.

6. An act to punish drunkenness in the army, the Congress of the Confederate States of America, April 21, 1862.

7. CSA, AOW #52.

8. GO #88, ANV, September 17, 1863, par. 1.

9. Jordan, *North Carolina Troops*, vol. 9, p. 512.

10. Winthrop, *Military Law and Precedents*, p. 146.

CHAPTER IV

1. CSA, AOW #55.

2. GO #28, ANV, February 27,1863, par. 3.

3. Riggs, *13th Virginia Infantry*, p. 141.

4. GO #126, ANV, November 12, 1862.

5. GO #21, Dept. S.C., Ga., & Fla., February 1, 1863.

6. SO #21, A&IGO, January 26, 1864, par. 26.

7. CSA, AOW #65.

8. GO #68, A&IGO, May 27, 1863.

CHAPTER V

1. CSA, AOW #65.

2. GO #9, Dept. S.C., Ga., & Fla., January 17, 1863, par. 8.

3. *Regulations for the Army of the Confederate States*, art. 18, par. 149.

4. NA, record group 109, M474, Letters Received by the Confederate Adjutant and Inspector General, 1861–1865.

5. DeHart, pp.198–99.

6. GO #91, A&IGO, June 27, 1863.
7. SO #158, A&IGO, July 9, 1862, par. 23.
8. SO #285, A&IGO, December 1, 1864, par. 22.
9. Riggs, *21st Virginia Infantry*, p. 76.

CHAPTER VI

1. CSA, AOW #67.
2. *Regulations for the Army of the Confederate States*, art. 41, par. 1069.
3. GO #75, Dept. S.C., Ga., & Fla., June 1, 1863, par. 4.
4. *Regulations*, art. 18, par. 153–54.
5. GO #1, A&IGO, January 3, 1863, par. 4.
6. SO #7, A&IGO, January 9, 1862, par. 10.
7. BPL, CSR, M311, film #63.
8. BPL, CSR, M311, film #30.
9. GO #105, AOT, May 16, 1863.
10. Footnote to Article of War #87 for the Government of the Armies of the United States.
11. CSA, AOW #87.
12. An act to prohibit the punishment of soldiers by whipping, Congress of the Confederate States, approved April 13,1863.
13. Jordan, *North Carolina Troops*, vol. 12, p. 202.
14. DeHart, p. 194.
15. AHC, CSR, M317, film #15.
16. NA, CSR, M322, film #92.
17. Ibid.
18. NA, CSR, M322, film #93.
19. BPL, CSR, M311, film #100.
20. DeHart, pp. 213–18.
21. Ibid., pp. 214–19.
22. Lee, *Vade Mecum*, sec. 265–67, pp. 190–95.

CHAPTER VII

1. GO #11, AOT, January 24, 1863.
2. Nine and Wilson, *The Appomattox Paroles*, p. 47.
3. WVAHL, CSR, M324, film #216.
4. Jordan, *North Carolina Troops*, vol. 13, p. 507.
5. Alexander, *Fighting for the Confederacy*, pp. 191–93.
6. NA, Confederate Court-Martial Records, chap. 1, vols. 194–199, film #2, vol. 197, p.169, #1565.
7. Rankin, *37th Virginia Infantry*, p. 136.
8. Howard, *Reflections of a Maryland Confederate and Staff Officer*, pp. 258–61.
9. MDAH, CSR, M269, film #188.
10. Alexander, *Fighting for the Confederacy*, p. 119.
11. GO #75, AOP, December 6, 1861.
12. Ibid.
13. Jones, ed.,*Civil War Memoirs of Captain William J. Seymour*, pp. 100–101.
14. UV, J. W. Daniel, "The Deserter," box 22, folder 1904–8, Daniel Papers.

15. Davis, ed., *Diary of a Confederate Soldier, John S. Jackman of the Orphan Brigade*, p. 112.
16. NA, record group 109, chap. 1, vol. 42, Letters, Telegrams, and Endorsements Sent Relating to Courts-Martial 1864–65, p. 20.
17. GO #81, AOT, April 22, 1863.
18. GO #37, ANV, May 2, 1864, par. 7.
19. Jordan, *North Carolina Troops*, vol. 5, p. 562.
20. Armstrong, *19th & 20th Virginia Cavalry*, p. 135.
21. Jordan, *North Carolina Troops*, vol. 14, p. 730.
22. Casler, *Four Years in the Stonewall Brigade*, pp. 188–90.
23. NA, CSR, M401, film #10.
24. Ibid.
25. Ibid.
26. Ibid.
27. Ibid.
28. Ibid.
29. NA, CSR, M401, film #11.
30. Ibid.
31. Ibid.
32. Ibid.
33. Ibid.
34. Ibid.
35. Ibid.
36. Ibid.
37. Ibid.
38. NA, CSR, M401, film #12.
39. Ibid.
40. Ibid.
41. Ibid.
42. NA, CSR, M401, film #13.
43. Ibid.
44. Ibid.
45. Campbell appears as Pvt. William H. Campbell, Co. K, 2d Ohio Infantry, in the Confederate Courts-martial records, but he was a civilian soldier of fortune who probably passed himself off as a member of the military hoping to be treated as a prisoner of war.
46. *Official Roster of Soldiers of the State of Ohio*, vol. 3, p. 543.
47. Ibid., vol. 2, p. 33.
48. Ibid., vol. 3, p. 23.
49. Ibid., vol. 2, p. 59, name appears as Shadrick, Charles P.
50. Ibid., vol. 3, p. 767.
51. Ibid., vol. 2, p. 39.
52. NA, CSR, M258, film #57.
53. OR, ser. 2, vol. 5, p. 862.

CHAPTER VIII

1. Livermore, *Numbers and Losses in the Civil War*, p. 63.
2. Lonn, *Desertion During the Civil War*, p. 231.

3. Sublett, *57th Virginia Infantry*, p. 85.

4. WVAHL, CSR, M324, film #249.

5. GO #139, A&IGO, October 28, 1863, par. 3.

6. *Blue & Gray*, June/July 1986, pp. 27–32.

APPENDIX 1

1. *Regulations for the Army of the Confederate States*, Richmond, 1863, pp. 407–20.

APPENDIX 2

1. OR, ser. 4, vol. 2, pp. 202–203.

APPENDIX 3

1. Winthrop, *Military Law and Precedents*, pp. 931–46.

Bibliography

Manuscript Sources

Alabama, Birmingham Public Library, Birmingham, Alabama. Index to Compiled Service Records of Confederate Soldiers who served in organizations from the State of Alabama (M374). Compiled Service Records of Confederate Soldiers who served in organizations from the State of Alabama (M311).

Arkansas History Commission, Little Rock, Arkansas. Index to Compiled Service Records of Confederate Soldiers who served in organizations from the State of Arkansas (M376). Compiled Service Records of Confederate Soldiers who served in organizations from the State of Arkansas (M317). Compiled Service Records of Confederate Soldiers who served in organizations raised directly by the Confederate Government (M258).

Georgia Department of Archives and History, Atlanta, Georgia. Compiled Service Records of Confederate Soldiers who served in organizations from the State of Georgia (M266).

Kentucky Department of Archives and Libraries, Frankfort, Kentucky. Index to the Compiled Service Records of Confederate Soldiers who served in organizations from the State of Kentucky (M377). Compiled Service Records of Confederate Soldiers who served in organizations from the State of Kentucky (M319).

Mississippi Department of Archives and History, Jackson, Mississippi. Index to Compiled Service Records of Confederate Soldiers who Served in organizations from the State of Mississippi (M232). Compiled Service Records of Confederate Soldiers who served in organizations from the State of Mississippi (M269).

National Archives, Washington, D.C. Compiled Service Records of Confederate General and Staff Officers (M331). Compiled Service Records of Confederate Soldiers from organizations raised directly by the Confederate Government (M258). Compiled Service Records of Confederate Soldiers who served in organizations from the State of Maryland (M321). Compiled Service Records of Confederate Soldiers who served in organizations from the State of Missouri (M322). Compiled Service Records of Confederate Soldiers who served in organizations from the State of Louisiana (M320). Compiled Service Records of Confederate Soldiers who served in organizations from the State of Florida (M251). Compiled Service Records of Volunteer Union Soldiers who served in organizations from the State of North Carolina (M401). Compiled Service Records of Confederate Soldiers who served in organizations from the State of Texas (M323). Consolidated Index to Compiled Service Records of Confederate Soldiers (M253). Endorsements on Court-martial Correspondence, Record Group 109, Chapter 1, Volumes 201. Court-martial Records, Record Group 109, Chapter 1, Volumes 194–99. General Orders and Circulars issued by the Department of Western Virginia, 1862–1864, Record Group 109, Chapter 2, Volume 62. General Orders and Circulars issued by the Military Department of the Trans-Mississippi, Department of Texas, New Mexico, and Arizona, 1862–1865, Record Group 109, Chapter 2, Volumes 74, 81. General Orders and Circulars of the Confederate War Department 1861–1865 (M901). General Orders Department of Texas, Record Group 109, Chapter 2, Volume 112. General Orders issued by the Army of Pensacola, May 1861–July 1861, Record Group 109, Chapter 2, Volume 83. General Orders issued by the Army of Tennessee, D. H. Hill's Corps and Hardee's Corps, 1862–1865, Record Group 109, Chapter 2, Volumes 89–92. General Orders issued by the Army of the Confederate States, 1865, Record Group 109, Chapter 2, Volume 64. General Orders issued by the Army of the Mississippi, 1862, Record Group 109, Chapter 2, Volume 97. General Orders issued by the Army of the Peninsula, May 1861–April 1862, Record Group 109, Chapter 2, Volume 229. General Orders Department of S.C., Georgia, and Florida, Record Group 109, Chapter 2, Volumes 41–43,182. Orders and Circulars issued by the Army of the Potomac and the Army of Northern Virginia, C.S.A. 1861–1865 (M921). Orders and Circulars issued by the Department and Army of Tennessee, C.S.A. 1862–1865, Record Group 109, Chapter 2, Entry #86, (Boxes #82 and #83). Orders and Circulars issued by the Department of East Tennessee 1862–1863, Record Group 109,

Chapter 2, Volume 85. Record of Court-martial cases submitted to the Secretary of War, Record Group 109, Chapter 1, Volume 200. Register of deaths and effects reported to the Adjutant & Inspector General's Office, Record Group 109, Chapter 1, Volumes 27–28.

North Carolina Department of Archives and History, Raleigh, North Carolina. Index to Compiled Service Records of Confederate Soldiers who served in organizations from the State of North Carolina (M230). Compiled Service Records of Confederate Soldiers who served in organizations from the State of North Carolina (M270). Compiled Service Records of Volunteer Union Soldiers who served in organizations from the State of North Carolina (M401).

South Carolina Department of Archives and History, Columbia, South Carolina. Consolidated Index to Compiled Service Records of Confederate Soldiers (M253). Compiled Service Records of Confederate Soldiers who served in organizations from the State of South Carolina (M267).

Tennessee State Library and Archives, Nashville, Tennessee. Index to Compiled Service Records of Confederate Soldiers who served in organizations from the State of Tennessee (M231). Compiled Service Records of Confederate Soldiers who served in organizations from the State of Tennessee (M268).

Virginia State Archives, Richmond, Virginia. Index to the Compiled Service Records of Confederate Soldiers who served in organizations from the State of Virginia (M382). Compiled Service Records of Confederate Soldiers who served in organizations from the State of Virginia (M324). Military service records, muster rolls. Special Orders issued by the Confederate War Department 1861–1865, UB 504.5 A3 Volumes 1–5 (Rare Book Room).

West Virginia Archives and History Library, Charleston, West Virginia. Index to the Compiled Service Records of Confederate Soldiers who served in organizations from the State of Virginia (M382). Compiled Service Records of Confederate Soldiers who served in organizations from the State of Virginia (M324).

Published Primary Sources

Alexander, E. P. *Military Memoirs of a Confederate*. New York: Charles Scribner's Sons, 1907.

Benet, Captain Steven V. *A Treatise on Military Law and Practice of Courts-Martial*. New York: D. Van Nostrand, 1862.

Casler, John O. *Four Years in the Stonewall Brigade*. Dayton, Ohio: Morningside Bookshop, 1971.

Clark, Walter. *History of North Carolina Regiments*. 5 vols. Raleigh and Goldsboro: E. M. Uzzell, 1901.

Confederate States War Department. *Regulations for the Army of Confederate States*. Richmond: J. W. Randolph, 1863.

Davis, William C., ed. *Diary of a Confederate Soldier; John S. Jackman of the Orphan Brigade*. Columbia: University of South Carolina Press, 1990.

DeHart, Captain William C. *Observations on Military Law and the Constitution and Practice of Courts Martial*. New York: Wiley and Halsted, 1859.

Goldsborough, William W. *The Maryland Line in the Confederate Army*. Baltimore: Guggenheimer, Weil & Co., 1900.

Hewett, Janet B., ed. *The Roster of Confederate Soldiers 1861–1865*. 16 vols. Wilmington, N.C.: Broadfoot Publishing Co., 1995.

Howard, McHenry. *Recollections of a Maryland Confederate and Staff Officer*. Dayton, Ohio: Morningside Bookshop, 1975.

Jones, Terry L., ed. *The Civil War Memoirs of Captain William J. Seymour: Reminiscences of a Louisiana Tiger*. Baton Rouge: Louisiana State University Press, 1991.

Journal of the Congress of the Confederate States of America, 1861–1865. 7 vols. Washington, D.C.: U.S. Government Printing Office, 1904.

Lee, Charles Henry. *The Judge Advocate's Vade Mecum*. Richmond: West and Johnston, 1864.

Livermore, Thomas L. *Numbers & Losses in the Civil War in America: 1861–65*. Bloomington: Indiana University Press, 1957.

Macomb, Major General Alexander. *The Practice of Courts Martial*. New York: Harper & Brothers, 1841.

Official Roster of the Soldiers of the State of Ohio in the *War of the Rebellion, 1861–1866*. 12 vols. Akron, Ohio: Werner Co., 1886–1895.

U.S. War Department. *War of the Rebellion: A Compilation of the Official Records of the Union and Confederate Armies*. 128 vols. Washington, D.C.: U.S. Government Printing Office, 1880–1901.

Worsham, John H. *One of Jackson's Foot Cavalry*. New York: The Neal Publishing Co., 1912.

Periodicals

Blue & Gray Magazine, 1986.

North Carolina Historical Review, 1989.

Secondary Sources

Alderman, John Perry. *29th Virginia Infantry.* Lynchburg, Va.: H. E. Howard, 1989.

Allen, Desmond Walls. *Index to Arkansas Confederate Soldiers.* 3 vols. Conway, Arkansas: Arkansas Research, 1990.

Amann, William Frayne. *Personnel of the Civil War.* New York: Thomas Yoseloff, 1968.

Andrus, Michael J. *The Brooke, Fauquier, Loudoun and Alexandria Artillery.* Lynchburg, Va.: H. E. Howard, 1990.

Armstrong, Richard L. *25th Virginia Infantry and 9th Battalion Virginia Infantry.* Lynchburg, Va.: H. E. Howard, 1990.

————. *7th Virginia Cavalry.* Lynchburg, Va.: H. E. Howard, 1992.

————. *11th Virginia Cavalry.* Lynchburg, Va.: H. E. Howard, 1989.

————. *19th & 20th Virginia Cavalry.* Lynchburg, Va.: H. E. Howard, 1994.

————. *26th Virginia Cavalry.* Lynchburg, Va.: H. E. Howard, 1994.

Ashcraft, John M., Jr. *31st Virginia Infantry.* Lynchburg, Va.: H. E. Howard, 1988.

Balfour, Daniel T. *13th Virginia Cavalry.* Lynchburg, Va.: H. E. Howard, 1986.

Bell, Robert T. *11th Virginia Infantry.* Lynchburg, Va.: H. E. Howard, 1985.

Boatner, Lt. Col. Mark M. III. *The Civil War Dictionary.* New York: David McKay Company, Inc., 1959.

Bohannon, Keith S. *The Giles, Alleghany and Jackson Artillery.* Lynchburg, Va.: H. E. Howard, 1990.

Booth, Andrew B. *Louisiana Military Records.* 3 vols. Spartanburg, South Carolina: The Reprint Company, 1984.

Brightwell, Juanita S. *Roster of the Confederate Soldiers of Georgia 1861–1865, an Index.* Spartanburg, South Carolina: The Reprint Company, 1982.

Brown, Louis A. *The Salisbury Prison.* Wilmington, North Carolina: Broadfoot Publishing Co., 1992.

Carmichael, Peter S. *The Purcell, Crenshaw and Letcher Artillery.* Lynchburg, Va.: H. E. Howard, 1990

Cavanaugh, Michael A. *6th Virginia Infantry.* Lynchburg, Va.: H. E. Howard, 1988.

————. *The Otey, Ringgold and Davidson Virginia Artillery.* Lynchburg, Va.: H. E. Howard, 1993.

Chapla, John D. *42d Virginia Infantry.* Lynchburg, Va.: H. E. Howard, 1983.

———. *48th Virginia Infantry.* Lynchburg, Va.: H. E. Howard, 1989.

Cole, Scott C. *34th Battalion Virginia Cavalry.* Lynchburg, Va.: H. E. Howard, 1993.

Collins, Darrell L. *46th Virginia Infantry.* Lynchburg, Va.: H. E. Howard, 1992.

Crews, Edward R. *14th Virginia Infantry.* Lynchburg, Va.: H. E. Howard, 1995.

Crute, Joseph H., Jr. *Units of the Confederate States Army.* Midlothian, Virginia: Derwent Books, 1987.

Davis, James A. *51st Virginia Infantry.* Lynchburg, Va.: H. E. Howard, 1984.

Delauter, R. U., Jr. *62d Virginia Infantry.* Lynchburg, Va.: H. E. Howard, 1988.

———. *18th Virginia Cavalry.* Lynchburg, Va.: H. E. Howard, 1985.

———. *McNeill's Rangers.* Lynchburg, Va.: H. E. Howard, 1986.

Dickinson, Jack L. *8th Virginia Cavalry.* Lynchburg, Va.: H. E. Howard, 1986.

———. *16th Virginia Cavalry.* Lynchburg, Va.: H. E. Howard, 1989.

Divine, John E. *8th Virginia Infantry.* Lynchburg, Va.: H. E. Howard, 1983.

———. *35th Battalion Virginia Cavalry.* Lynchburg, Va.: H. E. Howard, 1985.

Dornbusch, C. E. *Military Bibliography of the Civil War.* Dayton, Ohio: Morningside Bookshop, 1987.

Driver, Robert J., Jr. *52d Virginia Infantry.* Lynchburg, Va.: H. E. Howard, 1986.

———. *58th Virginia Infantry.* Lynchburg, Va.: H. E. Howard, 1990.

———. *1st Virginia Cavalry.* Lynchburg, Va.: H. E. Howard, 1991.

———. *2d Virginia Cavalry.* Lynchburg, Va.: H. E. Howard, 1995.

———. *10th Virginia Cavalry.* Lynchburg, Va.: H. E. Howard, 1992.

———. *14th Virginia Cavalry.* Lynchburg, Va.: H. E. Howard, 1988.

———. *Rockbridge Artillery.* Lynchburg, Va.: H. E. Howard, 1987.

———. *The Staunton Artillery-McClanahan's Battery.* Lynchburg, Va.: H. E. Howard, 1988.

Fields, Frank E., Jr. *28th Virginia Infantry.* Lynchburg, Va.: H. E. Howard, 1985.

Fitzhugh, Lester N. *Texas Batteries, Battalions, Regiments, Commanders, and Field Officers, C.S.A., 1861–1865.* Midlothian, Texas: Mirror Press, 1959.

Fortier, John. *15th Virginia Cavalry.* Lynchburg, Va.: H. E. Howard, 1993.

Frye, Dennis E. *2d Virginia Infantry.* Lynchburg, Va.: H. E. Howard, 1984.

———. *12th Virginia Cavalry.* Lynchburg, Va.: H. E. Howard, 1988.

Gallagher, Gary W., ed. *Fighting for the Confederacy: The Personal Recollections of General Edward Porter Alexander.* Chapel Hill: University of North Carolina Press, 1989.

Gregory, G. Howard. *38th Virginia Infantry.* Lynchburg, Va.: H. E. Howard, 1988.

Gunn, Ralph White. *24th Virginia Infantry.* Lynchburg, Va.: H. E. Howard, 1987.

Hale, Laura Virginia. *History of the Forty-ninth Virginia Infantry, C.S.A.* Lanham, Maryland: S. S. Phillips, 1981.

Harris, Nelson. *17th Virginia Cavalry.* Lynchburg, Va.: H. E. Howard, 1994.

Hartman, Davis W. *Biographical Roster of Florida's Confederate and Union Soldiers, 1861–1865.* 6 vols. Wilmington, North Carolina: Broadfoot Publishing Co., 1995.

Henderson, Lillian. *Roster of the Confederate Soldiers of Georgia.* 6 vols. Hapeville, Georgia: Longina & Porter, 1959.

Henderson, W. D. *12th Virginia Infantry.* Lynchburg, Va.: H. E. Howard, 1984.

———. *41st Virginia Infantry.* Lynchburg, Va.: H. E. Howard, 1986.

Jenson, Les. *32d Virginia Infantry.* Lynchburg, Va.: H. E. Howard, 1990.

Jordan, Ervin L., Jr. *19th Virginia Infantry.* Lynchburg, Va.: H. E. Howard, 1987.

Jordan, Weymouth T., Jr. *North Carolina Troops, 1861–1865: A Roster.* 14 vols. Raleigh: North Carolina Division of Archives and History, 1966–1998.

Keen, Hugh C. *43d Battalion Virginia Cavalry, Mosby's Command.* Lynchburg, Va.: H. E. Howard, 1993.

Kentucky Adjutant General, *Report of the Adjutant General of The State of Kentucky, Confederate Kentucky Volunteers, 1861–1865.* Frankfort: State Journal Company, 1915.

Koleszar, Marilyn Brewer. *Ashland, Bedford, and Taylor Virginia Light Artillery.* Lynchburg, Va.: H. E. Howard, 1994.

Krick, Robert E. L. *40th Virginia Infantry.* Lynchburg, Va.: H. E. Howard, 1985.

Krick, Robert K. *30th Virginia Infantry.* Lynchburg, Va.: H. E. Howard, 1983.

———. *9th Virginia Cavalry.* Lynchburg, Va.: H. E. Howard, 1982.

———. *Fredericksburg Artillery.* Lynchburg, Va.: H. E. Howard, 1986.

———. *Lee's Colonels: A Biographical Register of the Field Officers of the Army of Northern Virginia.* Dayton, Ohio: Morningside Bookshop, 1992.

Lambert, Dobbie Edward. *25th Virginia Cavalry.* Lynchburg, Va.: H. E. Howard, 1994.

Lonn, Ella. *Desertions During the Civil War.* Gloucester, Massachusetts: Peter Smith, 1966.

Lowry, Terry. *22d Virginia Infantry.* Lynchburg, Va.: H. E. Howard, 1988.

———. *26th Battalion Virginia Infantry.* Lynchburg, Va.: H. E. Howard, 1991.

Macaluso, Gregory J. *Morris, Orange, and King William Artillery.* Lynchburg, Va.: H. E. Howard, 1991.

Manarin, Louis H. *15th Virginia Infantry.* Lynchburg, Va.: H.E. Howard, 1990.

Markham, Jerald H. *The Botetourt Artillery.* Lynchburg, Va.: H.E. Howard, 1986.

Martin, David G. *The Fluvanna Artillery.* Lynchburg, Va.: H.E. Howard, 1992.

Moore, Robert H. II. *The Danville, Eight Star New Market and Dixie Artillery.* Lynchburg, Va.: H. E. Howard, 1989.

———. *The Charlottesville, Lee Lynchburg and Johnson's Bedford Artillery.* Lynchburg, Va.: H. E. Howard, 1990.

———. *The Richmond, Fayette, Hampden, Thomas, and Blount's Lynchburg Artillery.* Lynchburg, Va.: H. E. Howard, 1991.

Murphy, Terrence V. *10th Virginia Infantry.* Lynchburg, Va.: H. E. Howard, 1989.

Musick, Michael P. *6th Virginia Cavalry.* Lynchburg, Va.: H. E. Howard, 1990.

Musselman, Homer D. *47th Virginia Infantry.* Lynchburg, Va.: H. E. Howard, 1991.

————. *The Caroline Light, Parker and Stafford Light Virginia Artillery.* Lynchburg, Va.: H. E. Howard, 1992.

Nanzig, Thomas P. *3d Virginia Cavalry.* Lynchburg, Va.: H. E. Howard, 1989.

Neagles, James C. *Confederate Research Sources.* Salt Lake City, Utah: Ancestry Publishing, 1986.

Nine, William G., and Ronald G. Wilson. *The Appomattox Paroles.* Lynchburg, Va.: H. E. Howard, 1989.

O'Neill, Charles. *Wild Train.* New York: Random House, 1956.

O'Sullivan, Richard. *55th Virginia Infantry.* Lynchburg, Va.: H. E. Howard, 1989.

Olson, John E. *21st Virginia Cavalry.* Lynchburg, Va.: H. E. Howard, 1989.

Rankin, Thomas M. *23d Virginia Infantry.* Lynchburg, Va.: H. E. Howard, 1985.

————. *37th Virginia Infantry.* Lynchburg, Va.: H. E. Howard, 1987.

Reidenbaugh, Lowell. *27th Virginia Infantry.* Lynchburg, Va.: H. E. Howard, 1993.

————. *33d Virginia Infantry.* Lynchburg, Va.: H. E. Howard, 1987.

Riggs, David F. *7th Virginia Infantry.* Lynchburg, Va.: H. E. Howard, 1982.

————. *13th Virginia Infantry.* Lynchburg, Va.: H. E. Howard, 1988.

Riggs, Susan A. *21st Virginia Infantry.* Lynchburg, Va.: H. E. Howard, 1991.

Robertson, James, I. *4th Virginia Infantry.* Lynchburg, Va.: H. E. Howard, 1982.

————. *18th Virginia Infantry.* Lynchburg, Va.: H. E. Howard 1984.

————. *General A.P. Hill: The Story of a Confederate Warrior.* New York: Random House, 1987.

Robinson, William M., Jr. *Justice in Gray.* New York: Russell & Russell, 1941.

Ruffner, Kevin C. *44th Virginia Infantry.* Lynchburg, Va.: H. E. Howard, 1987.

Sally, A. S. *South Carolina Troops in Confederate Service.* Columbia: The R.L. Bryan Company, 1913.

Scott, J. L. *23d Battalion Virginia Infantry.* Lynchburg, Va.: H. E. Howard, 1991.

————. *36th Virginia Infantry.* Lynchburg, Va.: H. E. Howard, 1987.

————. *45th Virginia Infantry.* Lynchburg, Va.: H. E. Howard, 1989.

———. *36th and 37th Battalions Virginia Cavalry.* Lynchburg, Va.: H. E. Howard,1986.

———. *Lowry's, Bryan's, and Chapman's Batteries of Virginia Artillery.* Lynchburg, Va.: H. E. Howard, 1988.

Sherwood, G. L. *54th Virginia Infantry.* Lynchburg, Va.: H. E. Howard, 1993.

———. *20th and 39th Virginia Infantry.* Lynchburg, Va.: H. E. Howard, 1994.

———. *59th Virginia Infantry.* Lynchburg, Va.: H. E. Howard, 1994.

Sherwood, W. Cullen. *The Nelson Artillery, Lamkin and Rives Batteries.* Lynchburg, Va.: H. E. Howard, 1991.

Sifakis, Stewart, *Compendium of the Confederate States Armies.* 11 vols. New York: Facts on File, Inc., 1992–1995.

Stiles, Kenneth L. *4th Virginia Cavalry.* Lynchburg, Va.: H. E. Howard, 1985.

Sublett, Charles W. *57th Virginia Infantry.* Lynchburg, Va.: H. E. Howard, 1985.

Tennesseans in the Civil War. 2 vols. Nashville: Civil War Centennial Commission, 1964.

Trask, Benjamin H. *9th Virginia Infantry.* Lynchburg, Va.: H. E. Howard, 1984.

———. *16th Virginia Infantry.* Lynchburg, Va.: H. E. Howard, 1986.

———. *61st Virginia Infantry.* Lynchburg, Va.: H. E. Howard, 1988.

Wallace, Lee A., Jr. *1st Virginia Infantry.* Lynchburg, Va.: H. E. Howard, 1985

———. *3d Virginia Infantry.* Lynchburg, Va.: H. E. Howard, 1986.

———. *5th Virginia Infantry.* Lynchburg, Va.: H. E. Howard, 1988.

———. *17th Virginia Infantry.* Lynchburg, Va.: H. E. Howard, 1990.

———. *A Guide to Virginia Military Organizations.* Lynchburg, Va.: H. E. Howard, 1986.

———. *The Richmond Howitzers.* Lynchburg, Va.: H. E. Howard, 1993.

Warner, Ezra J. *Generals in Gray.* Baton Rouge: Louisiana State University Press, 1959.

Weaver, Jeffrey C. *63d Virginia Infantry.* Lynchburg, Va.: H. E. Howard, 1991.

———. *64th Virginia Infantry.* Lynchburg, Va.: H. E. Howard, 1992.

———. *22d Virginia Cavalry.* Lynchburg, Va.: H. E. Howard, 1991.

————. *The Virginia State Line and State Rangers*. Lynchburg, Va.: H. E. Howard, 1994.

————. *Thurman's Partisan Rangers and Swann's Battalion Virginia Cavalry*. Lynchburg, Va.: H. E. Howard, 1993.

————. *Goochland Light, Goochland Turner and Mountain Artillery*. Lynchburg, Va.: H. E. Howard, 1994.

————. *The Nottoway Artillery and Barr's Battery Virginia Light Artillery*. Lynchburg, Va.: H. E. Howard, 1994.

————. *45th Battalion Virginia Infantry, Smith and Count's Battalions of Partisan Rangers*. Lynchburg, Va.: H. E. Howard, 1994.

West, P. Michael. *30th Battalion Virginia Sharpshooters*. Lynchburg, Va.: H. E. Howard, 1995.

————. *The Gauley, Mercer and Western Artillery*. Lynchburg, Va.: H. E. Howard, 1991.

Wiatt, Alex L. *26th Virginia Infantry*. Lynchburg, Va.: H. E. Howard, 1984.

Winthrop, William. *Military Law and Precedents*. Washington, D.C.: U.S. Government Printing Office, 1920.

Wise, Jennings Cropper. *The Long Arm of Lee*. 2 vols. Lincoln: University of Nebraska Press, 1988.

Wright, John H. *Compendium of the Confederacy*. Wilmington, North Carolina: Broadfoot Publishing Co., 1989.

Young, William A., Jr. *56th Virginia Infantry*. Lynchburg, Va.: H. E. Howard, 1990.

Index